# The Fists of Righteous Harmony

# THE FISTS OF RIGHTEOUS HARMONY

A History of the Boxer Uprising in China
in the Year 1900

HENRY KEOWN-BOYD

Leo Cooper LONDON

First published in Great Britain in 1991 by
LEO COOPER
190 Shaftesbury Avenue, London WC2H 8JL
an imprint of Pen & Sword Books Ltd
47 Church Street, Barnsley, South Yorkshire

ISBN 0 85052 403 2
Cataloguing in Publication data
is available from the British Library

Typeset by Rowland Phototypesetting Ltd, Bury St Edmunds, Suffolk
Printed in Great Britain by
The Redwood Press, Melksham
and bound by Hunter & Foulis Ltd, Edinburgh

To the Memory of the Gallant
Defenders of the Peking Legations
and the Peit'ang Cathedral, who,
with a little help from their Enemies,
withstood the strangest Siege in History.

# Contents

# Maps
Drawn by Chester Read

# Acknowledgements

I am greatly indebted to the following, all of whose help has been invaluable in various ways:

Brigadier General E. H. Simmons and Mr J. Michael Miller of the United States Marine Corps Historical Centre; General Robert Bassac and the staff of *Le Service Historique de l'Armee de Terre*; Dr P. B. Boyden and Miss Claire Wright of the National Army Museum; Mr Norman Holme, Assistant Archivist of the Royal Welch Fusiliers; Major J. T. Hancock and Mrs M. Magnusson of the Royal Engineers Institution; Miss B. Spiers, Archivist of the Royal Marines; Mr J. D. Williams of the Japan Information Centre in London; Lord Dacre of Glanton; Brigadier Michael Lee; Commander M. H. Farr, RN; Merilyn Thorold; Captain R. Campbell, RN (retd); Major A. P. B. Watkins; Mr N. A. Gaselee; Major P. E. Abbott; Mr Richard Hill; Captain Thomas Dunne; Miss Olivia Nourse; Mr Dave Harvey; Miss Melanie Aspey of News International; Mr Garth Burden of the *Daily Mail*; Captain Chester Read, RN (retd) who drew the maps; Mr Tom Hartman who edited the book; Mr Ben Williams who very kindly read the typescript and checked all the Chinese proper and place names; Mr Hugh Fairey for help with the index; Miss Emma Scarborough who typed the manuscript and, last but by no means least, my wife, who not only put up with those nervous tantrums without which, we are told, no author can claim the name, but also translated a number of extracts from French books and documents.

Perhaps I should add that the only person from whom I sought information and who did not reply was the Cultural Attaché at the Soviet Embassy in London. I daresay the concepts of glasnost and perestroika are yet to reach Millionaire's Row.

I am also deeply indebted to all those who have provided the illustrations used in this book; the sources are shown after the captions.

*Author's Note*

The Chinese names and place names which appear in this book are romanized in accordance with the Wade–Giles system, as they would have been at the time these events took place.

Similarly, the spelling of the word 'Welsh' in Royal Welsh Fusiliers is in accordance with the official (War Office) practice of the time. Today, of course, this famous regiment is known as the Royal Welch Fusiliers.

# Introduction

No one has ever arrived at
understanding them [the Chinese]
thoroughly and no one ever will.

Captain A. A. S. Barnes,
1st Chinese Regiment

The Chinese, Europeans have told themselves for centuries, are inscrutable. However, the most cursory glance at the history of the relations between China and what were known in the 19th century as the Powers reveals that the inscrutability was mutual. They fenced blindfolded in a dark room, fearing one another yet regarding each other with contempt and incomprehension. The Chinese were, and still are, great xenophobes although today's foreign tourist in China is regarded as comic rather than dangerous and mirth has replaced anger. To them, and here one is generalizing as there were many exceptions, the foreigner was a coarse, smelly, greedy barbarian. Even their close genetic kinsmen, the Japanese, were referred to as the 'ugly dwarfs'.

Perhaps it is not surprising that the Chinese view of the foreigner should have been somewhat jaundiced. Postponing for a moment serious political, commercial and military issues, it must be said that few countries have attracted a more remarkable and generally distasteful array of adventurers, confidence tricksters, soldiers of fortune, crackpots and other assorted undesirables as did China in the 19th and early 20th centuries. To mention but a few of the more spectacular examples, we have General Charles Gordon, sword in one hand, Bible in the other, leading his Ever Victorious Army of European, American and Chinese desperadoes against the Taiping

1

rebels;* the English pirate known, no doubt aptly, as Fuckie Tom, plundering the China coast in his fleet of junks. Later there appeared 'Two-Gun' Cohen, gangster confidant of Sun Yat Sen and a brace of the world's most bare-faced conmen, Sir Edmund Backhouse, Bart., brilliant sinologue, forger, fantasist and obscene diarist, and Trebitsch Lincoln, Hungarian-Jewish Member of Parliament for Doncaster, spy, swindler and Buddhist monk.

And let us not forget the ladies. The bordellos of the Treaty Ports catered for all tastes and pockets. Voluptuous poules de luxe, often Russian and, after the Revolution, invariably of self-proclaimed blue blood, entertained in well-appointed apartments while the water-front bars swarmed with tarts of every race, colour and proclivity. There was much to be learnt and, we are told, among the most successful 'amateur' pupils of these skilled professionals was a certain Wallis Spencer, then the wife of an American naval officer, who later used her knowledge of the arts of love to seduce to her bed and from his throne the King and Emperor of the greatest empire in the world.

But to return to more serious matters, to the Powers China was both a milch cow for raw materials and a great profitable maw into which the products of Manchester, Dusseldorf, Lyons, Milan, Osaka and Milwaukee could be stuffed. It was also a chess-board upon which the diplomats accredited to the Imperial Court at Peking, the Consuls-General in the other great cities of China and their political masters at home could manoeuvre and posture in the great game of scoring points over one another and acquiring Concessions.

In the prosecution of these aims, they bullied, harassed and bribed the atrophied and degenerate Imperial Government remorselessly and from all directions. Their velvet gloves were thread-bare and through them distracted Manchu and Chinese officials glimpsed the iron fists of the Royal Navy and the Tsarist, Prussian and Japanese military machines. But to concede to the British was to excite the jealousy of the French and to give in to the Italians was to enrage the Germans and so on. It was a vicious circle. The demands of all had to be satisfied, at least up to a point, or the consequences from one quarter or another might be dire.

* See Appendix D.

2

To an extent, the Chinese managed to prevaricate behind their creaking, ponderous bureaucracy, immemorial protocol and all-pervading corruption. The 'squeeze' or bribe, reigned supreme across the entire political and social spectrum. To move a mule-cart from A to B required a tiny payment to some petty official or policeman; for a provincial viceroy to obtain entry to the Forbidden City called for the distribution of largesse to every kow-towing eunuch who managed politely but firmly to impede his path to the steps of the throne. The squeeze was not simply part of the system, it was the system itself. High mandarins and foreign officials like Sir Robert Hart, the long-serving Inspector-General of the Imperial Customs Service, amassed huge fortunes from peculation and what would today be described as insider dealing. The British industrialist, Lord Rendel, who, from time to time, played a delicate role as an honest broker on behalf of China, put it bluntly. '[Manchu] government,' he wrote, 'meant chiefly a system by which eighteen separate administrations bled eighteen provinces on the terms of furnishing each their quota to the principal blood-sucker at Peking.'

As distasteful to most Chinese as the diplomatic and commercial demands of the barbarians was their apparently fatuous but intrusive religion, Christianity, which their missionaries preached in vigorous competition with one another and with little regard for Chinese conventions and superstitions. Most disliked were the Roman Catholics whose bishops, through the persistent intervention of the French Government, had succeeded in acquiring for themselves the rights and privileges of the Mandarin class. While in the main the peasantry were disturbed by the possible effect of the missionaries' activities on the spirits of their ancestors, the official classes were more concerned with the secular aspects of the presence of these foreigners in the provinces. The diplomatic representatives of the Powers were concentrated in, and seldom emerged from, Peking and the Treaty Ports, while the missionaries acted as a kind of intelligence network, albeit frequently ignored, for them throughout the country, a state of affairs as offensive to officialdom then as it would be today.

To the most efficient and progressive administration, the governance of 19th century China would have presented many intractable problems. Its huge size, vast population, multiplicity of languages, extremes of climate giving rise to natural disasters on the grand scale, and lack of communications, posed administrative difficulties compared to which the problem of the rapacious Powers paled into insignificance. However, no such efficient and progressive administration existed. Instead, this enormous and unwieldy conglomerate had been ruled since the mid-17th century by the Manchu, or Ch'ing, dynasty, themselves foreigners to the native Chinese. Once warlike and irresistible, the Imperial family had degenerated over the centuries into effete, vicious and incompetent flabbiness. Hidebound by archaic ceremonial, semi-paralysed by the corrupt 'eunuch' system of palace administration, fearing all technological innovation, by the end of the 19th century the Manchus had become worthless as an engine of national government. By comparison with them, the Tsar of Russia was a model of dynamism and progressive thought. The British Minister in Peking at the turn of the century, Sir Claude MacDonald, described the mandarins of the Chinese government as being as ignorant as they were arrogant, epithets which, incidentally, the said mandarins themselves would probably have used in reference to Sir Claude and his colleagues of the other legations.

Only superstitious belief in the divinity of the Emperor and his terrible aunt, the Empress Dowager, and the conservatism of the masses allowed the Manchus, for a few more years and insofar as it could be imposed, to exercise authority over the land.

For the purposes of this book the incumbent Emperor Kuang Hsu, a crushed and feeble cypher, may be largely ignored. Responsibility for the events of the summer of 1900 lay with the Empress Dowager Tsu Hai who had been the de facto ruler of China for nearly forty years since the death of the Emperor Hsien-feng whose favourite concubine she had been.

To describe this extraordinary woman as an enigmatic figure is to understate the case. Although she ruled China for nearly half a century until her death in 1908, we know much less about her than about many insignificant western monarchs of the far more distant past. Much that has been written of her is based on rumour, speculation and forgery. What is incontestable is that her most highly developed sense was that of self-preservation. However, the Manchu dynasty itself was decayed beyond preservation and, in effect, died with her.

4

An idealized portrait of the Empress Dowager.

Her support for the Boxers must be seen as the most serious lapse in her life-long struggle for personal survival and dominance. Probably it came about as the result of that mutual inscrutability mentioned at the beginning of this introduction. It is doubtful if she had any real conception of the power of the Powers, particularly if they were to be temporarily united under a common threat. Probably she was so wildly misinformed by many of her advisers that she believed the destruction of the legations and their occupants would lead to the abandonment of European, American and Japanese ambitions in China. Also, for a while at least, she probably believed in the physical indestructibility which the Boxers professed, in which case she was simply sharing the credulity of many of her people and the strongest party at her Court.

The Boxers may not have possessed the mystical powers they claimed, but their origins, motive force and organization were certainly mysterious and, to this day, largely unknown. The rank and file were peasants, fanatically anti-Christian, anti-foreign and,

5

originally, anti-Manchu, whose combustion seems to have been spontaneous rather than planned. No distinct leaders emerged until the movement was unofficially adopted by the Imperial family and even then their structure remained apparently anarchical. Most importantly of all, they attracted little or no support outside the northern provinces of the Empire. Even their name is obscure, invented, it is said, by a British or American missionary wishing to abbreviate the English translation, The Fists of Righteous Harmony, of the equivalent Chinese words and to describe in everyday terms the weird callisthenics which formed a part of their ceremonial.

This, then, is the story of these strange revolutionaries, those who supported them and those whom they sought to destroy.

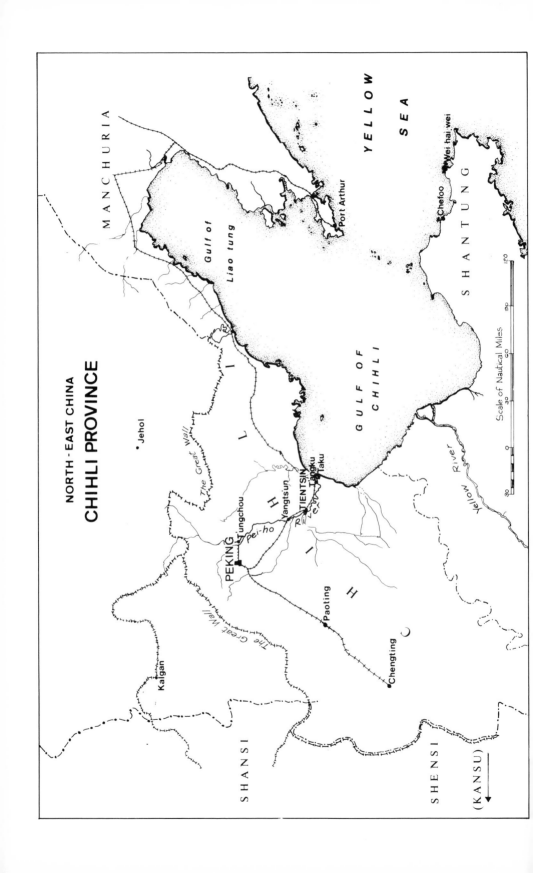

NORTH - EAST CHINA
**CHIHLI PROVINCE**

MANCHURIA

Gulf of Liao tung

YELLOW SEA

Port Arthur

Wei hai wei

Chefoo

SHANTUNG

GULF OF CHIHLI

Jehol

The Great Wall

C H I H L I

Yellow River

Tungchou

Yangtsun

Taku

Tangku

TIENTSIN

Pei-ho

Peiho River

PEKING

Paoting

The Great Wall

Kalgan

Chengting

SHANSI

SHENSI

(KANSU)

Scale of Nautical Miles

# 1

# The Barbarian Encroaches

To have friends coming to one
from distant parts – is this
not a great pleasure?

Confucius

To deal in one chapter with a subject so vast and fascinating as China's relations with the various Powers in the 19th century is an impertinence but one necessary for the provision of a backdrop to the main theme of this book.

Chinese produce reached the west in Roman times but there was no direct contact between the two great empires. It was from early Renaissance Italy that the explorer Marco Polo and the missionaries John of Monte Corvino and Odoric travelled to Far Cathay, returning with, or reporting, news which excited the interest of the merchants, churchmen and politicians of many nations.

The Portuguese were the first Europeans to exploit the Chinese coastal trade and were established in Macao by the middle of the 16th century, but by the end of the 18th century Great Britain, aggressive, forceful and enterprising, had asserted herself as China's most powerful trading partner. France, Russia, Japan and later Germany and the United States, jealous of each other and especially of Britain, began their respective encroachments upon Chinese territory and sovereignty spurred on by British successes and the fear of total British domination of the China trade.

By the mid-19th century all these Powers, usually at loggerheads with one another but sometimes in temporary coalition, were nibbling and nagging at the corrupt and crumbling Manchu dynasty, vying with each other for concessions and imperiously demanding

9

'most favoured nation' treatment. In these negotiations the Manchus and their mandarins were handicapped not only by their lack of military power but by their ill-concealed conviction of their racial, intellectual and material superiority over all 'barbarians'.

Western envoys, themselves often proud and arrogant men, did not take kindly to the endless prevarications and sometimes humiliating formalities of Chinese diplomacy which served only to fray tempers and harden attitudes. For example, George the Third and his ministers were unlikely to receive favourably the Emperor Ch'ien Lung's reply to His Majesty's fraternal message delivered by Lord Macartney in 1793, to wit, 'even were your envoy competent to acquire some rudiments of them [Chinese ways], he could not transplant them to your barbarous land. . . . As your ambassador can see, we possess all things . . . and have no use for your country's manufactures.' Hardly the language of diplomacy or the soft words which turn away wrath.

In order to present a coherent picture of China's relations with the Powers during the 19th century it is perhaps best to deal with each important nation individually, an opportunity which the unfortunate Chinese were seldom given as the various *desmarches* with various nations often took place more or less simultaneously.

## Great Britain

As the Industrial Revolution developed, so Britain sought wider and more distant markets for her manufactured goods. At the same time, as the standard of living and the buying power of the British people increased so a 'consumer' society evolved. China produced tea, silk and rhubarb root, the latter a purgative without which, it seems, no middle-class Englishman could face the day in comfort. These imports had to be paid for in silver and a trade imbalance, in China's favour, developed.

Since the 16th century the Chinese had acquired a taste for opium, originally for medical purposes, but, from the late 18th century onwards, addiction spread from the coast inland, while local production was prohibited.

British India, run virtually as a private trading concern by the mighty East India Company (known as John Company) was a major

10

grower of the poppy from which, of course, opium is derived. The Company, with a nudge and a wink from the home government, was not slow to seize the opportunity to redress the balance of trade. Thus, opium imports into China had, by the third decade of the 19th century, become a substantial contributor to the Company's profitability and to the prosperity of many Indian peasant farmers, as well as a source of indirect revenue to the British Treasury. The legitimacy or otherwise of this trade and the attitude of British and Chinese officialdom towards it are matters of much scholarly and moralistic discourse, but as this book is not intended as a social history it will be dealt with here in a somewhat peremptory and cold-blooded fashion. However, it must be said that few Englishmen who were not directly involved with this noxious commerce were other than disgusted by it. For example, the hard-headed industrialist, Lord Rendel, a close friend of Gladstone, wrote that the Chinese, in contrast to the British Indian government, by rigorously suppressing the production of opium gave 'evidence that even a corrupt oriental administration could respect the primary interest of humanity'.

Roughly, the business worked as follows. John Company purchased the raw material (poppy) from the Indian farmers, processed it and sold it at auction to local merchants. The 'chests' of opium were then shipped to Canton, usually in the Company's ships. The drug reached the Chinese addict through the media of British traders, chiefly Scotsmen such as Jardine and Matheson, whose warehouses (known as factories) were located on the Canton waterfront, and a syndicate of Chinese entrepreneurs called the Cohong. Later,* the trade expanded to other ports of entry and traders of other nationalities, mostly American, joined in.

During the first third of the 19th century the volume of opium imports increased from about 5,000 chests per annum at the turn of the century to over 30,000 in 1836. Despite various Imperial edicts banning the trade, the attitude of the Chinese authorities was ambivalent. Many mandarins were themselves addicted and many others profited greatly from the exaction of squeezes from the

* The East India Company's trading monopoly in the Far East was abolished by Parliament in 1833.

Cohong. Nevertheless, opium smoking was recognized as a serious social evil and, to give it its due, the ruling Manchu dynasty did attempt to combat it. These efforts led to conflict with Britain and in 1839 the First Opium War broke out following the destruction by the Imperial Commissioner at Canton of large quantities of the drug stored in British factories.

The war, consisting mainly of a series of combined naval and army operations which met with little serious resistance from Chinese forces, involved, at its height in 1840, some three and a half thousand British and Indian troops and about twenty ships of the Royal Navy, as well as many merchantmen, including steamers. It ended with the historic Treaty of Nanking and the lesser-known Treaty of the Bogue which were signed in 1842 and 1843 respectively.

The most significant aspects of these treaties were the ceding to Great Britain in perpetuity of Hong Kong island and the opening of five 'Treaty Ports', that is to say ports in which and from which foreigners would be allowed to trade. Also they included 'Most Favoured Nation' clauses under which Britain would be entitled in the future to concessions equivalent to those granted to any other country. These clauses were to have far-reaching consequences for the Chinese, who, from then on, found themselves in a diplomatic vicious circle of demands from all the militarily powerful nations of the world.

In the years following the signature of what the Chinese under-standably regarded as these 'unequal' treaties, entered into under duress, the British became increasingly dissatisfied with their im-plementation. The refusal of senior Chinese officials, notably the Governor of Canton, to receive and negotiate with British envoys and the general harassment of British merchants and merchant shipping exacerbated the situation. Thus, the Second Opium War (1857–60), often referred to as the Arrow War, was sparked off by the arrest, on the Governor's orders, of a Hong Kong-registered trading vessel called the *Arrow*, with a British captain and a Chinese crew, the excuse being that some of the latter were pirates (which they probably were).

This time the French became involved, as, though protesting neutrality, did the United States and Russia. In 1859, to the surprise and irritation of the Anglo-French, the Chinese stoutly defended the Taku Forts at the mouth of the Pei-ho River and gave the indignant Allies a bloody nose. The assault force, about one thousand strong, suffered 40% casualties and was forced to withdraw. However, a year later the Forts were taken with little resistance from the Chinese, most of whose troops were occupied elsewhere with the Taiping Rebellion, a neo-Christian uprising which raged for some fifteen years and is estimated to have caused twenty million deaths.*

When the Anglo-French eventually arrived in Peking they burnt the Emperor's magnificent Summer Palace, ostensibly in revenge for the ill-treatment and death† of Allied prisoners, in an act of grandiose vandalism, having taken the precaution of thoroughly looting its contents. In fact, this arson was a stroke of coolly calculated diplomatic terror designed to soften Manchu resistance to the Treaty of Tientsin‡ into which they had entered two years previously. One clause of this treaty is of special importance to our story as it provided for the establishment of permanent foreign legations at Peking.

While Great Britain was to remain the leading foreign Power in China for the rest of the century, the reverses inflicted upon her army by the Boers in 1899 were not lost on the Chinese. This may have influenced the anti-foreign faction at Court in their attitude to the Boxers. Of course, they knew little or nothing about the Boers but if the most feared of the barbarians could be chastised by one handful of peasants, so they could by another, particularly if that other was possessed of magical powers and immunities.

## France

French penetration of China was spearheaded by Jesuit missionaries and, until the downfall of the Manchus in the early years of the 20th century, France used the Roman Catholic Church in China as an arm of her diplomacy. Much anti-Christian resentment was engendered

---

* See Appendix D.
† For a description of the horrific circumstances of their imprisonment and lingering deaths, see H. B. Loch's *Personal Narrative*.
‡ Separate treaties of this name were also signed with France, Russia and the United States at about the same time.

among the Chinese of all classes by the privileges conferred upon the Catholic clergy and, by extension, upon native converts, under pressure from France. An admittedly hostile witness, the Reverend Arthur Smith, a Protestant missionary, wrote, 'Thus the [Catholic] bishops . . . adopt the rank of a Chinese Governor, and bear a button on their caps indicative of that fact, travelling in a chair with the number of bearers appropriate to that rank, with outriders and attendants on foot, an umbrella of honour borne in front and a cannon discharged upon their arrival and departure. . . . All this and much else is a part of the settled policy of the Church . . . and it is a policy which is in many ways repellent to Chinese pride and repugnant to their sense of propriety and fitness. . . . By the steady pressure of the French Legation, the claims which the [Catholic] Church had always made for itself were, on the 15th March 1899, officially granted by the Chinese Government.'

On the secular side, although trade and rivalry with Britain played significant roles, France's dealings with China in the 19th century were concerned mainly with her acquisition of the territories which became known as French Indo-China (Vietnam etc). Down the centuries these states had owed a tenuous kind of feudal allegiance to the successive ruling dynasties of the Chinese empire and the Manchus struggled, usually in vain, to prevent them from slipping into French hands.

In 1870 Chinese resentment against France as a nation and against her missionaries in particular exploded into violence at Tientsin. On 21 June, in a quarrel with the local magistrate, the French Consul lost his head and shot the magistrate's servant. The French Consulate and the Roman Catholic Church were attacked and put to the torch, several French priests and nuns and some other foreigners being killed. The Chinese authorities eventually apologized but the incident remained a bitter memory in the minds of the Christian clergy and the apology a humiliation and loss of face to the Chinese.

In 1884 a brief war broke out between France and China with the usual outcome and, in the following year, China was forced to sign a second Treaty of Tientsin with France accepting French acquisition of Indo-China.

## Russia

Trade across the often disputed Sino-Russian border had existed since long before any records of such activities were kept. Ambassadors from both countries visited each others' capitals from the 16th century onwards and in 1689 the Treaty of Nershinsk,* the first between China and any European Power, was signed. This treaty was concerned chiefly with frontier demarcation.

By the end of the 18th century Russia had realized the importance of the China coastal trade through Canton and had joined with Britain, France and the United States in the game of multilateral power play. The Arrow War gave Russia the chance to jump on the Anglo-French band-wagon and the Treaty of Tientsin allowed her access to the Treaty Ports and a permanent legation at Peking.

Throughout the 19th century the main bone of contention between these two clumsy giants was Manchuria, homeland of the Manchu, an issue complicated by Japanese interest in the same area. As Manchu power declined so Russian encroachment in Manchuria increased to the point where, during the Boxer uprising, she was in virtual occupation of the province. In due course, this led to the Russo-Japanese War of 1904–5 in which the Chinese were helpless onlookers on their own territory and in which the Russians were heavily defeated, both at sea and on land, after a breathtaking display of military and, particularly, naval ineptitude.

## Japan

The close racial kinship between the Japanese and the Chinese does not seem to have done much for good relations between the two over the centuries. Until fairly recent times, Chinese cultural and religious influence was strong in Japan, but since Japan's modernizing revolution of 1868 (known as the Meiji Restoration), she has moved light years ahead of China in military and technological development.

The Chinese of the 19th century appear to have regarded the Japanese with the same mixture of fear, hatred and contempt as

* At these negotiations the Chinese were assisted by two Jesuit priests, Gerbillion and Pereira, who acted as advisers and interpreters.

they did westerners. As the Manchus weakened, so Japan, like the other Powers, increased her pressure on China, particularly in Korea, a vassal state of China, and in Manchuria. In 1894 war broke out between the two countries in which China, hopelessly outmatched, was ignominiously defeated. The subsequent peace treaty resulted in the 'independence' of Korea under de facto Japanese control and other territorial concessions which greatly strengthened Japan's position in the area, although pressure from the other Powers forced her to hand over some of the prizes.

In the early stages of the Boxer troubles the Japanese legate in Peking was reluctant to make common cause with his Christian colleagues, advising his minister in Tokyo that it was a religious issue in which Japan was not involved and that by intervening she risked offending China for nothing. The Japanese Government, however, was unconvinced and, in any case, when one of her diplomats was murdered in Peking and the legation quarter attacked, Japan was dragged in willy-nilly.

As it turned out, the Boxers unwittingly helped Japan up the last few rungs of the ladder onto the platform of equality with the other Powers in China.

## The United States

Of course, the United States, a new nation, arrived late on the Chinese scene, although her commercial activities on the China coast opened up soon after (perhaps even before) her independence from Britain, and her merchants by no means disdained the opium trade. In 1844 she obtained from China under the Treaty of Whangia similar rights to those accorded to Great Britain under the earlier Treaty of Nanking. Then, in 1858, she too entered into a Treaty of Tientsin, enabling her, inter alia, to open a legation in Peking. However, it must be said that the United States did not join in the power play on the Chinese chessboard with quite the same gusto and enthusiasm as did the other western nations and Japan. She was alarmed by the prospect of the dismemberment of China and the sharing-out of her provinces among the Powers, notably Russia and Japan, which might prohibit large areas of the country to American trade. To some extent aided by Britain, she sought to use her influence, though far from what it is today, to protect Chinese territorial integrity.

On the other hand, American Protestant missionaries, although perhaps humbler in their attitudes than their French and Italian Catholic competitors, played no small role in exciting Chinese enmity towards Christianity and its propagators. Thus Americans, for all their relative restraint in their dealings with China, bore a measure of responsibility for the rise of the Boxers and its consequences.

## Germany

Although the Germans had played no great part in the history of China's foreign affairs, by the end of the 19th century Germany was her fourth largest trading partner, after Britain, Japan and the United States. Moreover, impressed by Prussia's easy victory over the French in 1870, the Manchus had sought and obtained German military aid in the form of both weaponry and instructors. However, this does not seem to have improved China's military performance, although in fairness to the Germans, this was largely due to the ruthless plundering of the defence budget by the mandarins responsible, and, above all, by the Empress Dowager.

At the time of the rise of the Boxers, opinion in China had turned sharply against Germany. Following the murder of two German missionaries at the end of 1897, the Kaiser and his government seized the chance to wrench major concessions and territorial leases from China, sparking off a new round of demands from the other Powers.

## Italy

In 1899 Italy acquired the dubious distinction of being the only European Power, up to that date, to be faced down by the Chinese.

Desperate to keep up with the other bullying Joneses, she demanded a lease on San Men Bay. However, as far as the Chinese were concerned, since the days of Marco Polo, Italy had faded into insignificance. Moreover, her defeat by 'black barbarians' (even more despised than white ones) at Adowa in 1896 had not passed unnoticed. So when the demand was presented to the Tsungli Yamen

(Foreign Ministry) by Italy's comic-opera legate in Peking, Signor di Martino, to everyone's astonishment it was curtly refused. Di Martino, who seems to have been devoid of all diplomatic qualities, failed to rise to the occasion. Distracted by the temporary absence of his Japanese mistress (who was also a Japanese spy) and ridden by superstitious fears of conducting business on certain days in March (the Ides, perhaps), he lost his head and, without reference to his government, issued an ultimatum and ordered Italian vessels to 'demonstrate' in the Yellow Sea.

The Imperial Government, accustomed to being threatened by mighty fleets, was unimpressed when told that the Italians had but two warships in the area, the *Marco* and the *Polo*. In fact, there turned out to be only one, the *Marco Polo*. In any case, the Tsungli Yamen was unable to identify the bay in question on its map and the whole farcical episode collapsed in a welter of absurdity.

However, this event did have a more serious side to it. Di Martino was recalled by his embarrassed government, thus giving a tremendous boost to Chinese morale. In a lecture many years later Sir Claude MacDonald suggested that the humiliation of Italy on this occasion had been one of the most important factors in bringing the Empress Dowager and her anti-foreign party down on the side of the Boxers. It led them to believe that their tormentors were not, perhaps, such invincible devils after all. Sir Claude may have had a point, but he was conveniently forgetting the Boers.

## Other Nations

At the turn of the century Austria-Hungary, Spain, Belgium and Holland were also diplomatically represented in Peking. None* of these nations was of any importance in the history of 19th century China and only Austria-Hungary produced a contingent of legation guards prior to the siege.

Having glanced at the nations which aroused the ire and the enmity of the Chinese people, their rulers and, ultimately, the Boxers, we

* Although the Dutch had traded with China for centuries.

18

must turn our attention briefly to the religion which was so closely associated with the European encroachment, Christianity.

There was nothing apologetic or hesitant about 19th century Christianity. There were no bishops who doubted the Scriptures, and the role of the priest, be he Catholic or Protestant, was to teach the Gospel and to save souls. The missionaries went to China and elsewhere with the intention of converting the heathen and setting him on the path of righteousness. The excellent secular work which they did in medicine, education and child-care was not an end in itself but part of the process of spiritual conversion. If they had to co-exist side by side with other religions, beliefs and traditions, they did so only because they had no choice.

The history of Christianity in China has been a chequered one. Although there are believed to have been Nestorian Christians from Central Asia in Peking in the 7th century, the first effective impact was made by Jesuits in the 16th century. The approach adopted by these remarkable men, the most notable of whom was the Italian,

Boxers desecrating a church and massacring Chinese Christians. (*Mary Evans Picture Library*)

Father Matteo Ricci, was pragmatic. Fluent Chinese linguists, skilled diplomatists, scientists and mathematicians, they aroused the interest and curiosity of the late Ming and early Ch'ing (Manchu) emperors and mandarins. With no hope or intention of ever returning home, the Jesuits managed to identify themselves with China and the Chinese as completely as any European can, but without losing sight of the true purpose of their holy mission. By the end of the 17th century they had become trusted to the extent that, as we have seen, two of their number, Fathers Gerbillon and Pereira, were employed by the Manchus as interpreters and advisers in their negotiations with Russia. However, for all their secular success, the Jesuits can hardly be said to have brought about mass conversion and the problems facing their proselytizing work, notably the conflict with Confucianism which regarded Christian rejection of emperor and ancestor worship as heretical, far outweighed the advantages they had so carefully and conscientiously constructed.

By this time other Catholic orders were at work in China but their failure to adopt Chinese dress and customs and their apparent neglect of the Chinese language tended to inhibit their activities and limit their success rate.

Until the mid-19th century so few were the missionaries, so vast China and so poor her communications that their political impact upon the country as a whole was negligible. However, in the early part of the century British, American, German and Scandinavian Protestant missionaries started to reinforce, if one may apply such a term to competitors, their Catholic forerunners. These newcomers believed more strongly than, for example, the Jesuits had, that the way to the pagan soul was through social welfare. Now not only churches but schools, orphanages and clinics began to spring up all over China, the various denominations in fierce competition with one another in the construction and management of the most attractive facilities. Unfortunately these good works were not regarded as unqualified blessings by all Chinese. Whereas the actual pupils, orphans and patients benefited enormously, far greater in number were the disjointed noses. Local officialdom saw the Christian-educated peasant as a threat to its traditional dominance over the toiling masses. In China every man knew his place and was expected to stay there.

The medical skill of the missionaries damaged the livelihood of the
native quacks and purveyors of potions and cures. The orphanages
affronted such gruesome traditions as exposure or sale of unwanted
children and, of course, provided a ready-made supply of new
Christians. The tall spires of the churches interfered with the free
passage of the aerial spirits, and Christians, it was rumoured, indulged in frenzied and indiscriminate copulation after church services; drank women's menstrual flow; used children's eyes and
testicles for the concoction of medicines and other parts of their
bodies as alchemic material for the production of silver.

It is interesting to recall that the Jews of medieval Europe were
frequently accused of similar blood-curdling perversions, which
sometimes sparked pogroms, not unlike Boxer attacks upon the
Christians.

Finally, we cannot ignore the impact of western technology and
'progress' upon a society as resistant to change as China. Foreign
businessmen, railway and mining engineers, were, in general, as
unpopular as the missionaries, although many shrewd Chinese en-

21

riched themselves immensely through clever investment and the squeeze. Western imports ruined many local industries, particularly in the cheap cloth trade. Railways were regarded by some educated Chinese as 'scissors' cutting up China into convenient sections for the Powers to swallow. As for the peasantry, the roaring locomotives affronted the spirits of their ancestors through whose cemeteries they puffed and snorted, while overhead the telegraph wires whistled and moaned in the wind with sinister but incomprehensible messages. Furthermore, all these devilish devices and contraptions threatened millions of coolies, chairmen, carters and bargees with unemployment and starvation.

By the last decade of the 19th century, all this had festered into a boil of hatred for the foreigners and, as the new century dawned, it burst.

# 2

# The Hundred Days
# and the Rise of the Boxers

> I have found that only reforms can save China
> and that reforms can only be achieved
> through the discharge of the conservative
> and ignorant ministers and the appointment
> of the intelligent and brave scholars.

Emperor Kuang Hsu 1898

After the death of her son in 1875, the Empress Dowager arranged for her nephew, who reigned as Kuang Hsu, to succeed as Emperor. This was unconstitutional but secured the Old Buddha's* position by depriving her widowed and pregnant daughter-in-law of the chance of becoming Empress Dowager should the child be a boy.

The new Emperor was a weak-minded youth and no match for his formidable aunt, who, despite ostensibly handing over power to him in 1889 when he achieved his majority, retained ultimate authority throughout his reign. However, for a few months in 1898 the well-meaning young man sought to assert himself.

As the pressure on China from the Powers increased after her defeat by Japan in 1895, it dawned upon some of the less reactionary members of the mandarin class that China must reform and modernize, as Japan had thirty years earlier, or perish as an independent nation. Dismemberment by the Powers was no longer a vague fear but an imminent possibility and the so-called Spheres of Interest† might soon become colonies.

---

\* A respectable and rather affectionate alternative name for the Empress Dowager.

† These were semi-officially defined areas in which the Powers had agreed, in principle, not to encroach upon one another's interests. They were divided roughly as follows:

Russia – all to the north of the Great Wall (not accepted by Japan)

A French magazine cartoon of the Empress Dowager. (*Mary Evans Picture Library*)

In January, 1898, a junior government official and scholar, K'ang Yu-wei, through the good offices of the Emperor's tutor, Weng Tung-ho, succeeded in submitting a memorial* to His Majesty recommending extensive and far-reaching reforms. In June of the same year K'ang was granted the rare privilege for a junior official of an Imperial audience, thus in effect inaugurating the Palace-inspired reform movement known to history as the Hundred Days.

The precise nature of these reforms, the means by which they were to be implemented and their practicability are beyond the compass of this book. Suffice it to say that they presented a serious threat to the power and prosperity of the mandarin hierarchy, particularly the ultra-conservatives, and to the influential eunuchs

---

Germany – Shantung Province and the Yellow River Valley
Great Britain – the Yangtze Valley and central China
Japan – Fukien Province and Formosa
France – south China, bordering on Indo-China
* Memorial is the word generally used to describe written reports or submissions to the Palace.

24

by whom the entire dynastic system was managed. The Empress Dowager may not have been unimpressed by some aspects of the suggested reforms, particularly those aimed at improving the efficiency of the armed forces; nor is she likely to have been much concerned with the interests of her reactionary courtiers. With one possible exception, which we shall meet later, there is no evidence that she ever gave a moment's thought to the interests or welfare of others, unless they happened to coincide with her own. Throughout her life she dedicated herself exclusively to the preservation of her own power, comfort and security. Her only misjudgement in this respect was her handling of the Boxer uprising.

Apart from these considerations, those aspects of the proposed reforms most likely to upset her would have been any tinkerings, especially those with spiritual connotations, with the traditions and ceremonials of her dynasty. Thus, her 'counter-revolution' was sparked off in September, 1898, by the Emperor's dismissal of the senior officials of the Board of Rites, one of whom had been guilty of blocking the submission to the Emperor of a reformist memorial.

Word reached the Emperor that he was to be arrested while inspecting troops at Tientsin, whereupon he appealed to one of the local commanders in the area, Yuan Shih-k'ai, to pre-empt the coup by arresting the leading opponents of reform and purging the entourage of the Empress Dowager. However, Yuan, a wily opportunist, though seemingly in agreement and sympathetic to the reformists, was doubtful of success and betrayed the plan to the Viceroy of Chihli and Commander-in-Chief of the northern armies, Jung Lu, the Old Buddha's closest confidant and, it was rumoured, her lover. She struck hard and decisively. On 19 September the Emperor was seized and held under indefinite house arrest. The Hundred Days were over.

For some time the Emperor's life hung in the balance. Rumours were circulated that his health was deteriorating and an official heir, a son of the ultra-reactionary Prince Tuan, was appointed. These obvious preparatory moves towards the Emperor's premature and unnatural demise were more than the powerful southern viceroys and the Corps Diplomatique could stomach. Their separate representations and barely concealed threats forced the Empress Dowager to postpone her nephew's rendezvous with his ancestors but, for the remaining ten years of his life, his role was purely formal.

Such reforms as had been affected during the Hundred Days were quickly thrown into reverse, reactionary officials reinstated, reformists executed or banished. Nevertheless, it was felt that urgent steps must be taken to preserve China from the further depredations and encroachments of the Powers and that the military measures proposed in the reforms should go ahead. Re-training, re-equipment and re-organization were essential, but, for this, large additional tax revenues were required and a burden even heavier than usual weighed down upon a groaning population.

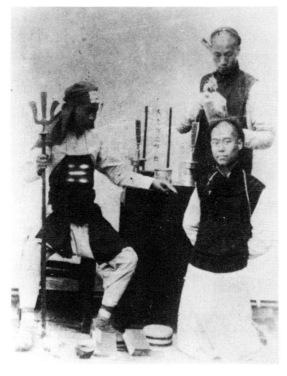

Boxers posing with various ritualistic artefacts. (*The late Mr Han Zhong Min/ Research Centre of Inscriptions and Documents*)

The peasantry knew little or nothing of the power struggles between the Emperor and his aunt or the reformers and the reactionaries. All they knew was that at the root of all their troubles lay the hated foreign barbarian, whose representative in the countryside was the Christian missionary and the railway engineer. Not only was the peasant called upon to pay higher taxes to keep the foreigner at bay but competition from foreign imports diminished his ability to pay those taxes. Also there was drought and famine, natural phenomena of which the tax-collectors took no cognisance, countering pleas of poverty with the bamboo rod, the cangue* and the fetid dungeon. But the foreign devil was to blame and he must be exterminated.

The genealogy of the Boxers is obscure and the subject of much scholastic debate. One theory, that they were deliberately recruited by the Chinese government as a kind of militia, does not stand up to scrutiny. According to Chester C. Tan, quoting a learned source in his *Boxer Catastrophe*, the I Ho Ch'uan – Fists of Righteous Harmony – were associated as early as 1808 with various secret societies such as the White Lotus society, the Eight Diagram Sect and the Red Fist Society, which he describes as 'heretical and revolutionary organizations'. Although largely suppressed at that time, the Fists of Righteous Harmony, or Boxers, maintained a more or less dormant existence for the rest of the 19th century in the northern provinces, principally Chihli and Shantung. They seem to have been recruited from the poorest classes of society – landless peasants, unemployed coolies, discharged soldiers and the like. The Boxer movement also had women members, called Lanterns (Red, Blue, Black and Green according to age) but the role of these ladies is unclear and no European eye-witness ever reported seeing them in action.

One of the most curious features of the Boxers was their apparent lack of leadership or command. In the light of their self-proclaimed immunity to bullets, perhaps they felt they needed none. They would prepare themselves for action by performing various rites and gymnastic movements, which appeared to observers to resemble boxing, hence the name.† Most Boxers wore something red – a sash, a scarf, turban or head-band. They were devoid of military training and possessed few firearms.

Their original aims were the overthrow of the Manchus, the destruction of the Christians and all their works and the total ejection of all foreigners from China. The first of these was dropped once

* A heavy wooden plank worn, as a punishment, like a portable pillory round the neck.
† There is some confusion here as the name 'Boxers' may also have been an attempt to translate from the Chinese 'I Ho Ch'uan' or 'I Ho Tuan'.

they had attracted the support of the dynasty. Of course there were other less altruistic motives for joining the movement such as banditry, pillage, rape, arson and murder. As the numerical size of the Boxers has never been established, it is impossible to say how many were genuine patriots and how many simply scallywags who jumped on a promising bandwagon. Nor is it certain that all the outrages committed against Christians, for example those in Shansi and Manchuria, were carried out by Boxers. Some of these may have been opportunist attacks by local people upon their Christian neighbours for a variety of motives.

A Boxer girl of Tientsin. Although reputedly expert in the martial arts there is no evidence that the Lanterns, as they were called, took part in warlike operations. (*As above*)

Some Boxers may have been active in Shantung Province as early as 1896 but they were not taken seriously until two years later when their existence was officially acknowledged under the name of I Ho Tuan.

From the beginning the attitude of the Court towards the Boxers was ambivalent. Viceroys, governors, generals, magistrates and even lowly head constables of villages, faced with conflicting edicts and instructions, found themselves in an impossible position. The Manchu dynasty, whimsical, corrupt and incompetent, is seen at its most absurd and dangerously indecisive during this crisis. The Boxers were good; no, they were bad; then they were good again. They must be restrained but they must not be punished. Well, maybe the leaders, if any could be found, should be punished but the rank and file should simply be 'dispersed'. If the missionaries and Chinese converts were attacked by the Boxers, then, it was argued, they had asked for it by their high-handed attitude towards the mass of unconverted peasantry and their insistence on privileges denied others. Nevertheless, Chinese Christians were Chinese and the local authorities were reminded of their duty to protect them and their property, but in the course of so doing, they must not be too hard on the Boxers . . . and so on.

Of course, the conflicting edicts issued by the Court, always in the Emperor's name, reflected the conflicts within the Forbidden City. While the reactionaries, blind to everything except their hatred of the foreigner, strove to protect and nurture the Boxer movement, their opponents, mindful of China's inability to resist the military might of the Powers should they be provoked, sought to bring it under control.

The Empress Dowager, though devious and cunning, knew little of the world outside. Although of uncertain origin, as an Emperor's concubine she had risen to supreme power through her skill at the ploy and gambit of palace politics, the playing off of one high personage against another and the constant intriguing and manoeuvring required to achieve and maintain her position. But her contact with foreigners had been minimal. She probably knew little of the history or even the geography of other nations, could speak no foreign language and had no comprehension of western philosophy or politics. However, it must be said in defence of her policy during the Boxer crisis that the Manchu dynasty had more to fear from internal upheaval than from foreign aggression. The foreigner could be 'soothed' – that had been Chinese policy for most of the 19th century – but revolutionaries could not. The Taiping rebellion had been touch and go for her dynasty and had been suppressed only with the aid of foreign officers like 'Chinese' Gordon and his motley crew of mercenaries and adventurers. Therefore, she may have reasoned, safer to join the Boxers than to attempt to crush them, particularly if there was anything to their claims of magical immunity. Certainly, this policy changed the Boxers' attitude to the dynasty and their 'Down with the Manchus' slogan was dropped.

Strong voices for moderation came from the south. The viceroys and governors of the central and southern provinces, far removed from the influence of the palace reactionaries and in closer touch with the foreign officials and businessmen of the Treaty Ports, consistently took an anti-Boxer line, pleading with the Imperial Government to take stern measures to suppress this potentially disastrous movement. But they were a long way away and without direct access to the ear of the Empress Dowager so their pleas and arguments were largely ignored.

Although the Boxers had powerful supporters within the dynastic family, such as Prince Tuan, father of the Heir Apparent, even more vital to their real success was the sponsorship of certain high officials in the provinces. The most notorious of these was Yu Hsien, Governor of Shantung. In October, 1899, 300 Boxers attacked Christians in the P'ingyuan district but, when confronted by government troops, a number were killed, despite their alleged invulnerability, and the rest put to flight. Yu Hsien was furious and sacked several senior officials, thus encouraging the Boxers in further outrages. By the end of the year, pressure from the legations led to his recall to Peking where he found that, if anything, he stood higher in the Old Buddha's esteem than before and was soon appointed to the governorship of Shansi where he was to encourage, indeed preside over, a horrific massacre of missionaries and their families.

His replacement in Shantung Province was General Yuan Shih-k'ai, he who had betrayed the Emperor's proposed coup in September, 1898. Yuan, far too intelligent to be fooled by the Boxers, cracked down on them hard. Despite remonstrative edicts from the Court, he succeeded in virtually eliminating Boxer activity in his province. On at least one occasion he had a number of them lined up and shot by firing squad, proving to his own satisfaction and, presumably to the on-lookers, that Boxers were as vulnerable to bullets as anyone else.

But in neighbouring Chihli Province the situation was very different. The Viceroy Yu Lu walked a tight-rope between the pro- and anti-Boxer parties at Court. Under constant pressure from Peking and from his own pro-Boxer subordinates, vacillating between policies of suppression and placation, by the spring of 1900 he had lost control over the Boxers. Smashing, burning and looting, tearing railway lines up and telegraph lines down, they marched inexorably upon that principal nest of the hated foreigner, Peking.

As warnings from the missionaries increased in frequency and volume, echoed and passed on to the foreign legates by the French Roman Catholic Bishop Favier, the diplomats awoke slowly from their complacent slumbers. The British Minister believed that a good shower of rain would do much to cool the atmosphere, both politically and meteorologically, while the doyen of the Old China Hands, Sir Robert Hart, Inspector-General of the Imperial Chinese Customs, refused to believe that the Boxers presented any real threat to the diplomats and foreign community in Peking.

Only the wise old Bishop Favier started to fortify his cathedral, stock up with food and buy up guns, precautions to which he and many of his flock were to owe their lives in the days to come.

# 3

# Bannermen and Braves

The Army of China presents
a curious example of the
survival of the unfittest.

Major A. Cavendish,
British Military Observer,
Sino-Japanese War 1894–5

If Sir Robert Hart and the diplomats expected the Chinese army to suppress or even control the Boxers, they were to be disappointed.

Despite the reforms of 1898 with which the Empress Dowager had ordered Jung Lu to press ahead after the Hundred Days, the Chinese army was still one of the least effective in the world. It was also then, as now, one of the most difficult to analyse in terms of its structure and organization. However, at least two western military observers of the time made the attempt. These were the Major Cavendish quoted above and Commandant Vidal, the French Military Attaché at Peking at the turn of the century. Cavendish dealt with the subject in general and in nationwide terms, while Vidal's more detailed observations were restricted mainly to the forces in northern China.

Like most other armies, that of China in the late 19th and early 20th centuries was divided into three broad categories: regulars, territorials and reservists. But there the similarity with the western concept of military organization ends, so the reader must indulge the writer who will inevitably flounder in his search for analogies with western military expressions and definitions.

As in all other aspects of Chinese life in the late Manchu period, the squeeze reigned supreme, draining the army not only of funds but of efficiency and morale. Generally speaking, the troops were badly paid, badly fed, badly housed, badly armed and badly trained.

Above all, they had bad officers. Although the conquering Manchus had been a warlike race, the profession of arms was despised in China and those who followed it were the dregs of society, regarded by the rest of the population as little better than bandits.

The purchase of modern foreign-made weaponry, of which there was a great deal available but unused in 1900, was seen by the mandarins responsible as a simple means of amassing fortunes and the western armaments manufacturers vied with each other in the handing-out of huge bribes and commissions. Seldom were the weapons used or the men trained in their use.

The junior officers, usually completely ignorant of their profession, were often the former servants, poor relations or toadies of the mandarins who masqueraded as generals. They were lazy, venal and incapable of instilling consistent discipline. Cavendish, only slightly tongue in cheek, remarked that he could only tell the difference between officers and men because the men's tea-kettles dangled from the muzzles of their rifles whereas the officers had servants to carry theirs! Serious offences would be ignored and then suddenly a man would be decapitated for some trivial misdemeanour. Beatings on parade, even of the junior officers themselves, were frequent but do not seem to have improved the men's turnout, drill or discipline, and, in any case, except where foreign instructors were available, there was no one to teach them any of these things.

Part of the army, known in English as Bannermen, was of a hereditary nature. These troops were the descendants of the Manchurian and Mongol units, or Banners, which brought the Ch'ing or Manchu dynasty to power in China in the 17th century. Originally there had been four Banners, roughly the equivalent of regimental colours: yellow, white, blue and red, which soon afterwards were increased to four more, known as the Bordered Banners: yellow bordered with red, with blue, and so on. In the late 1890s Cavendish estimated that there were some 460,000 of these men, of whom 160,000 were in Peking, aged between 16 and 60 and drawing pay and rice rations for life. He listed eleven different divisions of Bannermen, ranging from the 4,000-strong Guards of the Household Division, responsible for the security of the Imperial family, to the Peking Police or Gendarmerie of about 15,000 men.

It is not entirely clear what role the Bannermen played in the siege of the legations or in opposing the relief forces. Unfortunately, neither Vidal nor his British opposite number, a Colonel Browne, were in Peking during the siege and the legation guards, all of them new to China, had little idea who precisely they were fighting. The only foreign military attaché we know to have been present during the siege was Colonel Shiba of the Japanese Legation and regrettably his account has never been translated into a European language. However, Cavendish believed that the £4 million per annum spent on maintaining the Bannermen did not produce 'one efficient soldier'.

Imperial Bannermen. These were hereditary troops useless in war. (*As above*)

Vidal was equally dismissive of the Lu-ying or Green Regiments of Territorials. These were provincial troops owing their allegiance to the viceroy or governor rather than the central government. It was to them that the principal role of attempting to suppress the Boxers fell and one doubts that, even if they had been given the necessary support and leadership, they would have made much of a job of it. This force was reputedly about 650,000 strong but the true numbers were probably lower, so that the governors and commanding officers could pocket the difference between establishment and actual costs.

In an emergency, and in theory, these troops could be transferred from one province to another, but this required a spirit of co-operation between provincial authorities which seldom existed. If any serious fighting was to be done, then the men called upon to do it were the Chuang-Yung or Fighting Braves, and the Lien-chun or Disciplined Troops. Although Cavendish refers to these two separately, according to Vidal the latter were an elite selection of the former.

The Fighting Braves, many of them Moslems from Kansu, had their origin in the Taiping Rebellion, which was in reality a civil war. Later they had been used to suppress their co-religionists in Kansu and had acquired a reputation for extreme brutality. They played an important role in the siege of the legations and their commander there, Tung Fu-hsiang, was regarded, even by his fellow reactionaries, as a savage ruffian.

The dreaded Kansu Braves. During the Boxer campaign their bark proved to be worse than their bite. (*As above*)

The peacetime establishment of this force was roughly 30,000 men but this could be rapidly increased, as it was during the 1898 re-organization, by the recruitment of every hungry but able-bodied man whom the authorities could entice with the promise of a rice ration and a few taels. These rapid expansions and contractions of numbers were highly profitable to the officials concerned as the Board of War had little or no knowledge of the number of men actually recruited or discharged. However, the regulars appear to have been better paid and rationed than the other elements of the Chinese military establishment. Also, they were rather better equipped, although in the mid-1980s some eighty men out of each 350-man battalion were armed only with a trident, spear or flag. The gingal, or two-man gun, was still widely used, as indeed it was during the siege of the legations. This huge weapon, of one-inch calibre and nine feet in length, must have been unique in the discomfort which it caused to those who fired it until the appearance of the Boyes anti-tank rifle forty years later! Some, though, were simply dummies as the barrels had not been bored out.

The 1898 reforms carried out by Jung Lu seem to have concentrated upon the Disciplined Troops and Fighting Braves and here again there comes to our notice one of the most important figures

Chinese 'Disciplined Troops', probably Moslems. (*Illustrated London News*)

of the late Manchu and early republican era in China. Aged forty, General Yuan Shih-k'ai was a progressive and capable soldier but above all an adept politician. By his betrayal of the Emperor, he had ingratiated himself with both the Empress Dowager and Jung Lu and over the next two years he succeeded in taking a strong anti-Boxer line and in keeping his troops out of the fighting with the foreigners, without losing the good-will of his patrons at Court, a remarkable feat of political dexterity. 'Without scruples and without fear . . . [Yuan is] a man to follow who will probably leave his name in the history of his country,' wrote Vidal with considerable prescience.

The reforms and re-organization involved the redeployment and, to a limited extent, the retraining of approximately 60,000 men in Chihli Province. It appears that only the Disciplined Troops and Fighting Braves were involved and that the Bannermen and Green Regiments were unaffected. The troops concerned were divided into five divisions as follows:

| Commander | Strength | Location |
| --- | --- | --- |
| 1st Division | 14,000 | Shanhaikwan |
| General Sung Ching | | |
| 2nd Division | 14,000 | Lutai |
| General Nieh Shih ch'eng | | |
| 3rd Division | 7,000 | near Tientsin |
| General Yuan Shih-k'ai | | |
| 4th Division | 13,500 | T'ungchou |
| General Tung Fu h'siang | | |
| 5th or Headquarter Division | 10,000 | Peking |
| General Jung Lu (CinC Northern Army) | | |

In addition there were a number of independent units, garrisoning forts and other strong points amounting to about 20,000 men. These were probably Greens and/or Bannermen.

The above were the dispositions in January, 1899. By the summer of 1900 strengths may have increased and some of the locations changed. Also by then General Ma Yu-kun seems to have assumed command in the field of 1st Division as General Sung was too old for active service.

As commander of the only well-trained Chinese Army division, General Yuan Shih k'ai played a crucial role during the seige of the legations and the Allied invasion by doing absolutely nothing. (*Mitchell Library*)

Vidal scored these divisions in order of potential effectiveness on a scale of 1–5, placing only Yuan's 3rd Division in the first category and then only with reservations. Although Yuan's troops took no part in either the siege of the legations, the fighting around Tientsin or in opposing the Allied relief forces, it may be interesting in the light of the overall performance of the northern army in these coming events to record some of the French officer's comments regarding Yuan's division. Yuan, incidentally, was better disposed towards foreigners than most Chinese of his class and during the Boxer period seems to have had particularly close links with the French.

Vidal was a great believer in the Napoleonic maxim that there are no bad soldiers, only bad officers and his comments on Yuan's senior subordinates are scathing. 'Worthless', 'cowardly', 'ignorant', 'obstructionist' are adjectives with which his reports are liberally peppered. The troops, however, he found 'excellent' – a view shared, incidentally, by the British officers who served with the 1st Chinese Regiment during its short life from 1898 to 1906. For example, he

38

found that Yuan's men were good shots and their drill on a par with that of the Prussian Guards in Berlin. The cavalry were fine horsemen and performed skilfully with sabre and lance. The artillery, though slow, fired accurately and the gunners were able to read the European numerals on the gun sights.* For all this, Vidal did not believe the troops would perform well in battle due to the complete absence of good, professional leadership. If Yuan's men were technically proficient, this was due entirely to the expertise and dedication of the European instructors. According to Cavendish, prior to the Jung Lu reforms, these men, former junior officers or senior NCOs of various European armies, were often ignored or held up to ridicule by the Chinese officers, but Yuan was determined that his men should learn from them and they did. The same does not seem to have been the policy of the other divisional commanders.

In any case, these instructors were woefully few. In Yuan's division there were five: Captain Basens, a Belgian artilleryman; Munte, a Norwegian NCO who spoke Chinese and was held in high regard; and three German NCOs, one of whom was an ordnance artificer.

As for establishments, in order to avoid repetition, we will take Yuan's division as an example.

It consisted of the following elements:

| Infantry | 5 'camps' (battalions) | of 1,000 men each | 5,000 |
|---|---|---|---|
| Cavalry | 1 camp | of 500 men | 500 |
| Artillery | 1 camp | of 1,000 men | 1,000 |
| Pioneers | 1 camp | of 425 men | 425 |
| Total (January, 1899)† | | | 6,925 |

As for weapons, particularly small arms, the variety was infinite. German Mannlichers and Mausers were the most commonly found and a number of American Remingtons and French Hotchkiss rifles were also in use. The gingal has already been mentioned. Many up-to-date Maxim machine-guns had been imported but we do not hear of them being used during the Boxer campaign and the Allies

* We will find this to be in sharp contrast to the very poor performance of the Chinese gunners during the siege of the legations.
† By the summer of 1900 this total had risen to about 12,000.

found a number, brand new, stored in arsenals. Presumably they had been purchased simply for the sake of the commissions payable by the manufacturer.

The artillery consisted of both imported and locally produced German Krupp guns as well as British Armstrongs, including some of the most modern versions.

At the turn of the century there were theoretically 1.75 million men under arms in China, but it is quite impossible to say how many there were in practice. Nor has any serious attempt ever been made to calculate the number of Boxers. However, owing to the attitudes of most of the central and southern provinces and the huge distances involved, the likelihood of any reinforcements reaching Chihli during the Boxer campaign was always extremely remote. Therefore the total number of armed men by whom the Allies might have been confronted in north China* never exceeded about 100,000, of whom perhaps the majority were ineffective and some, probably the best, were deliberately kept out of the fighting.

Chinese horsemen on their hardy Mongolian ponies. However, Chinese cavalry did not play a large part in the Boxer campaign. (*Illustrated London News*)

* Not including Manchuria where the Russians fought a completely separate campaign.

# 4

# A Rude Awakening

The [Boxer] movement may
become serious especially if
a leader can be found.

Professor F. Huberty James
(shortly before his murder
in June, 1900)

As it turned out, it was fortunate for the foreign community in
Peking that the British Minister, Sir Claude MacDonald, was a
rather better soldier than he was diplomatist. Indeed, by background
and training, he was a military man, having served nearly twenty
years in the army before entering the Foreign Office.

Commissioned in the 74th Regiment (Highland Light Infantry) in
1872, he had taken part in the expedition to Egypt against Arabi
Pasha in 1882 and, attached to the Black Watch, he had fought at
the Battles of El Teb and Tamai in the Sudan against the famous
Mahdist emir, Osman Digna, in 1884.

After a few years as military attaché at the British Residency in
Cairo under the great pro-consul Sir Evelyn Baring (later Earl of
Cromer) he transferred to West Africa where he participated in a
number of small military expeditions against recalcitrant tribesmen.
But it may have been as a result of his experience on Baring's
staff that he acquired a taste for diplomatic rather than military
manoeuvres. At all events, by 1898 we find him, at the age of 46,
now married with two small daughters, as Her Britannic Majesty's
Minister to the Imperial Court of China in Peking.

Among his senior colleagues were the ministers of France, Germany and the United States. M. Stephen Pichon, the French Minister, was a left-wing politician in his early forties and a close associate
of Clemenceau. Temporarily out of office through the ups and downs

41

Sir Claude MacDonald, the British soldier turned diplomat who commanded the defence of the legations. (*Illustrated London News*)

of electoral fortune, he spent several years as a diplomat and colonial administrator. Later he was twice Foreign Minister and in 1918 was to play a leading role in the negotiations leading to the disastrous Treaty of Versailles. He had been in Peking since 1897 and, although no sinologue, he was probably the most intelligent and best-informed of all the foreign legates. Much of his information came from the Roman Catholic missionaries through their bishop, Monseigneur Favier.

Perhaps the most important role historically, albeit both short and unwitting, in the events surrounding the siege of the legations was played by the bombastic German Minister, Baron Klemens von Ketteler. Another former soldier in his mid-forties, Ketteler had considerable experience in China and some knowledge of the language, but cannot be said to have been sympathetic to the country or its people. He was a man of great courage but little finesse, who doubted the necessity or wisdom of covering the iron fist with the velvet glove.

The American Minister, Mr Edwin Conger, like his British and

42

German colleagues, was a man of military background who had served with some distinction in the Civil War. Older than the others, he was sound and steady, but unimaginative. His wife, on the other hand, was a lady of some eccentricity, who, during the siege, informed anyone who cared to listen that the bullets whistling round their ears were figments of their imagination.

Of the others, we have only vague descriptions, most of which we owe to the acerbic Dr George Morrison, the *Times* correspondent in Peking. He had no great opinion of any of them, although some at least had an amusing side. The Marquese di Salvago Raggi, who had succeeded the disastrous di Martino as the Italian representative, largely ignored the undignified military proceedings by which he was surrounded noisily during the siege and he and his beautiful wife continued to dress elegantly for dinner every night.

Morrison has little to say of Baron Nishi of Japan except that he 'resembled an anthropoid ape'.

But Morrison himself, although by no means a diplomat, is worthy of some attention. An Australian in his thirties of Scottish descent, he regarded himself as an 'Englishman' working for 'England's' interest, an attitude which today would doubtless excite both ridicule and indignation, but which, ninety years ago, was regarded as perfectly normal. He had spent an adventurous youth in the South Seas and elsewhere and had qualified as a medical doctor at Edinburgh. But his heart and livelihood were in journalism and he was among the lions of his profession in his day. His relationship with China and the Chinese was one of fascination rather than affection. Strangely, he seems to have made little effort to learn the language and was thus often dependent on unreliable sinologues like Backhouse for information gleaned from the vernacular press or informed Chinese. Nevertheless, he was seldom hoodwinked and if he was not always right he was usually less wrong than the diplomats.

Life in Peking, though rather circumscribed, was very pleasant for the Corps Diplomatique and the more senior members of the foreign community. There was the usual round of receptions, luncheons and race meetings where the diplomats and their ladies mingled and gossiped to the strains of Sir Robert Hart's not-untalented Chinese orchestra. However, social contact with the Manchus and Chinese, even with the most exalted mandarins, was

Baron Klement von Ketteler, the German minister at Peking. Impulsive and belligerent, by his death he unwittingly saved the lives of his diplomatic colleagues. (*Illustrated London News*)

Mr Edwin H. Conger, the American minister at Peking. No live wire but a steadying influence during the siege of the legations. (*Illustrated London News*)

minimal. The foreigners were not entirely to blame for this. Friendly intercourse with barbarians was discouraged by Chinese tradition and could involve loss of face. That sensitive and intelligent observer of the Chinese scene, the Reverend Arthur Smith, noted, for example, that even Chinese language teachers would ignore or endeavour to avoid their foreign pupils if they met them in the street.

Each legation had its 'Chinese' Secretary, a national of that legation with long experience in China and the ability to speak, read and write Mandarin fluently. He acted as official interpreter and translator to his minister but, in most cases, does not seem to have been particularly well-informed.

The best sources of intelligence for the foreign representatives were the missionaries. They lived and worked in the countryside, many adopted Chinese dress and, to some extent, the Chinese way of life. They even ate Chinese food which, in those days, was usually shunned by the rest of the foreign community. A number of them spoke various dialects fluently, looked upon China as their home and many, particularly the Catholics, never contemplated returning to their native lands. But they were not highly regarded by the diplomats (except the French), who thought them a rum lot, not quite gentlemen, and instigators, albeit unwittingly, of much of the ill-feeling against foreigners. As we have seen, they were not entirely mistaken in this latter belief, but were in error when they ignored the steady flow of intelligence and warnings which the missionaries provided.

Admittedly, there was nothing particularly unusual about reports from the interior of the persecution of Christian converts, the destruction of church property or even the occasional murder of a missionary. Complaints would be filed with the Tsungli Yamen (Foreign Ministry), local troops would eventually be dispatched to quell the disturbances, which would often be over before they arrived, and a few heads, usually the wrong ones, would be chopped off. Such events were fairly commonplace and it has been suggested wryly, though perhaps with some truth, that the reality of the situation in the summer of 1900 was not brought home to the diplomats until the grandstand of their beloved Peking racecourse had been burnt down by the Boxers and, incidentally, a Chinese Christian roasted alive in the conflagration.

Chinese sources suggest that these two missionaries (left and centre) may have been Frederick Brown, an Englishman, and Alexander Martin, an American, both attached to the Allied Relief Expedition as intelligence officers. (*The late Mr Han Zhong Min/Research Centre of Inscriptions and Documents*)

The fact that Sir Claude MacDonald and his ponderous American colleague, Mr Conger, allowed their womenfolk and children to travel to their summer villas in the hills near Peking at the end of May and in early June, with the countryside ablaze around them, gives us an idea of the depth of their complacency. The reasons for this attitude have never been fully explained. Sir Claude, in one of his few public statements on the subject, a lecture to the Royal United Services Institute in 1914, attempted to excuse himself by pointing out that even the Old China Hands 'did not see the Boxer movement on the horizon nor yet comprehended it when it was at their doors',* so how could he and his colleagues, mere 'birds of passage', have foreseen the horrors to come?

For all that, Sir Claude had less excuse than his colleagues for his complacency. As we have seen, he had been in Egypt and the Sudan

* He was quoting the Reverend Arthur Smith.

in the 1880s when the Mahdi, Mohamed Ahmed, and his rebel 'ansar' drove the Egyptian Army, a body of men about as far down the league table of military distinction as the Chinese, from the Sudan, besieged General 'Chinese' Gordon at Khartoum and eventually slew him, his staff, garrison and a large number of civilians both foreign and native. Of course, there are no exact parallels in history but the Boxer movement ought to have had a ring of familiarity about it to MacDonald.

But we must be fair to the diplomats and even to the Old China Hands. If they failed to recognize the Boxers as a special threat to foreigners, it must be borne in mind that China was in a constant state of turmoil and subject to frequent outbreaks of insurrection. Moreover, they believed that even the third-rate Chinese Army would be able to control such a tatterdemalion mob of untrained and badly-armed peasants. No competent leaders of the Boxer movement were discernible – no Spartacus, no Wat Tyler, no Hung Hsiu ch'uan (the Taiping leader), no one who inspired fear or respect. Their very claims to invulnerability, together with their weird incantations and exercises, made them ridiculous in most western eyes. Above all, it was inconceivable that a cunning old bird like the Empress Dowager would set any store by, let alone support, such a rabble. To what end? What could she and even the most xenophobic of her clansmen and mandarins hope to profit from the destruction of their own capital and the slaughter of the representatives of all the greatest Powers on earth?

Furthermore, once the ministers had decided collectively to summon contingents of legation guards from their respective fleets in Chinese waters and these men had arrived, the consensus of opinion (even including Bishop Favier) was that their mere presence would be enough to deter aggression by both Boxers and, if they had thoughts of joining in on the wrong side, Imperial troops. This belief was based on the knowledge of the ferocious reputation of the European soldier (or sailor) in China. He had seldom been defeated by Chinese forces and then only temporarily. He was invincibly armed and equipped and never failed to live up to the name of 'fierce and untameable barbarian'. Such was this reputation that after the arrival of the legation guards one mandarin wrote, 'If the foreign troops sally forth during the night, one soldier would be as strong as a hundred and a hundred as strong as a thousand.' On this occasion, however, rage, hatred and superstition were about to overcome fear.

On the other hand, it has been suggested that the arrival of the legation guards was the spark which ignited the attack on the legations. But the opposite may be argued with equal, or greater, force. Had the guards been summoned sooner and in larger numbers, the deterrent effect might have been sufficient to prevent any assault upon the legations. But it is futile to labour this point, as it is not what happened.

In the event, on 26 May, the foreign legates, having obtained the consent of their own governments, sought permission from the Tsungli Yamen to summon the guards from their fleets which lay at anchor in the Gulf of Chihli. Although at that date the President of the Yamen was still the moderate Prince Ch'ing, that worthy body prevaricated, in keeping with its time-honoured custom in dealings with foreigners. On this occasion, however, its deliberations were probably already infected by the influence of the arch-reactionary, Prince Tuan, who, a fortnight later, was appointed President in place of Prince Ch'ing.

There was no need for foreign guards, the Yamen argued, as steps were already in hand to ensure the security of the legations and foreign property and needed only a little time to take effect. Anyway, 'the Boxers were not worth a smile'. The appearance of a few lightly armed but well-dressed youths, probably Bannermen, did nothing to reassure the diplomats who reiterated their request on 30 May. This time, the Yamen reluctantly gave its consent, setting a limit of thirty men for each legation. No doubt as expected by the Yamen, the limit was ignored and the next day a total of approximately 450 officers and men were summoned from the Allied fleets.

This must have been something of a set-back to the plans of the 'war party' at Court. We will never know in any reliable detail what took place then, or at any other time during the crisis, within the Forbidden City, but it is unlikely that even the most rabid anti-foreign and anti-Christian faction wished the Chinese Army to be seen as the main element of the assault upon the legations and the slaughter of the foreigners and native Christians. It must have been hoped that the virtually unopposed Boxers, provided they were not

48

The Tsungli Yamen, the Chinese Foreign Ministry, whose opinions and advice carried little weight with the Empress Dowager and the anti-foreign party at Court. (*Illustrated London News*)

actually hindered by the regular army, would be able to do the job unaided. Thus, in the aftermath of the gruesome affair, the Imperial Government would be able to evade the responsibility and plead that the atrocity had been perpetrated by revolutionary elements beyond its control. Of course such nonsense would have cut no ice with the enraged Powers, but, it must be remembered, in the words of the Foreign Editor of *The Times*, 'A more hopeless spectacle of fatuous umbecility . . . than the central government of the Chinese Empire . . . is impossible to conceive.'

5

# The Defenders

In present days there is a little band
Of gallant men who hail from England's land
Whose valour great compares with Spartans brave
For such they've shown on land and on the wave.

Sergeant David Hobbs,
Royal Marine Light Infantry, 1900

The above excruciating lines were penned at the time of the siege as part of a poem entitled 'A Gallant 79' in honour of the British contingent of legation guards consisting of three officers and seventy-six men of the Royal Marine Light Infantry and three Royal Navy ratings.*

Had it not been for Russian objections, they would have been 'A Gallant 100', the original number sent from the fleet at Taku to Tientsin, but, at the last minute before their departure by rail for Peking, the senior Russian officer at Tientsin, Colonel Vogack, presumably unable to muster more than seventy-three men himself (there were already six Cossack guards at his Peking Legation), insisted that the British reduce their contingent accordingly. Even in the face of imminent collective destruction, a small and futile card in the Great Game had to be played. There can be no better illustration of the frayed ropes by which the so-called Allies in this crisis were bound together.

As we have seen in the previous chapter the legation guards were summoned to Peking on 30 May, the majority arriving on the evening of the 31st and the rest on 3 June. Of the eleven Powers represented in the Chinese capital, seven were able to produce contingents of

---

* Evidently, Sergeant Hobbs did not consider the three naval ratings as worthy of inclusion in his poem.

Russian Legation guards and friend! All but the 'friend' are probably men of the East Siberian Regiment. (*Institution of Royal Engineers*)

Austrian Legation guards. Most of these sailors came from what is now Yugoslavia. (*National Army Museum*)

fighting men, the exceptions being Holland, Belgium and Spain who had no warships in Chinese waters (and not many anywhere else) from which to draw them.

The Allies were doubtful, assuming the trains arrived at all, of the reception their contingents would receive at the railway terminus outside Peking and how they would fare on the seven-mile march from there to the legations. In the event they were unhindered, but Captain Bowman McCalla,* US Navy, the most senior officer accompanying the first train, feared that the city gates might be closed in their faces and US Marine Private Oscar Upham recalled his detachment breaking into double time in order to avoid this embarrassing and potentially dangerous possibility.

The combined force was made up of the following elements:

| | *Officers* (including Midshipmen) | *Men* |
|---|---|---|
| Austria | 7 | 30 |
| France | 3 | 75 |
| Germany | 1 | 51 |
| Great Britain | 3 | 79 |
| Italy | 2 | 39 |
| Japan | 1 | 24 |
| Russia | 2 | 79 |
| USA | 2 + 1 M.O. | 53 |
| Total | 22 | 430 |

(See Appendix A for nominal roles of some of the contingents)

From the French contingent were detached one officer and twenty-nine men and from the Italian one midshipman and ten men to guard the Peit'ang Cathedral.

Most of the guards were either marines or sailors but the Russian contingent seems to have included a few soldiers of the East Siberian Regiment as well as the Cossacks mentioned above.

In addition, all the able-bodied European and Japanese male civilians and officers who happened to be on leave or duty in Peking were 'called-up' as armed auxiliaries. There were over a hundred of

* He returned to Tientsin next day

these, including Captain Francis Poole, whose brother Wordsworth was the British Legation doctor. Although a self-confessed sinophobe, Captain Poole had been sent out to Peking by the War Office to learn the language.* He had arrived only a few days before the legation guards and kept a diary throughout the siege. He played a significant role in the defence of the legations and was awarded the Distinguished Service Order.

Witnessing the entry into Peking of the various contingents of legation guards Poole's comments were fairly predictable. 'Ours [Royal Marines],' he wrote in his diary, '[were] naturally the smartest.' The Americans were 'a serviceable-looking lot' but the Russians and Italians were 'very dirty'.

However, the Reverend Arthur Smith, although an anglophile American, while not disputing the smartness of the British contingent, was unimpressed in other respects. Some of those who saw them, he wrote, 'were enabled to comprehend something of the reasons for the disasters in the South African campaign . . . the 79 British marines were patient, brave and always ready for duty . . . but officers and men alike were young and without the smallest experience of the kind of warfare in which they were now to engage.' While it is true that no member of the contingent had ever seen a shot fired in anger, it is not clear where the reverend gentleman might have expected them to have gained experience of the rare, possibly unique, ordeal which they were about to face. Even the most battle-hardened of the detachments, namely the Americans who had come from the campaign in the Philippines, and those Japanese who had served in the recent Sino-Japanese war, would never have come face to face with such a situation before and nor, incidentally, were they ever likely to again.

Impartial assessment of the qualities of each national contingent is hard to find. The judgement of military virtue is, apparently, in the eye of the beholder and the extent of that virtue, or lack of it, depends upon the nationality of the eye. The various witnesses, in an age of fervent patriotism, seldom criticized their own men and seldom praised the 'competition'. However, as Dr Johnson

* In the immemorial, and probably immortal, tradition of the British Army, no sooner had Poole qualified as an 'interpreter' in Chinese than he was immediately posted to Egypt!

The NCOs of the British Legation guard. Seated centre is Sergeant Murphy and to his left (with leg in plaster) is Corporal Gregory. Sitting on the ground is probably Leading Signalman Swannell but the others cannot be individually identified with any certainty. (*Royal Marines Museum*)

suggested, the prospect of imminent and violent death concentrates the mind. Thus, to the natural fighting spirit and professional pride of these men was added the certain knowledge that defeat or surrender could lead only to death, and probably a horrible and lingering death at that. Furthermore, in a more romantic and chivalrous era than ours, the fact that the many women and children under their protection would suffer a similar fate no doubt increased their resolve and determination to fight to the last.

It should also be borne in mind that their opponents were not only their enemies in war but the enemies of their religion. Ninety years ago Christianity had a stronger hold on the minds of the peoples of Europe and North America than it does today. Of course the Japanese would have been unaffected by the religious implications of the Boxers' anti-Christian crusade but most of the men of the other contingents, particularly the Russians, French (mostly Bretons) and Italians recruited from peasant and sea-faring stock, would have felt a powerful resentment that their ancient religion should be threatened by a people they regarded as benighted heathens.

Perhaps the most outstanding example of inspired Christian courage was that of Enseigne de Vaisseau (Lieutenant) Paul Henry, the

54

young Breton naval officer assigned to command the defence of the Peit'ang or North Cathedral. A *'chevalier sans peur et sans reproche'*, he led, fought and died with a selfless heroism reminiscent of the knights of Arthurian legend. But his story will come later.

Certainly the guards were not armed or equipped to withstand a long siege. Apart from their rifles and a few hundred rounds per man, they had no reserve ammunition, no heavy weapons and only three machine-guns; the Americans had a light Colt 236, the Austrians a Maxim and the British an obsolete and highly unreliable multi-barrelled Nordenfeldt .45. The only artillery was a little one-pounder gun belonging to the Italians for which they had 120 shells. The Russians were supposed to have brought a heavier weapon with them but they forgot it at Tientsin railway-station, although they remembered its ammunition.

Presumably it did not occur to those who sent them that a lengthy siege was in the offing. After all, mighty fleets with thousands more sailors and marines lay at anchor only a hundred miles from Peking and it took but a day to get there by rail. Furthermore, in those early days at the end of May and the beginning of June, it had not yet dawned upon the foreigners that the Chinese Army, far from protecting them, would play a much greater role in attacking them than the Boxers themselves.

However, as the month of June matured so the security situation in and around Peking deteriorated. As Sir Claude MacDonald put it, 'Christian establishments were burnt down; the summer residence of the British Minister and his staff, just completed at the cost of £10,000, was similarly treated; two devoted English missionaries (Robinson and Norman) were murdered near the Peking–Tientsin line and the anti-foreign party at Court seemed to have obtained a complete ascendancy over the Empress Dowager.'

Many years later one of the Royal Marine Light Infantrymen, Corporal Gowney, recalled asking a Chinese employee of the British Legation as they marched into the city if they would be returning by the same route. Lifting his eyes up to Heaven, the man replied comfortingly, 'No, no – you go up top'!

Why Corporal Gowney, all his comrades and those whom he had been sent to defend, did not 'go up top' remains the abiding mystery of the Siege of the Legations.

# PEKING~TARTAR CITY

Hsi
Chih
Men

Tung
Chih
Men

T   A   R   T   A   R

Tianan Men

IMPERIAL
CITY

Ch'ao
Yang
Men

Peit'ang
Cathedral

FORBIDDEN
CITY

Winter
Palace

Tsungli
Yamen

(Foreign Ministry)

C   I   T   Y

LEGATIONS

Tung
Pien
Men

T   A   R   T   A   R     W   A   L   L

Shun
Chih Men

Chien
Men

Hata
Men

Scale of Yards
500    O    500   1000   1500   2000

C   H   I   N   E   S   E       C   I   T   Y

## 6

# The Diary of a Chinese Summer

I have a rendezvous with Death
At some disputed barricade

From 'Rendezvous' by Alan Seeger

### Peking, 1st June 1900

M. Stephen Pichon telegraphed the Quai d'Orsay with the information that the main body of legation guards had reached Peking
the previous evening. Someone, perhaps M. Delcassé, the Foreign
Minister, noted optimistically on the file copy of the telegram, 'Now
we can consider calm at Peking as assured'.

If anyone was calm at Peking it was not M. Pichon. Gifted
with rather more imagination than such diplomatic colleagues as
MacDonald, Conger or von Ketteler and closer to the well-informed
Favier, as the situation deteriorated so did Pichon's morale. Anglo-
Saxon observers were shocked at the absence of a stiff upper lip in
such a senior man who should have been setting an example to his
juniors. 'A craven hearted cur,' was how George Morrison saw him
and to Francis Poole he was 'a funkstick', while one of his fellow
countrymen went further, remarking that '*il ne fait que pisser dans
ses caleçons*'.

### 2nd June

Lieutenant Baron von Raden, commander of the Russian contingent
of legation guards, discovered that he had left his artillery piece and
nearly half his rifle ammunition behind at Tientsin railway station.
This meant that his men would have only 140 rounds of ammunition

57

each. Such oversights were not unusual in the Tsarist navy and von Raden regarded them as no more than 'unfortunate'.

Sir Claude MacDonald decided that his sister-in-law, Miss Armstrong, and his two small daughters might be in some small need of protection at the legation summer retreat (soon to be burnt to the ground) in the hills near Peking, so he sent one of the three Royal Marine officers, Captain Wray, and a party of eleven marines to guard them. Wisely, Wray brought Miss Armstrong and the children back to Peking on the 4th.

## 5th June

With Chinese Christian refugees pouring into the legation quarter seeking foreign protection, somewhat belated defensive preparations were put in hand.

M. Pichon reported to Paris the apparently wild and unaccountable behaviour of his German colleague, Baron von Ketteler, who, it seemed to Pichon, was deliberately trying to provoke the Chinese. Was he attempting to precipitate a situation in which the Imperial dynasty would fall? Had he such instructions from Berlin? On one occasion, Pichon reported, von Ketteler had proposed 'marching on the Summer Palace'. It is interesting to speculate what the outcome of such a bold initiative might have been. In view of the later performance of the Chinese Army, it seems quite likely the Palace guards would have surrendered without much resistance to the dreaded barbarians, but what would have happened thereafter, both locally and internationally, is anyone's guess.

## 6th June

Sir Claude MacDonald proposed to the assembled foreign legates that an audience with the Empress Dowager and the Emperor be sought. This may have been a move to dampen von Ketteler's enthusiasm for precipitate military action but seems to have come to nothing. The German was unable to persuade his colleagues as to the wisdom of violent measures but took a unilateral, if minor, step by seizing and thrashing with his walking stick a Boxer youth whom he had caught sharpening his sword in Legation Street.

## 8th–9th June

Both Captain Poole and Lieutenant von Raden recorded arrivals of large numbers of Fighting Braves and Disciplined Troops in Peking. At first it was thought that these had been brought in for the protection of the legations but when a Russian professor at Peking University was attacked by Braves and forced to escape at the gallop it became evident whose side the troops were on.

Off Taku, the Allied admirals were receiving increasingly urgent signals from their respective ministers at Peking, although some of these were contradictory. For example, M. Michael de Giers, the Russian legate, is reputed to have sent three telegrams in one day, the first calling for immediate reinforcements, the second cancelling the request and the third reinstating the first. The admirals, as ever trammelled by the conflicting requirements of their political masters at home, were not of one mind. St Petersburg was anxious that the other Powers, particularly the British and the Japanese, should be seen by the Chinese as aggressors and thus emerge from the crisis in bad odour. But, at the same time, the Tsarist government did not want to miss any opportunities of increasing their power and influence, particularly in Manchuria. We do not have access to the signals which sped between the Russian fleet commander, Admiral Alexeiev, to St Petersburg and back, but we may assume that they were muddled and ambiguous.

Meanwhile, the Japanese government was torn between the advice it was getting from Baron Nishi in Peking, which was to stay out of what he saw as a Euro-Christian problem, and the pressure it was under from the British Legation in Tokyo to join in wholeheartedly. Unwilling to offend Britain, whom it regarded as an ally against Russia, it came down eventually on the side of intervention.

Similarly, Washington was in a quandary. President McKinley, a Republican, was seeking re-election and did not wish to upset the Right by failing to protect American lives and property in China, especially the missionaries. However, he feared accusations from the Left of collaboration with 'imperialist' Powers in the bullying of China. No doubt Secretary of State Hay felt he had overcome this dilemma by letting it be known that the United States was prepared to involve itself in a rescue mission to Peking, if necessary, while

59

remaining aloof from the diplomatic machinations of the other Powers. Perhaps he had, as McKinley won the election, only to be assassinated in the following year.

The British, bogged down in South Africa, sought to minimize their military commitment in China and their main diplomatic thrust was aimed at ensuring maximum Japanese involvement. France tended to follow Russia's line, while Germany saw the chance to throw her weight about in the Far East. The Italians blew trumpets and waved flags.

Remarkably, by the evening of 9 June some sort of consensus had been reached and contingents of seamen and marines of various nationalities were landed at T'angku (where the railway started) for the twenty-five-mile journey to Tientsin on the first leg of their mission to reinforce or relieve the Peking legations.

In command of this hastily assembled force was Vice-Admiral Sir Edward Seymour,* an old salt whose China experience went back

Admiral Seymour (seated right) and Captain Jellicoe (seated left) with the fleet in the Gulf of Chihli off Taku. (*National Maritime Museum*)

* Admiral of the Fleet Sir Edward Seymour, OM GCB (1840–1929).

60

forty years when, as a young midshipman serving under his uncle, Admiral Sir Michael, he had landed at Taku during the Arrow War.

Commandant Vidal, arriving in Tientsin a few days later after a routine tour of Korea, commented that this was the first and last time that a single officer exercised undisputed and undivided command over an Allied operation during the campaign. Immediately under him were two other able and resolute officers, Captains McCalla* and von Usedom respectively of the United States and Imperial German navies. Also under his command were some famous names of the future: his Chief of Staff, Captain Jellicoe, Commander Beatty and Lieutenant Keyes.†

The Seymour Expedition consisted of the following elements of sailors and marines:

| British‡ | 915 | American | 111 |
|----------|-----|----------|-----|
| German | 512 | Japanese | 54 |
| Russian | 312 | Italian | 42 |
| French | 157 | Austrian | 26 |
| Total | | | 2,129 |

The assembly of the force and its transiting arrangements through Tientsin were fraught with difficulties, involving the Allied naval and consular authorities, often at loggerheads with each other, Chinese officialdom, in receipt of confused and conflicting instructions from the Forbidden City, and railway staff of various nationalities. However, apparently with the permission of the Viceroy of

* Rear Admiral Bowman McCalla (1844–1910).

† Admiral of the Fleet Lord Keyes GCB, KCVO, CMG, DSO (1872–1945) did not take part in the Seymour Expedition but remained with the fleet in command of the destroyer HMS *Fame*.

‡ The British contingent comprised the following:

62 naval and marine officers
640 naval ratings
213 marines

3 nine pounder guns
1 six pounder gun
2 .45 Maxim machine-guns
6 .45 Nordenfeldt machine-guns

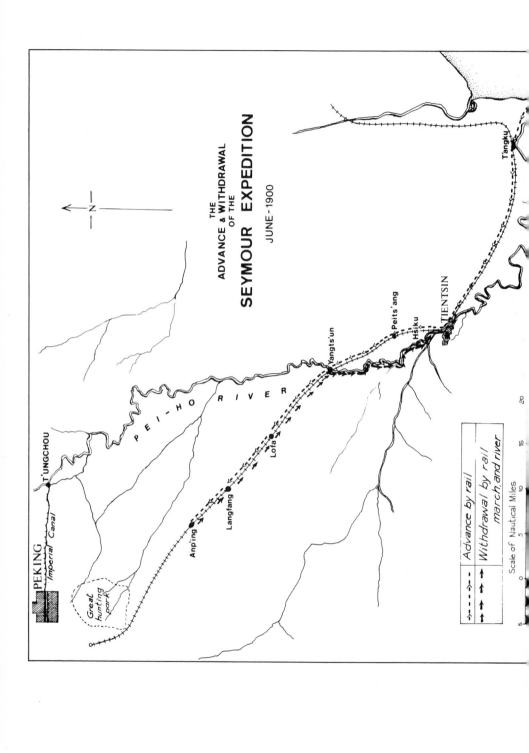

THE
ADVANCE & WITHDRAWAL
OF THE
SEYMOUR EXPEDITION
JUNE - 1900

PEKING

T'UNGCHOU

Imperial Canal

Great hunting park

Anp'ing

Langfang

Lofa

PEI-HO RIVER

Yangts'un

Peits'ang

Hsiku

TIENTSIN

Tangku

|  | Advance by rail |
| --- | --- |
|  | Withdrawal by rail |
|  | march, and river |

Scale of Nautical Miles

0    5    10    15    20

Chihli, five loaded trains chuffed out of Tientsin station at mid-morning on the 10th.

## 10th June

At this stage no one, not even the Chinese commanders themselves, knew where the Chinese Army stood, both literally and metaphorically. There had been no time for reconnaissance and the only 'Intelligence Officer' with the expedition was a young former Grenadier Guards officer called Clive Bigham, who was on his way to take up a post at the British Legation in Peking. This debonair young gentleman had been to China once before and therefore must 'know the form'. Anyway, Sir Edward Seymour would have reasoned, his father was a damned good chap and a member of the Reform Club.

Seymour has been criticized for 'behaving like a midshipman' and charging off into the blue without any knowledge of what awaited him along the railway line between Tientsin and Peking. This is all very well but it is wisdom with hindsight. Urgent if confusing summons had been reaching the admirals from Peking; they and most of their governments had agreed that a rescue mission should be mounted without delay and that Seymour, as commander of the largest single national element, should lead it. It was only about eighty miles, a three- or four-hour rail journey, which he had no firm reasons to assume would be interrupted. And how were the men on the spot to explain themselves if they simply hung about at sea or in Tientsin waiting for something to happen in Peking? Also, it is worth recalling that only fifteen years before, the officer commanding the expedition to rescue Gordon from Khartoum, Colonel Sir Charles Wilson, had been castigated for delaying his departure from Metemmah for two days in order to carry out reconnaissance and to re-victual his steamers. Thus, it was said, he was responsible for the fall of Khartoum and the death of General Gordon. The arm-chair critic usually likes to have his cake and eat it.

Ironically, according to Captain McCalla, no sooner had the trains steamed out of Tientsin station than the British Consul received a telegram from Sir Claude MacDonald revoking the urgent pleas for help of the previous day. However, there is no reason to set too much store by this as the message itself might well have been revoked later in the day, if not by MacDonald then by one of the other legates. The idea of working in concert was not coming easily to the Allies-through-necessity.

## Peking, 11th June

In confident expectation of the arrival of the Seymour expedition at the railway terminus, some distance to the south of the Chinese City, a number of legation officials and other foreigners set out to meet their deliverers in the afternoon. Unfortunately they were about two months too early and, far from receiving their friends, they were attacked by their enemies. The Chancellor of the Japanese Legation, Mr Sugiyama, was hauled from his Peking cart and cut to pieces. It is unclear if his assailants were Boxers, soldiers or simply roughs as it was not always easy to tell the difference, but they were probably soldiers as it was rumoured that they had cut out his heart and sent it to their commanding officer.

Shocked and disappointed, the various reception committees returned apprehensively to their legations, counting themselves lucky in avoiding Mr Sugiyama's fate. Corporal Gowney's hopes for the immediate future were not improved when he learnt from some missionaries that, according to Chinese sources, the Boxers had fixed 19 June, the 30th anniversary of the Tientsin massacre, as the day on which all foreigners would be exterminated.

## With the Seymour Expedition

In fact, at the time of Sugiyama's murder, the Seymour expedition was only half-way to Peking at Langfang. It had progressed smoothly as far as Lofa, having passed through General Nieh's 2nd Division garrison at Yangts'un without incident. But after Lofa the line was found to be damaged and track re-laying slowed the train convoy to snail's pace. At Langfang it ground to a temporary halt.

## 12th June

The dates of particular events vary in participants' accounts but at Langfang messengers from the legations brought warnings to

64

Seymour that he was likely to be seriously opposed in the Great Hunting Park south of Peking, probably by elements of both the 4th and 5th Divisions. Then, in the afternoon, the Boxers launched their first attack on the expedition, attacks which were to be repeated over the next few days.

Sub-Lieutenant Maurice Cochrane of HMS *Centurion*, in charge of one of the Maxim machine-gun detachments,* recognized the Boxers immediately. 'Their distinguishing feature is red,' he wrote to his parents afterwards, 'red caps, red socks, red sashes, and very formidable swords and spears with red on them.' Also he found them hard to stop: 'they work themselves into an extreme state of hypnotism and certainly do not for the moment feel body wounds. We have all learnt that they take a tremendous lot of killing and I myself put four man-stopping revolver bullets into one man before he dropped.' However, the more prosaic Captain McCalla was inclined to blame the lack of stopping power of the 6mm rifle, with which the United States Navy was equipped, for the Boxer's apparent invulnerability to bullets.

McCalla has left a vivid account of one Boxer attack on the trains. 'They reached the water tank . . . and several of the leaders were killed within a few feet of the train . . . recognizing Captain Jellicoe's† clear voice calling for the Maxim and looking out of the car [railway carriage] window I saw the Boxers in a wedge led by a very large Chinaman who was wielding a two-handed sword. Grasping a rifle from one of my men I sprang to the ground . . . opening fire myself at the flank of the enemy. . . . I almost immediately heard the sound of Captain Jellicoe's Maxim, which cut down the head of the on-rushing column. The leader escaped the fire from the Maxim but, turning at a right-angle, he came directly towards me. At this critical moment, I was seized by one of my men, a coloured Oiler, Smith, who at first was more intent in endeavouring to haul me towards the steps of the car than on using his own rifle. It required

---

* Commander M. E. Cochrane, DSO, RN (1879–1943). When Cochrane brought his detachment up from T'angku to Tientsin by rail in early June, the Chinese ticket-inspector charged him $1.50 for transporting the Maxim, described on the ticket as a 'cannon', although Cochrane had tried to conceal the weapon under a rug!

† Admiral of the Fleet the Earl Jellicoe, OM, KCVO (1859–1935).

several seconds for me to extricate myself from my would-be rescuer and direct him to open fire on the few remaining Boxers. By that time, a gallant young English signal boy armed with a rifle had also come to my assistance . . . the Boxer leader was within thirty yards of us, advancing gallantly and though my first shot hit him it was not entirely disabling but the second shot from my rifle proved fatal.'

In this action, among other casualties, five Italian sailors were killed and the Boxers left eighty-eight dead on or near the railway line, having taken the precaution of cutting the throats of their own wounded so that they should not fall into the hands of the foreign devils. Two of the Italians were stragglers but the other three, on picket duty several hundred yards from the train, had been caught napping by the Boxers. The countryside between Tientsin and Peking was dead flat and intensively cultivated with maize and millet, which, at that time of year, was well grown, affording excellent cover right up to the railway embankment.

## 13th June

Seymour was now in serious difficulty and, despite Vidal's contention that the British admiral's command was undisputed, his orders began to be challenged by the senior officers of some of the other nationalities.

It was impossible to eliminate, even in the face of deep crisis, the mutual suspicions which had plagued the European Powers for centuries, so when Seymour requested the French and German commanders to move their trains back to Yangts'un in order to secure the station, communications with Tientsin and thus a line of retreat, they refused, assuming that here was a British trick to enable Seymour to get his own men to Peking before the others. However perfidious Albion may be, it is highly improbable that the harassed and beleaguered Admiral had any such thought in the circumstances, but the episode typified the uneasy relationships which remained between the Allies throughout the Boxer campaign.

McCalla believed that the Franco-German refusal had a crucial effect on the campaign as a whole. While admitting that he himself would have been reluctant to remain at Yangts'un with his American contingent, if there was any prospect of the others reaching Peking, he maintained that had the French and Germans accepted Seymour's request, communications with Tientsin, both by rail and telegraph, and by extension, with the fleets in Chinese waters, would not have been interrupted. It was, he wrote, Seymour's enforced silence and their alarm at the possible fate of his force which caused the Allied admirals to seize the Taku forts and thus precipitate a state of war with China.

By the next morning it was too late. A train attempting to return to Tientsin for supplies found the line irreparably cut beyond Yangts'un and that night Yangts'un station (and presumably the telegraph office) was destroyed by the Boxers, without any interference from General Nieh. Seymour had lost his line of retreat.

## 14th June

From Peking to Taku chaos and confusion was spreading. Nobody knew what anybody else was doing or had had done to them. In the absurdly short distance between Tientsin and Peking, on a rail journey which normally took three and a half hours, Seymour and two thousand men had disappeared into thin air.

In the legation quarter of Peking, the foreign and Christian communities waited, wondered and trembled. In the Forbidden City the deadly debate as to what should be done with them rumbled on. The moderates and the reactionaries, ever watchful of the Empress Dowager's mood, fenced and parried, their very lives at stake; a wrong word, too mild or too bold, might bring a whispered death sentence or the hint that the speaker should take his own life and count himself lucky.

The Chinese generals too must play their own game of survival. On whose side should they be? Was Imperial support moving for or against the Boxers? Should the foreign devils be slain or succoured? Should their armies be opposed, aided or ignored? Every man had to make his own decision and bear the consequences.

At Tientsin, divided into a walled native city and the French and British 'Concession' Settlements to its south-east, tensions were rising. Rumours that the invincible barbarian had been checked increased the boldness and confidence of the bitterly anti-foreign

Russian troops marching through the Foreign Concessions at Tientsin. Mostly conscripts, they were badly led and trained but possessed immense powers of endurance. (*National Army Museum*)

Chinese population. The foreign garrison* of about 2,500 men, the majority Russian, was placed on full alert. The danger, as the admirals off Taku saw it, lay in the isolation from each other of four separate concentrations of foreigners, both military and civilian: they and their fleets off Taku; the Tientsin Settlements; the Seymour expedition; and the Peking legations. In order to relieve the last of these, Seymour had set out hastily and unprepared; now the reliever must be relieved and in order to do that, they reasoned, the Taku forts must be neutralized and Tientsin held secure.

In Canton the Grand Old Man of Chinese politics, Li Hung-chang, received a last desperate appeal by telegram from his old friend Sir Robert Hart. The previous night fires blazing unchecked throughout Peking had caught Sir Robert's house and burnt it to the ground, destroying the accumulated treasures of a lifetime. Fortunately for posterity, his journals survived, all seventy volumes being rescued from the conflagration by a young Customs officer, Leslie Sandercock. Sir Robert's telegram read: 'You have killed missionaries; that

---

* These had been moved in earlier in the Boxer crisis and were not a permanent garrison at that time.

is bad enough but if you harm the legations you will violate the most sacred international obligations and create an impossible situation.' Later that day telegraphic communication between the legations and the outside world was cut.

In due course appeals for intervention were to reach Li from another quarter, from no less a personage than the Empress Dowager herself. But the ever-cautious Li lingered in the south, using one excuse after another, reserving his energies (and possibly his head) for the inevitable nemesis which he knew would eventually overwhelm his imperial mistress, whatever the outcome of the siege of the legations.

Li Hung-chang, the Elder Statesman whose skilled negotiations with the victorious Allies saved the Empress Dowager from humiliation and loss of face. (*Institution of Royal Engineers*)

## Peking, 15th–19th June

Boxer activity in Peking was reaching a crescendo. Great palls of smoke hung over the city as they rampaged through the streets, burning, looting and murdering. The legation guards mounted several sorties to rescue beleaguered Christians, killing a number of

Boxers in savage hand-to-hand fighting. The 'fierce and untameable barbarian' was already living up to his reputation.

George Morrison accompanied one of these sorties and afterwards snatched a few moments to scribble a rather garbled, but nevertheless blood-curdling, account of it in his diary. 'Up early very much refreshed,' he wrote, 'had a chit from Sir Claude MacDonald asking, will I go out? Captain Wray, 20 British, 10 Americans and 5 Japanese with an officer and Captain Shiba. Damned poor not knowing his own mind. We made a raid on a temple 30 yards from the Austrian outpost; the Austrians coming up afterwards. 45 killed – butchered. Christian captives with hands tied being immolated while actually massacring, 5 already dead. Rescued three. One accidentally killed. All Boxers killed; only one dared to face us. I killed myself at least six. Back tired having paraded city and witnessed devastation in many places.'

'Damned poor not knowing his own mind' is more likely to refer to Wray than to Colonel (not Captain) Goro Shiba, the Japanese Military Attaché, who was acknowledged as an outstanding officer. Wray, on the other hand, was later described by Poole as an

Fires over Peking started by Boxers shortly before the beginning of the Siege of the Legations. (*National Army Museum*)

70

'excitable, irresponsible chap'. '45 killed' refers to Boxers, not Austrians.

Morrison's last dispatch to *The Times* before the siege closed in on the legations was published in London on 18 June. It was a measured, restrained account of a deteriorating situation, describing the burning of the East Cathedral, much other Christian property and the Maritime Customs buildings. It had left Peking by special (and highly paid) messenger for Tientsin on the 14th and was telegraphed from there.

These were days not only of terror but of uncertainty and doubt. Where was Seymour? Had he been forced back or was his arrival imminent? No one knew. Nor was it yet clear where the various elements of the Chinese army stood. Would they, at last, deal firmly with the Boxers? They, the regular troops, were to be seen in large numbers around the legation quarter, but in what capacity were they there, as attackers or defenders? Again, no one knew. But perhaps clarification was at hand.

On the morning of the 18th Sir Claude MacDonald was informed that a high-ranking delegation from the Chinese Government waited upon him. Two of its members, officials of the Tsungli Yamen, were known to Sir Claude, but the third, Li Shan, Comptroller of the Imperial Household, was not. The spokesman for the trio was Hsu Ching-cheng, formerly minister at Berlin and St Petersburg, and his approach was oblique. His delegation, he said, had come directly from the Empress Dowager with a message for Lady MacDonald expressing regret that she and the other foreign ladies and members of the legations had been incommoded by the activities of various bandits and that their summer holiday arrangements in the western hills (where their country residences were located) had been disrupted. These ruffians, however, would soon be dealt with and all would return to normal. Sir Claude replied that the Empress Dowager's message would be conveyed to Lady MacDonald, adding, perhaps with a touch of mild asperity, that the foreign legates had repeatedly warned the Tsungli Yamen of the state of affairs which was now causing such concern to all.

Having delivered himself of these polite preliminaries, Hsu Ching-cheng came to the point. What, he asked, were the intentions of Her Britannic Majesty's Government towards the Manchu dynasty

Lady MacDonald, who was the object of the Empress Dowager's entirely bogus concern. (*Illustrated London News*)

and towards China as a whole? Did the Powers seek to partition the country among themselves? No, replied Sir Claude, his government was well disposed towards the dynasty and had no plans for the dismemberment of the Chinese Empire, but, owing to the destruction of the railway and telegraph lines, he was now totally isolated in Peking and was therefore unable to convey to the delegation his government's current position in detail. However, he added, he felt it unlikely that it would be reassured when it learnt of the state of anarchy into which Peking had been allowed to drift. With this Hsu Ching-cheng and his colleagues had to be satisfied and after some further discussion along the same lines they proceeded to similar meetings with the Russian and American ministers from whom they received similar reactions.

The delegation's purpose had been to allay the fear and rage which the Empress Dowager had felt upon receiving a Note, purporting to come from the Powers but in reality forged by Prince Tuan, setting out several unacceptable demands which would, in effect, strip the Imperial Government of most of its authority. Their timing, however, was fatal to the unfortunate members of the delegation. At the very moment when they were reporting their findings and impressions to the Old Buddha news of the threat to the Taku forts by the Allies reached the Forbidden City, news which hardly lent credence to the rather vague assurances with which the delegation had returned from the legations. Rather, the seizure of the forts would add substance and fact to the imperious demands contained in the forged Note.

One of the Taku Forts captured by the Allies. (*The late Mr Han Zhong Min/ Research Centre of Inscriptions and Documents*)

At the time of their meetings with the delegation the existence of this forgery was unknown to the foreign legates; nor were they, or the delegation, aware that the Taku forts had already been stormed and put out of action by the Allies. The arrogance of the forged Note and the 'unprovoked' aggression at Taku provided the excuses which the Empress Dowager and the anti-foreign party at Court needed to declare war on the Powers. They also led to the downfall and eventual execution of the trio of 'appeasers' whose assurance of the goodwill of the Powers could now be interpreted as false.

Thus, on 19 June, every foreign legate (and Sir Robert Hart) received a document timed and dated 'Four hours after noon on the 23rd day of the 5th moon, 23rd year of the Emperor Kuang-Hsu (i.e. 4 pm, 19 June 1900)'. In short, this demanded that the recipients, their staffs and the legation guards should leave Peking under escort within 24 hours and proceed to Tientsin as, following the Allied aggression at Taku, the Imperial Government could no longer guarantee their security in Peking. No mention was made of the missionaries, other foreign nationals or the Chinese Christians, nor was any explicit declaration of war made in it.*

Ignorant of events at Taku and in the wake of the apparently successful visit of the mandarins on the previous day, this ultimatum was received by most but not all of the legates with, to use MacDonald's word, stupefaction. An immediate conference was called at the French Legation but on the way there MacDonald met the Russian minister, de Giers, who, to the Scotsman's surprise, expressed his satisfaction with the Note, which, he said, indicated that the Chinese Government had come to its senses and was behaving correctly. MacDonald, however, offered the opinion that the Note was a ruse to lure them from the comparative security of the legations and massacre them in the open, a point of view to which he did not adhere very firmly over the next few hours.

The diplomats deliberated long and hard. The problem of language must have lengthened the debate. Although most diplomatists of the day spoke passable French, the lingua franca of diplomacy, the Japanese Minister, Baron Tokujiro Nishi, spoke only his mother tongue and Russian. Therefore, he could communicate directly with none but de Giers who then translated what Nishi said (or perhaps what he, de Giers, wanted them to hear) to the others and vice versa. It is not clear where Nishi stood in the matter – earlier he had counselled his own government against co-operation with the Christian Powers but the murder of his Chancellor may have altered

---

* There is some uncertainty on the question of a formal declaration of war by China against the Powers. No such declaration ever seems to have reached any of the legations or their home governments. However, according to Chester C. Tan in *The Boxer Catastrophe*, an edict, presumably for internal circulation within the Imperial Government, was issued declaring war on 25 June, 1900.

his view – while de Giers, Pichon and Conger were for accepting the Chinese ultimatum. MacDonald seems to have sat on the fence and only von Ketteler was for refusing, probably for the wrong reasons although he was undoubtedly right. By midnight a formula had been agreed. The order to depart was to be accepted in principle but a meeting with the Tsungli Yamen was to be sought for 9 o'clock the following morning to discuss the details of their departure and to arrange a delay in its implementation. Observing the proper protocol, a reply to this effect was sent over the signature of the Spanish minister, Cologon, as doyen of the Corps Diplomatique.

By the time this communication had reached the Tsungli Yamen a new and fateful day was dawning, a hideous day, the sunrise obscured by palls of smoke and the cock-crow drowned by the war-cries of the Boxers and the screams of their victims.

## Taku, 16th–17th June

We must now retrace our steps a few days in time and a few score miles across north China to Taku.

Here the admirals of the Allied fleets had issued an ultimatum of their own to the Viceroy of Chihli at Tientsin dated 16 June. It read as follows:

'The Allied Powers since the beginning of the troubles have landed detachments without opposition for the protection of their nationals and Diplomatic Body against the rebels who are known by the name of Boxers.

'At first the representatives of the Imperial authority seemed to understand their duty and made apparent efforts to re-establish order but now they clearly show their sympathy for the enemies of the foreigners by placing troops on the railway lines and by placing torpedoes at the entrance of the Pei-ho [River]. These acts show that the Government forgets its solemn engagements towards the foreigners and as the commanding officers of the allied forces are bound to remain in constant communication with the detachments on land, they have decided to occupy provisionally by consent or by force the Taku Forts.

'The limit of the time for their surrender to the allied forces is 2 o'clock in the morning of 17th June 1900.'

The style of this communication must have been as distasteful to the Chinese as its message. The gruff sailors who had drafted it were not subtle men. The demand was blunt and incapable of misunderstanding. It left no room for manoeuvre, delay or prevarication. Hand over the forts or else, it said.*

But perhaps the admirals did not feel quite the confidence which their ultimatum implied. The larger ships of the combined Allied fleet in the Gulf of Chihli could not cross the sand-bar which effectively blocked the entrance to the Pei-ho River to all but shallow-draft vessels. The destruction of the forts by heavy naval bombardment from the big ships was ruled out. In the first place several of the Allies, notably the Russians and the Americans, wanted this to be a low-key affair and there are few more spectacular or sensational manifestations of war than lengthy and concentrated shelling by large-calibre naval guns. Furthermore, at this stage, the Allies wished to occupy the forts temporarily rather than destroy them.

At the time when a copy of the ultimatum was delivered by a Russian officer to the commander of the forts, at about 10 pm on the 16th, the Allies had ten small vessels already over the sand-bar in the river. These were:

HMS *Fame*, a British destroyer, mounting one 12-pdr QF gun and five 6-pdr QF guns.
HMS *Whiting*, an identical vessel.
HMS *Algerine*, a British sloop, mounting six 4-inch QF guns and a number of machine-guns. She was old and unarmoured.
HIMS *Iltis*, an old German sloop similar to *Algerine*.
HIRMS *Gilyak*, a new Russian gun-boat, heavily (perhaps over-) armed with one 4.7-inch QF gun and six 12-pdr QF guns.
HIRMS *Bobr*, an old Russian gun-boat, mounting one 9-inch BL gun and one 6-inch BL gun.
HIRMS *Koreytz*, similar to the above with heavier guns. A British naval officer noted, 'this ship had the heaviest, although probably the least efficient, armament of any of the Allied squadron'.

* The American Admiral Kempff, presumably under instruction from his government, disapproved of the ultimatum and declined to sign it.

76

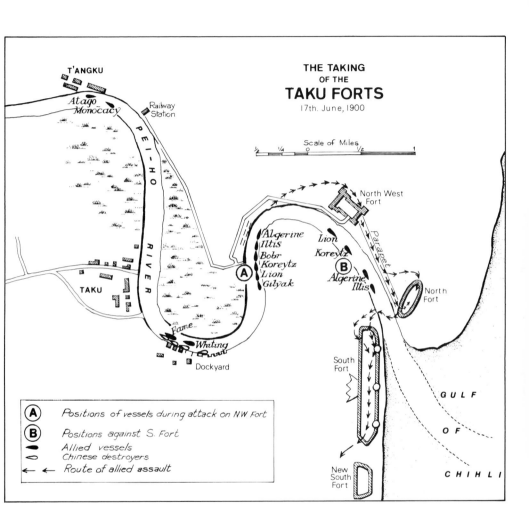

THE TAKING
OF THE
**TAKU FORTS**
17th. June, 1900

Scale of Miles

T'ANGKU

*Atago*
*Monocacy*

Railway
Station

PEI-HO RIVER

TAKU

A

*Algerine*
*Iltis*
*Bobr*
*Koreytz*
*Lion*
*Gilyak*

*Lion*
*Koreytz*

B

*Algerine*
*Iltis*

*Fame*

*Whiting*

Dockyard

North West
Fort

Parapet

North
Fort

South
Fort

GULF

OF

CHIHLI

New
South
Fort

A   *Positions of vessels during attack on N.W. Fort*

B   *Positions against S. Fort*

▬   *Allied vessels*
◠   *Chinese destroyers*
←←   *Route of allied assault*

The *Lion*, a very old French gun-boat mounting two 5.5-inch guns and several obsolete machine-guns.

HIJMS *Atago*, an old Japanese gun-boat, similarly armed to the *Lion*.

USS *Monocacy*, an ancient American paddle-steamer with two muzzle-loader guns and several Colt machine-guns.

Several civilian craft were also pressed into service.

On board these vessels, in addition to their crews, were a total of about 900 sailors and marines, consisting of 320 British, 240 Japanese, 160 Russians, 130 Germans, 25 Italians and 20 Austrians. Under instruction from Admiral Kempff, the USS *Monocacy* and her crew took no part in the operation.

This far from formidable task force was required, if the ultimatum were to be rejected, to take by assault four massive fortresses, fairly recently modified by German engineers, defended by an array of modern artillery pieces, mostly supplied by Messrs Krupp, and surrounded by moats and parapets. Faced with a modicum of 'bottom' and average gunnery, the puny flotilla could be blown out of the water before the landing parties could be put ashore. Similarly, the assaulting troops could easily be mown down as they advanced across the featureless mud-flats towards their objectives.

Theoretically, overall command of this uninviting operation was entrusted to Captain Dobrovolsky of the Russian Navy but in practice the major contributors of vessels and men acted more or less independently in accordance with a pre-arranged plan. In any case, once the operation got under way in the dark, there could be little or no communication between the various ships and landing parties. The senior British officer was Commander Cradock and in command of HMS *Fame* was the 28-year-old Lieutenant Roger Keyes, later famous as one of the great exponents of amphibious warfare of which the taking of the Taku forts was to be his first experience.

The ultimatum was neither accepted nor rejected (the Chinese seldom accepted or rejected anything outright), the commander of the forts indicating that he personally would be quite willing to hand them over but permission to do so would have to come from higher authority, presumably the Viceroy. In any case, he said, there was no intention of impeding Allied shipping in the Pei-ho. Why then, asked the Russian officer, had torpedoes been prepared for firing? No need to worry, he was told, they would not go off anyway.

In the event, no written or verbal reply to the ultimatum was ever received but the Allies got their answer when every gun on every fort opened up simultaneously at about 1 am on the 17th. First blood went to the Chinese. For reasons known only to her commander, the searchlight on the Russian gun-boat *Gilyak* was switched on, providing a target which the Chinese gunners could not miss. The result was that both she and her sister ship, the *Koreytz*, were hit several times and seriously damaged. Two officers and sixteen ratings were killed and about sixty-five wounded.

As soon as hostilities commenced, the British destroyers *Fame* and *Whiting* steamed up-river, staying well out in mid-stream as though bound for T'angku railway station, but in reality to attack and seize four German-built destroyers of the Chinese Navy which were moored at Taku dockyard.

Drawing level with their targets, the British ships suddenly swung to port, ran alongside and boarded all four destroyers simultaneously. There was little resistance from the crews but there was

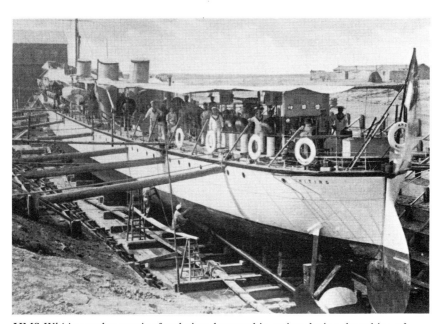

HMS *Whiting* under repair after being damaged in action during the taking of the Taku Forts. (*National Maritime Museum*)

some sniping from the dockyard which Keyes ordered cleared. The Chinese vessels were then towed to T'angku as prizes, the *Whiting* receiving a hit on the way.

Meanwhile, the assault force had landed about 1,300 yards to the west of the North-West Fort, while the gun-boats pounded all the forts with covering fire. Communication between the landing party and the ships was impossible in the dark, so Cradock, who by common consent had been 'elected' to command the assault, decided to delay the attack until first light for fear that his men would come under fire from their own guns.

The Allied bombardment was largely ineffective as the light shells made little impression on the massive gun emplacements. However, a chance shot, claimed by the French gun-boat *Lion*, pierced the magazine in the South Fort causing a huge explosion which put several of its guns out of action. At 4.30 am the bombardment was lifted and the assault went in, the British, Japanese and Italians in the first wave, supported by the Russians, Germans and Austrians, in a series of rushes and volleys. A young British naval officer, Lieutenant C. C. Dix, has described the attack on the North-West Fort. 'Fix bayonets! And away we all dashed converging on the NW corner of the fort. The area over which the attack passed was hard mud, quite flat without a vestige of cover. At about 200 yards from the moat, there was an extensive stretch of impassable ground necessitating a certain amount of crowding . . . it was here that most of the casualties occurred, but without a check the British and Japanese gave several cheers and went at them bald-headed, soon finding themselves in possession of the outer fort . . . it was some minutes before the inner fort was gained.' In the course of this action Dix used his pistol for the first (and probably the last) time in his career, 'bagging a brace' of Chinese.

Within fifteen minutes, the Allied flags having been run up on the North-West Fort, the victors were moving swiftly along the parapet towards the North Fort, whence came another deafening explosion as its magazine was hit, this time by HMS *Algerine*. However, the Chinese gunners continued to work the remaining guns scoring hits on the German sloop *Iltis*, killing her commander, another officer and four ratings. *Algerine* was also lightly damaged and several of her crew wounded.

Despite this, the assault force met little opposition as it stormed the North Fort which was soon in Allied hands. Turning the captured guns onto the South Fort the Allies engaged in a brief artillery duel with the South Fort's only remaining undamaged gun, a 6-inch Armstrong. When this was silenced, the assault force crossed the river in small craft and seized its two final objectives, the South Fort and the New South Fort, without encountering any further resistance.

The causeway along which the Allied assault force dashed to take the North-West and North Taku Forts. (*Illustrated London News*)

A remarkable amphibious operation in which five major objectives (including the destroyers at Taku dockyard) had been taken in six hours was complete. This, perhaps the most important action of the whole Boxer campaign, had been achieved by largely untrained personnel – Keyes says that the British contingent, the Marines apart, consisted of 'quartermasters, boatswains, armourers, blacksmiths, stokers, boys and bandsmen' – hastily assembled, working to a sketchy plan, under ad hoc command. Luckily for the Allies, although the Chinese gunnery may have been of a higher standard than they had expected, the defenders had no stomach for close-quarter fighting, thus enabling the assault force to seize objectives which, given spirited resistance, would have been untakeable.

The Allied casualties speak for themselves. The ships' crews, with twenty-four killed and eighty-nine wounded, suffered considerably

81

more than their comrades on land with only seven dead and twelve wounded. About six months later, Lieutenant Myakishev of the Russian Navy wrote an account of the action which understandably emphasizes the role played by the Russians. Certainly they suffered the heaviest losses, but this was due largely to the incident of the *Gilyak*'s searchlight. On land, they had one man killed and another wounded, the Japanese one officer and four men killed and four wounded and the British one man killed and six wounded. The landing parties of the remaining nationalities do not seem to have suffered any casualties. Among the ships, the exploits of *Fame* and *Whiting* were especially daring and skilful, and elsewhere the honours seem to have been shared more or less equally. As mentioned earlier, much to the chagrin of her crew, the old USS *Monocacy* played no part in the capture of the Taku forts. McKinley's

A fanciful German depiction of the Allied assault on the Taku Forts. In reality the Germans played a very minor part in the land operations. (*National Army Museum*)

government, in a spasm of pre-election jitters, had decided that the operation smacked of 'imperialism'.

Estimates of Chinese casualties vary wildly between 100 and 800. Similarly, it is unclear by which part of the Chinese Army the forts were garrisoned, or, indeed, whether the men were soldiers or sailors, or both. If anyone took the trouble to find out, they did not consider it worth recording.

The mouth of the Pei-ho and therefore the channel of supply and reinforcement for Tientsin and, eventually, Peking was now secure.

## Peking, 20th June

By 9 o'clock in the morning the legates had received no reply from the Tsungli Yamen. Rumours were rife in the foreign community and among the Chinese Christians. The Corps Diplomatique, concerned only to save its own skin, was about to desert, it was said. Morrison tackled Cologon. 'The Chinese [referring to the Christians] will be massacred to a man,' he remonstrated, receiving the heartless and ungrammatical but nonetheless honest reply from the doyen, 'That does not regard us!' There can be little doubt that this was the general attitude of the diplomats. The Europeans, if they wished, could go with them on the hazardous journey to Tientsin, trusting either to the Chinese Government's worthless guarantee of safe conduct, or to the ferocious reputation of the legation guards, to see them through. The Chinese Christians must stay and take their chances undefended. Above all in the minds of the diplomats was the hope of meeting Seymour and his men on the way, and the nearer and sooner the better. Little did they know the desperate straits in which the worthy Admiral's expedition now found itself.

## With Seymour

We left the expedition on 14 June with its trains spread out along the line between Langfang and Yangts'un. The leading train had reached Anp'ing station, about six or seven miles beyond Langfang, under Captain McCalla on the 16th but was ordered to withdraw the same evening. The Admiral felt, and the other contingent commanders seem to have agreed with him, that further advance was too risky without having re-established contact with Tientsin. The reality was that the expedition was trapped. The extent of damage to the line and the bridges meant that there could be no movement by train except on the stretch between Yangts'un and Langfang.

Although, on first moving out of Tientsin on the 10th, the Allies had found the bodies of several Boxers decapitated and mutilated, presumably by General Nieh's troops, it was becoming clear that, under pressure from the Forbidden City, the General was changing sides. During the first week or so attacks on the trains had come exclusively from Boxers but now, from time to time, the expedition was coming under artillery fire and the Boxers had no artillery. What should Seymour do? Short of food and ammunition, encumbered by wounded and without transport, a march on Peking was out of the question. Messengers from the legations had already warned of the opposition the expedition could expect in the Great Hunting Park to the south of Peking and the Admiral did not fancy his chances of fighting his way through to the legations.

All doubts as to where the Imperial Army, or at least part of it, stood were dispelled when Captain von Usedom's men guarding Langfang station were attacked by several thousand Braves of Tung's

A railway bridge on the Tientsin–Peking line destroyed by Boxers. (*Institution of Royal Engineers*)

(4th) Division on 18 June. The attack was beaten off with light casualties to the Allies, although von Usedom himself was wounded, and severe losses to the enemy. Nevertheless, the German officer realized that his position was untenable and withdrew his 1,200-strong force to Yangts'un by train while he still could. That night the decision was taken to attempt a retreat to Tientsin on foot, using the Pei-ho River to transport the wounded and heavy equipment. The following morning junks were expropriated, loaded and, under continuous artillery fire, the battered column started to tramp, paddle and sail back to what it hoped was safety, a mere thirty miles downstream, perhaps the longest thirty miles in the lives of the survivors.

## Peking

For the diplomats, and for those whose lives depended upon their decisions, 20 June was a long and nerve-wracking day. The legates had met early to await the Tsungli Yamen's reply but by 9.30 am Baron von Ketteler had decided to wait no longer. 'I will go and sit

Seymour's expedition struggling back along the Pei-ho River having failed to reach Peking. When published this picture was euphemistically captioned 'Admiral Seymour's Advance on Tientsin'. In fact, of course, it was a retreat. (*Illustrated London News*)

there until they come if I have to sit there all night,' he growled. But some of the others tried to restrain him: MacDonald on the grounds that it would be undignified and de Giers that it would be dangerous. Why did not the baron send his Chinese Secretary instead? suggested the Russian, although why he should have imagined the mission safer for the Secretary than for the Minister is unclear. Perhaps he regarded Secretaries as expendable. In any case, although von Ketteler appears to have agreed to this suggestion, he was not the man to send another to face a risk alone which he himself was not prepared to run. So, a little while later, he set out for the Tsungli Yamen in his official 'chair' accompanied by his Chinese Secretary, Herr Cordes, and two liveried Chinese flunkies on horseback. It may be a cliché, but what happened then changed the course of history.

The bearers whisked their master and his Secretary through the burnt and plundered streets in separate chairs, their swift, sidling gait gently rocking the Baron as he puffed on his cigar and glanced through the pages of the book he had brought to while away the hours he expected to wait before being received by the mandarins of the Tsungli Yamen. Suddenly shots rang out. A uniformed Bannerman had dashed from the throng of pedestrians, opened fire with a rifle, killing the Baron outright, seriously wounding Cordes and then, pausing only to steal von Ketteler's watch, disappeared back into the crowd. The chairmen and outriders bolted but, miraculously, Cordes managed to escape, though shot through both thighs, and take refuge in the American Methodist building which had not yet been evacuated.

George Morrison was one of the first to hear of the outrage when his servant burst into his office shouting in pidgin, 'Any man speakee have makee kill German Minister!' The die was cast. By his unintended sacrifice, von Ketteler had saved the lives of his colleagues, the foreign community and most of the Chinese Christians who had taken refuge in the legation quarter. His death confirmed what he and he alone of the Corps Diplomatique had believed unreservedly, namely that the only hope of survival was to remain where they were and, if necessary, to defend themselves until help arrived. To set out for Tientsin under the 'protection' of the Chinese Army would be fatal. MacDonald, even if he had not actually favoured departure,

The murder of Baron von Ketteler. Brave but reckless, the German Minister was one of two foreign diplomats to be murdered during the Boxer uprising. (*Mary Evans Picture Library*)

had hitherto lacked the force of character to oppose the majority view but now de Giers, Pichon, Conger and the others needed no persuasion to stay.

But we cannot leave the matter there. Von Ketteler's murder was, and is, one of the impenetrable mysteries of this story. Was it premeditated, and, if so, why and by whom? The consensus of opinion at the time was that it had been organized and paid for by Prince Tuan, the leader of the anti-foreign, pro-Boxer party at Court. This view seemed to be confirmed when, through some clever Allied detective work after the siege, the murderer, a Bannerman corporal called En Hai, was arrested, sentenced to death and executed. He died, it was said, complaining that he had been cheated of his full fee and inveighing against the perfidy of princes. Furthermore, the murder had been reported in the Chinese and European press several days before it actually took place, indicating a leak and, generally speaking, in order for there to be a leak there has to be a plan. Of course, the diplomats, cut off from the outside world in Peking, knew nothing of these reports, although they had caused some stir in the capitals of Europe where enquiries at the various Chinese legations had met with blank and, perhaps understandable, incomprehension.

But what possible motive could Prince Tuan and the other reactionaries have had in arranging and procuring the premature murder of a single senior diplomat if they were planning to lure the whole Corps Diplomatique into the open where they could be butchered on the line of march to Tientsin?

Of course it is conceivable, if improbable, that the murder was planned by the 'progressive' party, including Prince Ch'ing, perhaps to prevent the main body of diplomats and foreigners from emerging from the legations to their deaths. Von Ketteler might well have been, to their minds, a most suitable victim. If, as we have seen, Pichon believed that the German minister was trying to bring about the downfall of the Manchu dynasty, perhaps the progressives were of the same opinion. Progressives they may have been, but few were republicans or wished to depose the Emperor, however much they may have desired to cut his ferocious aunt down to size. Perhaps they believed that by bringing about von Ketteler's death they might be saving both the dynasty and the foreigners. In any case he was personally unpopular with the Chinese and Germany as a nation was particularly disliked for the high-handed arrogance of her diplomacy and her unconcealed readiness to use force in the extraction of concessions. When, a few weeks later, the Kaiser addressed his troops as they departed for the 'pacification' of north China he made his attitude clear with the following words: 'Just as the Huns a thousand years ago under the leadership of Attila gained a reputation by virtue of which they live in historical tradition, so may the name of Germany become known in such a manner in China that no Chinese will ever dare again look askance at a German.' In the decades which followed, the Chinese were not the only people to recall this sinister instruction.

However, we have moved into the realms of speculation and there is no jot or tittle of evidence to support this theory. The plain fact is that we do not know why von Ketteler was murdered nor who, if anyone, instigated his death. We do not know if En Hai *really* made the remarks attributed to him at his execution. Perhaps he had murdered the German for his watch. Few political assassins pause to rob the bodies of their victims. Perhaps the premature press reports arose through inspired journalistic speculation based on the possible consequences of von Ketteler's known wild and unrestrained behaviour. Whatever the truth, he was the victim of mad times in a place gone mad, but in his death he rendered a greater service to his colleagues and thousands of others than ever he could have done by remaining alive.*

Hitherto preparations for the defence of the legation quarter had been patchy and half-hearted but now efforts were redoubled. It was clear that the British Legation and its compound, being the biggest, was the most suitable centre for the defence of the area as a whole. The large number of non-combatant Europeans, particularly women and children, could best be accommodated and protected there. As for the other legations, generally speaking these were to

The Italian Legation at Peking photographed in 1989. The last survivor of the original legations, it survived the siege more or less intact despite, or perhaps because of, being outside the defended area. (*Merilyn Thorold*)

* After the relief of the legations a memorial to von Ketteler was raised on the spot where he was murdered. This was, however, somewhat counter-productive as most Chinese believed the memorial honoured the man who had heroically slain a prominent foreign devil! It was demolished in November, 1918, after China had entered the war against Germany in the previous year.

be occupied by fighting men only. Four, the Austrian, Italian, Belgian and Dutch, were to be abandoned at an early stage of the siege as untenable. The layout of the legations and the area surrounding them is extremely difficult to describe in words, so careful scrutiny of the plan opposite is recommended.

With swift efficiency various committees were set up to deal with such vital matters as the rationing and distribution of food, the allocation of labour (the large number of Chinese Christian refugees provided most of this) and hygiene. Perhaps the most important job was given to the resourceful American engineer turned missionary, the Reverend F. D. Gamewell. The defended area at the beginning of the siege covered approximately 90.5 acres with a perimeter of 2,541 yards. As time went on this was reduced to 59 acres and 2,152 yards. With only 400 regulars and about 100 poorly armed civilian volunteers to man the perimeter, a fighting strength which would diminish daily through death, wounds and sickness, the need for adequate fortification under constant repair and improvement was obvious. Such was Mr Gamewell's task, one at which he and his gangs of Christian Chinese artisans and labourers toiled heroically and unceasingly throughout the siege, often under heavy fire.

A number of wells within the defended area provided a virtually unlimited supply of clean water. Food, for the feeding of over 3,000 people, roughly 900 Europeans and the rest Chinese Christians and local staff, would have presented an insurmountable problem had it not been for a stroke of good fortune. Early in June a convoy of 'tribute' grain destined for the Imperial Court from Honan Province had rumbled into Peking. Some 230 tons of this grain, mostly milling wheat, were found stored in the warehouse of the Broad Prosperity Grain Shop at the corner of East Legation Street by the Canal Bridge and expropriated by the Food Committee. After the siege the proprietor rendered his invoice to the British Legation which passed it on to the Chinese Government for payment! As for meat, the legation stables housed a number of racing ponies and draft mules (including fifteen of the latter which had belonged to the Broad Prosperity Grain Shop and had been used to transport the grain) and most of these, to the dismay of their owners, were to be consumed before relief came.

Living space was nearly as important as food as serious overcrowd-

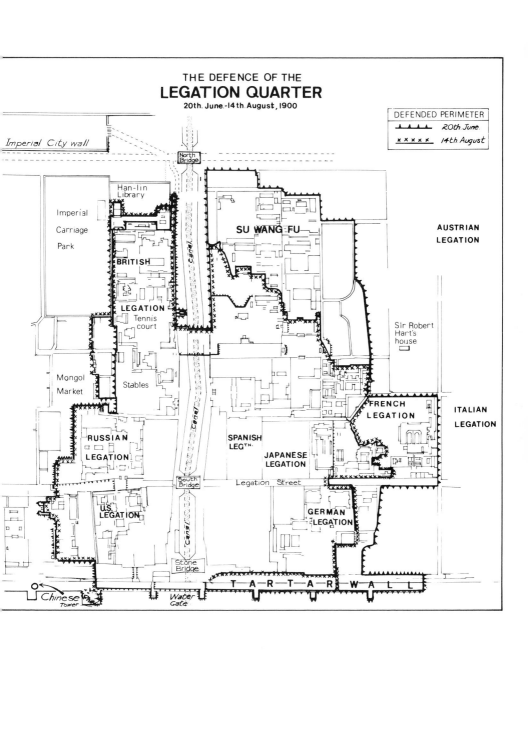

THE DEFENCE OF THE
# LEGATION QUARTER
20th. June.-14th. August, 1900

DEFENDED PERIMETER
▲▲▲▲ 20th. June.
✕✕✕✕✕ 14th. August

Imperial City wall

North Bridge

Han-lin Library

Imperial
Carriage
Park

SU WANG FU

AUSTRIAN
LEGATION

BRITISH

LEGATION
Tennis court

Sir Robert Hart's house

Mongol Market

Stables

FRENCH
LEGATION

ITALIAN
LEGATION

RUSSIAN
LEGATION

SPANISH
LEGᵀᴺ

JAPANESE
LEGATION

South Bridge

Legation Street

U.S.
LEGATION

GERMAN
LEGATION

Canal

Stone Bridge

T-A-R-T-A-R W-A-L-L

Chinese
Tower

Water Gate

ing might have led to outbreaks of disease. For this reason, as well as for tactical advantage, the mansion and extensive grounds (about 13 acres) known as the Su Wang Fu, lying across the canal to the east of the British Legation, was occupied by the Allies. Its owner, a Manchu grandee called Prince Su of known anti-foreign proclivities, wisely withdrew elsewhere for the duration of hostilities. Here were accommodated the majority of the Chinese Christian refugees.

In the early afternoon of the 20th two communications from the Tsungli Yamen were received by the legates. The first, without mentioning the murder of von Ketteler, regretted that it would be unsafe for them to visit the Yamen for further discussions for the time being, and the second, sent to the German Legation, demanded to know who were the two Germans, one of whom had been killed, who had fired into the crowd. No reply was sent to either of these cynical and insulting documents.

Perhaps Sir Claude MacDonald has left the clearest picture of the last hours of the 'phoney war' which had smouldered between the divided Chinese Government and the uncertain Allies since the end of May. 'The afternoon of the 20th dragged slowly on,' he recounted many years later, 'and the shadows had begun to lengthen. There was an ominous stillness and amongst the charred and blackened ruins which the Boxers had left to the north of the legations not a living soul was to be seen. It will be remembered that our (sic) ultimatum expired "four hours after noon". A few minutes before that time I strolled out of the main gate together with the constable* of the Legation – an ex-member of A Division of Police – we stood under the trees looking towards where the sun glinted on the yellow tiled coping of the Imperial City wall and lit up the blackened ruins in the Street of Permanent Peace as the street running north of the British Legation is called. It must have been on the stroke of the hour when "whiz", the almost forgotten sound, followed by another and yet another, and then some summer leaves from the trees above fell slowly to the ground, then a bullet struck the coping of the canal a few inches from where I stood and with as much dignity as we could command we walked back into the kindly shelter of the main gate.'

* Probably Sergeant R. D. Herring

92

Whatever qualities Her Britannic Majesty's Minister to the Imperial Court of the Middle Kingdom may have lacked, he undoubtedly possessed *'le sang froid ecossais'*.

Although a variety of rumours had been reaching the legations as to the whereabouts and fortunes of the Seymour expedition, the beleaguered diplomats had no reason to assume that the Admiral's predicament was at least as bad as their own.

The main gate of the British Legation through which Sir Claude MacDonald strolled minutes before the opening of hostilities. (*The late Mr Han Zhong Min/Research Centre of Inscriptions and Documents*)


## With Seymour, 21st–26th June

With McCalla leading the American, British and French contingents along the left bank of the Pei-ho and the wounded von Usedom in command of the Germans, Austrians, Japanese and Italians on the right, Seymour's men (the Admiral himself commanding the rearguard) were retreating slowly towards Tientsin, scouting and skirmishing yard by yard. Neither side was anxious to get to grips with the other and on one occasion McCalla witnessed a fairly rare occurrence in war – both sides running away from each other at the same time.

Observing a number of Chinese troops advancing on the van of his column, he sent a sergeant to bring up reinforcements; these, a

93

mixed force of British and Americans, came up at the double in dead ground unobserved by the Chinese who continued advancing to within fifty yards of the Allies. A brisk fire fight then ensued in which McCalla was slightly wounded and one of his Petty Officers killed. The Chinese soon took to their heels, led by their officers on horseback, but to McCalla's surprise and mortification most of his own men, far from following up this advantage, proceeded to retreat precipitately whence they had come. Understandably, this gave Seymour in the rear the impression that they had been driven back by superior Chinese forces, so he sent Bigham, his Intelligence Officer, to order McCalla to fall back with his remaining men and the wounded so that they could 'try to hold the village next in rear'. Realizing that this order was based on a misconception, McCalla remained where he was and the retreat was eventually able to continue.

Progress was painfully slow as the junks carrying the wounded were constantly grounding in the shallow river and unable to keep up with the marching men, who, in turn, dared not leave them unprotected. By sundown on the 21st they had covered only four miles on that day to within one mile of Hsiku Arsenal, the existence of which they had been quite unaware and from which they came under heavy and fairly accurate shell-fire. Earlier in the day, Captain Jellicoe, Seymour's Chief of Staff, had been seriously wounded and was not expected to live. His duties were assumed by Captain von Usedom.

The fact that Seymour had no idea of the existence of this huge forty-acre arsenal complex, probably the largest in north China, illustrates the disgraceful absence of military intelligence available to him and the other Allied commanders. A young French officer visiting China earlier in the year had remarked in his report to the Ministry of War in Paris upon the astonishing lack of interest which the foreign communities took in their surroundings and had noted in particular that even the western military attachés were completely ignorant of Chinese dispositions, fortifications and weaponry in the Tientsin area. This may not have been entirely fair to Commandant Vidal, the French Military Attaché, who does seem to have been fairly active and observant, bicycling and riding about the countryside, but he had not been in Tientsin when the Seymour expedition had set out. As a result, the intrepid Admiral had sallied forth on his hazardous mission without the slightest idea of what he was likely to encounter on the way or, come to that, on the way back.

As the arsenal was an unknown quantity in terms of its defensive capability, it was decided to by-pass it on the opposite (east) bank of the river. As the front of the column drew level with the arsenal, there was a shouted exchange between a British Consular official, Mr Campbell, who was acting as chief interpreter to the expedition, and some Chinese troops or Boxers on the other side of the river. Whatever was said, and there are various versions, the Chinese soon opened fire, the first shell narrowly missing Campbell. Ahead of the column were a series of defended villages which would have to be cleared if the Tientsin Concessions, now only about three miles away, were to be reached. McCalla, commanding the vanguard, sent back for the Royal Marines – perhaps surprisingly for an American officer he has recorded that 'if there were anything to be done, the British Marines were sent to do it' – only to find that Seymour had changed his mind and decided to storm the arsenal rather than allow it to menace his right flank and, in particular, the helpless junks, loaded with increasing numbers of wounded, floating or being towed sluggishly down the Pei-ho. On the face of it, this seemed a pretty tall order, which, apparently both the French and Russian commanders declined. So, in the small hours of the 22nd, Major J. R. Johnstone with a force of Royal Marines and bluejackets crossed the river on a pontoon of junks and stormed the arsenal from the north. A half-hearted defence was soon dealt with at the point of the bayonet and, once again as at the Taku forts, resolute men had succeeded in taking a virtually impregnable position thanks largely to the feebleness of the opposition. By this time the Germans had crossed the river down-stream of the arsenal and hastened the withdrawl of the Chinese* fleeing to the south. Soon they were joined by the rest of the expedition which found itself in an Aladdin's Cave of ordnance, consisting, inter alia, of at least 250 field-guns, an assortment of 14,000 rifles and millions of rounds of ammunition, much of which

---

* It is not clear whether the arsenal was occupied by Imperial troops or Boxers or both.

fitted the variety of small arms with which the column was equipped. As most of their heavier weapons had been dumped in the river along the way, as they had no transport animals and more space was required on the junks for the wounded, all this came to them as a priceless windfall. There were also medical supplies and enough rice to last them for several weeks if needed.

Despite this success, which had not been achieved without increasing his casualties, Seymour was still in desperate straits.

His men were exhausted and morale was low. The Tientsin Concessions were, as heavy gunfire from that direction told him, themselves under siege and the garrison there had no means of knowing where his column was or even if it still existed. He was faced with two urgent and conflicting problems: a. how to hold his position in the arsenal and b. how to get out of it. Opposed to him were elements of at least two divisions, the 1st and 2nd, plus the Boxers and, for all he knew, Yuan Shih-k'ai's crack 3rd Division might soon be joining the fray. The weather too was against him, hot strong winds buffeting his men with blinding dust storms.

Over the next few days a series of attacks were launched on the arsenal complex. One theory was that General Nieh, perhaps under some absurd order from the Forbidden City, had handed over the arsenal to the Boxers and, now that they had lost it, was determined to recover it. Nieh was personally opposed to the Boxers and was one of the few commanders who had mounted serious and successful operations against them before they had been taken under the Imperial wing. Fortunately, whoever was attacking showed little tactical skill or resolution and was repeatedly driven off. During one assault young Maurice Cochrane and his Maxim team were placed under the command of Captain von Usedom, whose second-in-command had just been killed. Together with an American lieutenant called Gilpin, who was firing shrapnel shells from an unspecified weapon, Cochrane's Maxim had inflicted severe casualties upon a body of two or three hundred Boxers which had joined the attack. This threw von Usedom into transports of delight, 'and', wrote Cochrane, 'he kept dancing about in a sort of ecstasy saying, "Eet ees lofely – beeautiful – I never haf seen anything like eet!"'

But Allied casualties continued to mount. In the course of one sortie, Captain Beyts of the Royal Marine Artillery and two of his men were separated from the rest of their party. Beyts was killed outright but when the bodies of the other two were recovered, they were found to have been tortured and mutilated before death.

On the afternoon of the 23rd Admiral Seymour decided to send out a patrol-in-strength in an endeavour to reach the Concessions. At first, it seems, he asked McCalla to lead sixty of his men in this attempt but, for unspecified reasons, in the event the task was given to Captain Doig and a hundred Royal Marines to be guided by Mr Currie, a British railway official, who was reputed to know the area well. However, according to one of the marines in the patrol, in the darkness Currie started off in the wrong direction and they came under fire from Russian sentries who fortunately missed. Eventually Currie got his bearings and brought the patrol to within a mile and a half of Tientsin railway station, but here they came under such heavy fire that they were forced to withdraw, leaving five casualties, presumably dead, on the railway line.

After this failure it was felt that Chinese civilian messengers rather than groups of armed men might have a better chance of getting through.

The first such attempt was made by Mr Campbell's Chinese servant who penetrated the enemy lines only to be shot dead by an Allied sentry on the outskirts of the Concessions. Then two railway coolies, probably pressed men, were sent on the same hazardous mission and, not surprisingly, simply disappeared. Captain McCalla was indignant. 'It is quite certain,' he wrote later, 'that these two China-men thought only of their own safety and it is not unlikely that they sympathized with the Boxers!'

At last, on the 24th, a reliable messenger was found in the shape of Clive Bigham's servant, one Chao Yin-ho. Chao was a type of gentleman's retainer whom we occasionally glimpse in the pages of history. Bold, resourceful, reliable but probably insubordinate, he is sometimes a better man than his master – a Gunga Din. In this case he was an ex-seaman who had already served in two navies, the Chinese and the British, and would later serve in another, the American. Setting out, presumably after dark, with an American escort as far as the river bank, he swam the river alone and set off for Tientsin. Soon he was stopped by Boxers who wanted to know why he was wet. He had been travelling down the west bank of the

Pei-ho to visit his relatives in Tientsin, he replied, but upon reaching the arsenal complex he found it occupied by foreign barbarians and in order to avoid these devils he had swum across the river. His brother had already been killed in the fighting and as soon as he had visited his family, who were tinsmiths, and acquired a gun he would return to join the Boxers, he added. The bit about his relations being tinsmiths was true and some of them were known to his interrogators so he was allowed to pass. Later he had to spin the same yarn to Imperial troops who arrested him, tied him to a tree and threatened to chop off his head. Again he was believed.

As he approached Tientsin railway station, like his unfortunate predecessor, he was fired on by Allied sentries but on this occasion they missed. Having learnt semaphore during his service in the Royal Navy he was able to signal the gist of his message (he had swallowed Bigham's note before being arrested by the Boxers) and was taken to see the senior British officer of the garrison, Captain Bayley, RN. Bayley, impressed by Chao's knowledge of matters naval, believed his story, although the general opinion was that the Seymour expedition had been slaughtered to a man.

Early the following morning, the 25th, a relief column of about 2,000 men, mostly Russian under Colonel Shirinsky but including two companies of the newly arrived Royal Welsh Fusiliers and some American marines and sailors, set out for the arsenal which they reached at 10 am after some brief skirmishing with the Chinese army. It is not clear whether Seymour's battered but thankful men reached the Tientsin Concessions that day or the next, but in either case they were carrying no less than 232 wounded with them, having buried sixty-two of their comrades along the way.*

There is an amusing sequel to the story of their saviour, the intrepid Chao Yin-ho. For his resourceful daring he received a payment of $1,000, an enormous sum for a man of his station in those days, but Bigham, unable to reach Peking for the time being, returned to England and had no further need of Chao's services. Therefore McCalla arranged for him to be enlisted as a steward in his own ship, the USS *Newark*, but a year or so later, having given up the command, received the following letter:

* British casualties were 29 killed and 89 wounded.

Captain M. C. Callah

U.S. New York Navy Yard

Sir,

I beg to inform you that I am very sorry leave US Navy but the
Japanese steward he sarcasm give me very hard so I had to apply
off position and I give to thank you for the kindness you have
rendered for my claim which I have received a paper of $1,000.
I hope you are very well at Home which I have got a small job
as a Clerk in the Imp Chinese Post Office at Newchwang.

I have the honor to be

Sir

your obedient servant

Chao Yin-Hoo

## Tientsin, 26th June

The Concession Settlements to which the Seymour expedition had
returned 'had altered most enormously', wrote Maurice Cochrane
to his parents. 'It was under shell-fire from the Chinese for five days.

The ruins of the French Concession at Tientsin after days of continuous
bombardment. (*Institution of Royal Engineers*)

All the French Concession is in bits and our Concession is knocked about a bit.' The room in the house where he had lodged after arriving from Taku had received a direct hit and he had lost all the kit he had left there. Forlornly, he hoped that 'the Admiral will pay compensation for all we have lost'.

There was confusion everywhere and on both sides. If the Imperial troops and the Boxers were ill at ease with one another, so were the Allies. Although in the last week of June the trickle of reinforcements of Russians from Manchuria, Americans from the Philippines and British from Hong Kong and Wei-hai-wei became a flood, there was no overall command or unified headquarters staff.

Commandant Vidal, arriving at Chefoo from Korea in transit to Taku and eventually Tientsin, received such gloomy reports of the situation from the officers of the British battleship *Orlando* and from the French Consul at Chefoo that he immediately telegraphed the Ministry of War in Paris. 'Consider necessary to send to China expeditionary force comprising two infantry regiments with strong proportion of mountain artillery and some cavalry. Bring all from France. I am joining the troops at Taku.' The reference, 'Bring all from France' was probably intended to prevent the Ministry from sending low-grade colonial battalions from Indo-China – so they sent low-grade colonial battalions from Indo-China!

HMS *Orlando* had arrived at Chefoo from Taku to collect the most curious of the Allied units to take part in the campaign, the 1st (and last) Chinese Regiment, recruited and based in the British concession territory of Wei-hai-wei. This concession had been obtained two years earlier as a counter-balance to German power and influence in Shantung Province and the Russian presence at Port Arthur. It had a particularly agreeable climate and was used as a place of rest and recreation for the China Station fleet. Except for its British officers and senior NCOs the regiment was recruited entirely from the local inhabitants. Among the first British officers to join it was Captain Charles Wood, son of the celebrated Field-Marshal Sir Evelyn Wood VC, a former Sirdar of the Egyptian Army. Wood Junior was no stranger to unconventional soldiering as he had fought at the Battle of Omdurman as one of only two British officers with the anti-Mahdist tribal levies.

100

Vidal followed up his telegram with a long situation report*
confirming heavy fighting around Tientsin. The Royal Marines under
Major Luke had seized the Chinese Military College; the Russians
had sustained heavy casualties in a stubborn and so far successful
defence of the railway station; the bombardment of the Concessions,
particularly the French, which had been almost totally destroyed,
was unceasing.

On the 19th James Watts, a British civilian, and three Cossacks
rode and fought their way through to Taku with news of the situation,
as both rail and telegraph links with the outside world had been cut,

Men of the 1st Chinese Regiment from Wei-hai-wei equipped with the obsolete
.45 Martini-Henry rifle. The British officer is carrying what appears to be a .22
sporting rifle. (*National Army Museum*)

* In his report, Vidal claims that a Madame d'Anthouard, going to Peking
to join her husband, had accompanied the Seymour expedition. This
seems highly improbable as the presence of a woman in the desperate
circumstances in which the expedition found itself would surely have been
mentioned in one or more of the letters, diaries and memoirs of the
participants.

There were, nevertheless, 'hitch-hikers' on the expedition. One of these,
an ex-sergeant of Royal Marines on his way to join the British Legation
as a constable, was remembered by Captain McCalla as an expert with
both rifle and bayonet, transfixing six Boxers in one hand-to-hand fight
and shooting a Chinese officer off his horse at 1,000 yards!

and demanded reinforcements. These, as we have seen, started to arrive during the last week of June, among them two companies of the Royal Welsh Fusiliers under Major F. Morris, the only British infantry battalion to take part in the campaign. Over the past five years this battalion had led a somewhat gypsy-like existence. After a long spell at home it had sailed for Malta in 1896 but since then had done two tours of duty in Crete, where it had had to deal with the rebellious Turkish community, and one in Egypt where it had replaced a resident battalion which had joined Kitchener in the Sudan. Early in 1899 it arrived for garrison duty in Hong Kong and with the outbreak of the Boer War found itself disappointingly remote from the scene of action. However, the Boxer uprising came as a welcome bonus to its more ambitious and warlike members.

From the remarks of some of his subordinates it would appear that Major Morris was neither ambitious nor warlike. In the skirmishing which took place during the advance from Taku to Tientsin Morris was slightly wounded, as a result of which one of his officers reported a fortnight later, 'Major Morris has broken down altogether and is being sent home to England today.' Another was more outspoken. 'Major Morris has been returned to store,' wrote Second-Lieutenant Owen* to his aunt, 'thank God he has gone. He was the most awful chap to have near when anything was on.' After Morris's departure the commanding officer of the battalion, Lieutenant-Colonel the Hon. R. H. Bertie, arrived in Tientsin with the battalion head-quarters and another company. The twelve officers and 460 men who took part in the campaign achieved a mixed reputation. The Americans, particularly the Marines, thought highly of the Welsh and have maintained links with them to this day; the great Sousa even wrote a march for them. But George Morrison, who witnessed their eventual arrival in Peking, aimed one of his most poisonous darts in their direction. 'They were worse than the Boxers,' he wrote some years later, 'only not so courageous, bigger thieves and bigger liars, men who rob graveyards. . . . Colonel Bertie was given the Companionship of the Bath for meritorious service in bringing his troops into Peking without a casualty except for drink.' This outburst

* Brigadier-General C. S. Owen, CMG, DSO (1879–1959) served with the battalion for many years. In 1914 he was adjutant and famous for his command of soldierly language.

102

was probably inspired by Morrison's dislike of the Welsh as a race rather than of the Royal Welsh Fusiliers (most of whom were not Welsh anyway) in particular. In any case, it was at least partly untrue as the battalion lost twelve men killed in action and twenty-two from other causes, none, so far as we know, from drink.

Dr George Morrison, the abrasive *Times* correspondent at Peking, posing in Chinese dress which he seldom wore. (*Mitchell Library*)

The Fusiliers did not perform, nor were they required to perform, any great feats of derring-do in China. With the exception of the Japanese who, whether by design or chance, did most of the fighting and suffered the most casualties, there seems to have been something uniformly second-rate about the Allied contingents which took part in the battle for Tientsin and the relief of Peking. That quality of leadership at the top, which might have brought out the best in the officers and men at regimental level, was lacking. Indeed, until the arrival at Tientsin towards the end of June of Acting Brigadier-General Arthur Dorward, there was no co-ordinated leadership at all. Dorward was a 52-year-old Royal Engineer who had spent most of his service in India, had fought in Afghanistan and had won the Distinguished Service Order in the Burma campaign of 1885–8. As

103

a relatively junior officer (substantively he was only a colonel) with no great prestige, he did his best under extremely difficult circumstances and succeeded, up to a point, in getting most of the commanders to work togetħer. He failed most noticeably with the Russians, who continued to play the Great Game with Britain and were at loggerheads with Japan. Russia and Japan were to produce the largest contingents, the latter under pressure and persuasion from Britain, and continued to snarl round each other like two powerful male dogs seeking to establish a pecking order without actually resorting to their teeth.

But by mid-July Dorward would have under his theoretical command an international force sufficiently large to enable him to launch the counter-attack against the walled city of Tientsin which was the essential preliminary to the advance on Peking, to which city we must now return and fall back a few days in time.

## Peking, 21st June

The day following the 'official' commencement of the siege was taken up with tremendous efforts to fortify the defended area. Hundreds of sandbags, some made of the expensive curtains and table cloths which adorned the legations, were filled and many barricades were constructed. Walls were reinforced, gates strengthened and trenches dug. But on the very next day all this work was nearly brought to nought by a potentially catastrophic and inexplicable decision on the part of the senior Allied officer, an Austrian naval captain called Thomann who happened to be in Peking.* Such was diplomatic devotion to protocol and precedence that this man, with no experience or training in land operations (and probably not much at sea), had been automatically accepted as the overall commander of the legation guards, purely on the basis of his seniority.

At about 10 am **on the 23rd**, to the horror of the on-lookers, all the national contingents of legation guards, except the British who were already there, began to pour into the British Legation compound having abandoned their various defensive positions on the

---

* He was captain of the ship from which the Austrian contingent of legation guards was drawn.

104

perimeter, not in panic but under orders to do so. Had the Chinese realized what had happened, they could have surrounded and completely dominated the British Legation in a matter of minutes and the siege would have been over almost before it had started. In his account of this episode, Sir Claude MacDonald is circumspect in ascribing blame to any individual officer, but most other witnesses specifically name Thomann. For example, according to Poole, 'the Austrian Captain lost his head.'

The ministers reacted with the speed of desperation and immediately ordered their respective contingents to re-occupy their positions. This was swiftly done, although two Germans, probably the first fatalities of the siege, were killed in the process. It had been a narrow squeak and one which must never be repeated. At a hastily convened ministerial conference, MacDonald was asked to take over as 'Commander-in-Chief'.

This appointment was made for three reasons. One, the British Legation was the nerve centre of the defended area and came

Peking ablaze during the siege. (*National Army Museum*)

automatically under MacDonald's control anyway. Two, as the representative of the leading foreign Power in China at that time, he was grudgingly accepted by his colleagues as the most authoritative figure, and thirdly, as a former regular army officer (in fact his name was still on the Army List) he was deemed to have had greater military experience than any of the others. On this point, he himself commented that because of the nature of the fighting, 'house to house, barricade against barricade and loophole to loophole . . . my military knowledge was therefore of no great advantage, but the fact that I had been a soldier acted as a species of link with the young commanders of detachments, who obeyed my orders although they often hesitated to carry out the wishes of their own ministers.' The latter part of this statement may be taken with a pinch of salt, as, in reality, the arrangement was not greeted rapturously by all 'the young commanders', or even some of their men. The Russian Lieutenant Baron von Raden described the appointment as 'unpleasant' although he accepted it as a 'necessity'. The American marines heartily disliked MacDonald (as they did most of the British civilians), on one occasion telling him that 'his orders didn't go on the Wall'.* But, on the whole, he seems to have handled a difficult job with skill, tact and common sense. The British officers and most of the civilian volunteers were, of course, delighted, always referring to him as the Chief.

On the afternoon of the same day the British suffered their first casualty when Private Scadding was shot dead on the west wall of the legation. In these early days the guards had not yet learnt the art of this type of fighting and Scadding had already been warned for exposing himself unnecessarily to enemy fire.

A serious danger lay to the immediate north of the British Legation in the shape of the Han-lin or Great Library of China. Captain Strouts, the commander of the British contingent, had pointed out to Sir Claude that, were the Chinese of a mind to set fire to the library while a north wind was blowing, this might spread to the legation and he urged that the Han-lin be occupied. Sir Claude was unwilling to commit his very limited manpower to extending the

---

* The southern perimeter of the defended area, the Tartar Wall, was held mainly by the Americans, Germans and Russians.

defended area. Moreover, he was assured by sinologues that the Dynasty would never permit such an act of vandalism as the library contained many priceless works of literature including the great Chinese encyclopaedia of nearly a million pages. But whatever instructions the Boxers or Imperial troops may have had from the Forbidden City, if any, cultural considerations did not inhibit them from putting the Han-lin to the torch as soon as the wind veered round to the north, which it did on the morning of 23 June.

Firing a machine-gun from the defences of the British Legation. The man on the right is a Royal Marine. The other is probably Gunner's Mate Mitchell, USN. Chinese coolies shore up the platform from below. (*National Army Museum*)

## 23rd–25th June

These days saw some of the heaviest fighting, against both fire and the enemy, of the entire siege – 'days and nights of hell' Poole described them – which left even the tough, vigorous young marines and sailors in a state of dazed exhaustion: days and nights in which they suffered serious losses, including one of their most valuable officers, Captain Lewis Halliday* of the Royal Marines. On the 23rd Halliday, Poole, Morrison and a detail of marines breached the Han-lin wall to enable parties of volunteers to get in and tackle the fire. Some attempt was made to save the literary treasures but the fire-fighters had enough to do to stop the flames spreading and to save themselves. Fire was also raging to the south of the legation among some Chinese houses and with the wind shifting and blustering this too presented a serious threat. The whole area resembled a scene from Dante's Inferno. Men, women and even children, both European and Chinese, scurried hither and thither, faces streaked with soot and sweat, forming bucket chains and dousing flames, all the while under heavy small-arms fire and occasional shelling. Among the casualties was the first US Marine to be killed in action, Private King. Nevertheless, the fires were eventually brought under control.

On the morning of the 24th Halliday and some of his marines were involved in an action following which Halliday was awarded the Victoria Cross.

The ruins of the student-interpreters' (fledgling diplomats and customs officials) quarters near the Han-lin. (*Illustrated London News*)

* General Sir Lewis Halliday, VC, KCB (1870–1965).

108

His citation read as follows:

'On June 24th the enemy, consisting of Boxers and Imperial Troops, made a fierce attack on the west wall of the British Legation, setting fire to the west gate of the south stable quarters and taking cover in the buildings which adjoined the wall.

'A hole was made in the legation wall and Captain Halliday in command of 20 Marines led the way into the building and almost immediately engaged a part of the enemy. Before he could use his revolver, however, he was shot through the left shoulder at point blank range, the bullet fracturing the shoulder and carrying away part of the lung.

'Notwithstanding the extremely severe nature of his wound, Captain Halliday killed three of his assailants and, telling his men "to carry on and not mind him", walked back unaided to the hospital refusing escort and aid so as not to diminish the number of men engaged in the sortie.'

Sixty-five years later, Halliday, by then the oldest living holder of the VC, decided the time had come to correct a few errors in the citation, which he described as 'wildly inaccurate'. 'Actually,' he

Captain Lewis Halliday, Royal Marine Light Infantry, was awarded the Victoria Cross and severely wounded in defence of the legations. (*Royal Marine Museum*)

wrote to the journal of the Royal Marines, 'I arrived at the west wall of the legation to report to Strouts that the Japanese did not need any help. I had been sent to see Colonel Shiba. Strouts had had a hole made in the wall and he told me to make a sortie with five men and a corporal *not* 20 men.

'I went down a narrow alley and ran into a group of five Boxers armed with rifles. The first shot was fired without bringing his rifle to the present. I then shot him and three others. The fifth ran away round the corner.

'I then told the men to carry on and I got back unaided to the wall. I was helped through the hole and Dr Rooke [probably Dr Poole] helped me to the hospital. Strouts then took out 20 or 30 men and pulled down the small building and cleared the field of fire.

'He told me next morning that my pistol had had a misfired round so I merely had pressed the trigger at the fifth man and he had escaped. It will be seen that I was acting under orders and I think that anyone must have done as I did.'

The reader must judge for himself whether this exploit, as described in either version, was sufficiently outstanding to have been rewarded with the Victoria Cross today. It may be cavalier but nonetheless realistic to suggest that Halliday would now have received the lesser award of a Military Cross which did not exist at that time.

Be that as it may, Halliday had been critically wounded (as had one of his men, Sawyer, who died later) and did not return to duty for the remainder of the siege.

Meanwhile, Colonel Goro Shiba with a mixed force of Japanese and Italians was fighting desperately to save the Fu and its occupants. The Chinese attacks were unusually persistent and pressed home with such exceptional vigour that the women and children refugees had to be temporarily evacuated. Indeed, it is surprising that Shiba had declined Halliday's proffered help. The battle raged all day, died down in the evening, only to be resumed on the following day, the 25th; but at about 4 pm there occurred the first of several strange interruptions to the siege.

A man appeared on the North or Imperial Bridge of the canal bearing a board with a legend which could be read through binoculars. MacDonald ordered a temporary cease-fire (apparently the

110

Chinese had already halted their attack) and a sinologue was called to interpret the message which read as follows: 'In accordance with Imperial commands to protect the foreign ministers, firing must stop. A despatch will be delivered at the Imperial Canal Bridge.' A Chinese messenger was sent out equipped with a similar board announcing that 'In compliance with the Imperial demand the despatch will be received.'

However, before reaching the bridge the messenger's nerve, understandably, failed him and, leaning his board against a post at an unreadable angle, he bolted back into the British Legation. Soon after that some mandarins escorted by soldiers appeared on the scene, perhaps with the intention of recovering and reading the legation's board or even delivering the promised despatch themselves. But whatever they may have intended it was not to be. Firing suddenly broke out and the little group scurried for safety.

MacDonald believed at first that the shots had come from the Fu, the guards there being unable to resist the temptation of 'bagging' a mandarin or two, but later he discovered they had been fired by Imperial troops to discourage any further communication between besiegers and besieged. Presumably, therefore, this episode was just another manifestation of the struggle between the moderate and reactionary parties within the Imperial Government.

## Shanghai, Paris, London, 26th June and later

The French Consul-General at Shanghai, M. Bezaure, reported to the Quai d'Orsay that in his opinion the foreign legates had been removed from Peking and were being held hostage in Shansi [Province] or Jehol. It was quite impossible, he believed, that Old China Hands like Sir Robert Hart and Bishop Favier could not get messages out of Peking if they were still there and alive. His colleague at Chefoo, M. Guerin, was another mine of misinformation. The Tientsin Concessions had fallen, he reported, Seymour had been captured, and the foreign legates had been removed from Peking to – he knew not where. But these worthy officials did sometimes get it right. For example, Guerin predicted that Yuan Shih k'ai would not intervene either for or against the foreigners unless it was obviously in his personal interest to join one side or the other, and

Bezaure assured Paris that the southern Viceroys were vehemently opposed to the Boxers.

But it was not only Chinese actions and intentions which exercised the minds of French diplomats and politicians. Those wretched English were fishing in troubled waters as usual: planning to seize Shanghai, Nanking and the Yangtse valley, using as an excuse the threat to British lives and property. This view was held not only by the French consular service in China but by no less a personality than M. Cambon, the Ambassador to the Court of St James and an architect of the Entente Cordiale. Although the Marquess of Salisbury, who was both Prime Minister and Foreign Secretary at the same time, had given him assurances to the contrary, Cambon was unconvinced. 'Your Excellency,' he wrote to Minister of Foreign Affairs Delcassé, 'should convince yourself that the time has come to make preparations unless we wish England to appropriate the richest areas of the Middle Kingdom.'

Soon France's worst suspicions were to be sharpened by the news that Admiral Seymour, far from languishing in a Chinese dungeon, had arrived in Shanghai for secret negotiations with the Viceroy. Equipped not only with his own pleasant and persuasive personality and backed by the threatening power of the Royal Navy, he was carrying with him a mouth-watering £75,000 worth of 'squeeze' money. Furthermore, an Indian brigade, at least 2,000 strong, was arriving in Hong Kong, more than was required to replace the Royal Welsh Fusiliers and other small British units which had been sent to north China.

These reports were based on fact but misinterpreted. Seymour visited Shanghai to investigate the security position in south China, to ascertain the attitudes of senior Chinese officials, to be briefed by the British consular authorities and to recommend a course of action, if any, to Her Majesty's Government. M. Bezaure had himself reported serious unrest in Shanghai with government employees unpaid and business at a standstill. He had suggested the despatch of two French warships to the port so it would have been imprudent of the British not to have made similar contingency plans against any upheaval in central and south China. As for the £75,000, naïve indeed the foreign emissary in China who failed to take account of the squeeze system. This money seems to have been handed over

112

to the powerful Viceroy at Hankow, Chang Chih-tung, in the form of a 'loan for the payment of troops'. We may assume that the intention was to ensure that none of Chang's troops took part in anti-foreign operations, paid or unpaid.

Less than two years after the Fashoda incident on the Nile, which had severely dented French prestige and national pride, British foreign policy throughout the world was regarded with almost paranoic suspicion by France. But it is highly improbable that the ageing Lord Salisbury, a cautious and pragmatic statesman, would have wished to embark upon another military adventure in China or even that he had the resources to do so, deeply embroiled as his country was in the South African War. What was happening in Peking was quite worrying enough and he had assured Cambon of his desire to maintain the status quo in the Middle Kingdom. He was no toppler of dynasties and preferred the devil he knew.

## Peking, 27th June

The siege had been under way for only a week and already eighteen Allied servicemen had been killed and at least that number wounded, some of whom would never return to duty. These were deeply worrying statistics. At this rate of attrition, if the siege lasted even for a few weeks, the garrison would be so depleted as to end all effective resistance. The most dangerous areas were the Tartar Wall,* held by the Americans, Germans and Russians, and the Fu held by the Japanese and Italians. The British and French contingents were primarily responsible for the defence of their own legations but they and the Austrians were also used as mobile reserves.

The Chinese system of attack was one of movable barricades, behind which they would advance, dismantling, pushing forward and rebuilding.† Continuously they battled for control of the Tartar Wall and the Fu and sometimes the respective barricades of besiegers and besieged would be within a few yards of one another.

Every now and again a gun would be trundled up to batter an Allied strongpoint but one of the many mysteries of the siege was

---

* 60 feet thick at the base, 52 feet wide at the top and 40 feet high.

† According to McCalla, who was not actually present during the siege, they used steel screens to cover their building operations.

113

A Chinese gun-platform erected against the Tartar Wall overlooking the Legation Quarter. (*National Army Museum*)

the ineffectiveness of the Chinese artillery. Usually the guns were over-elevated and most of the shells would whistle harmlessly over their targets. Barrages were seldom prolonged and rarely, if ever, followed up by a determined infantry assault. As, after the first few days, the diminishing number of defenders were in a permanent state of exhaustion, without heavy weapons and forced to conserve ammunition, a resolute and co-ordinated Chinese offensive against two or more sectors simultaneously would have ended the siege within a matter of hours. But this did not happen.

**The 27th** had been a hot, muggy day and that night a tremendous storm broke. US Marine Private Upham and his mates, on duty on the Tartar Wall within 100 yards of a Chinese barricade, spent a wet, uncomfortable and dangerous night. 'The rain coming down in torrents,' he recorded in his diary, 'a cold wind was blowing, the lightning was blinding, the Chinks seemed to go wild with delight and poured in a ton or two of lead at us.' But next morning he was able to note that 'dead Chinamen are getting very numbrous (sic) up here'.

114

## 28th–30th June

It was not until the end of June that all hope of Seymour's arrival had been abandoned and by then rumour and expectation had combined to dream up new rescue attempts. The Reverend Arthur Smith recorded that on the 28th it was being put about that a Chinese messenger had arrived from Tientsin with the news that an expedition would be setting out for Peking 'next Monday (2nd July) in three columns'. In reality, of course, the Allied garrison at Tientsin, although rapidly building up in numbers, was itself under siege and in no position to go anywhere, nor would it be for another fortnight or so.

On the evening of the 28th the Chinese opened up a terrific bombardment upon the British Legation stables. MacDonald and a Marine corporal who happened to be on the upper storey of the stable building 'made a record descent down the stairs and into the open'. The shelling did considerable damage and killed two mules and a pony (which of course were eaten) but in the process the Chinese gunners who were firing from the nearby Mongol Market suffered heavily from the small arms fire of the garrison and never repeated this particular performance.

The marksmanship of the various contingents was the subject of some comment both at the time and afterwards. The Americans were generally regarded, not least by themselves, as streets ahead of the others in this respect, although the small-bore Lee Straight-Pull rifle with which they were equipped required a high degree of accuracy to be effective. The British, who were armed with the excellent Lee-Metford .303, were considered bad shots by the Americans. When it came to sniping, those Royal Marine NCOs who had been trained as recruits with the old Martini-Henry .450 preferred this weapon, of which some had been found in the legation arms stores, as they were more likely to make a 'kill' with it. It had a kick like a mule but MacDonald, who had been a musketry instructor in his day, also enjoyed having a crack with one every now and again.

The French and Italians were regarded as profligate with their ammunition and the Japanese as handier with a bayonet than a rifle.

The bayonet came into its own during the various sorties against

Chinese barricades and gun positions. Less heroically, and in order to save ammunition, it was also used to despatch prisoners once they had been interrogated. One French sailor was credited, if that is the right word, with sending fifteen Boxer prisoners to meet their ancestors in this primitive manner. But not many prisoners were taken by either side. Few, perhaps only four, Europeans fell into Chinese hands during the siege; one, an eccentric English academic with the improbable name of Professor Huberty James, and another a Norwegian lunatic called Nestergard. James was murdered, probably after torture, and his severed head displayed for the amusement of the population. Nestergard, having voluntarily given the Chinese all the information about Allied dispositions, food supplies, etc. which his muddled head contained, was released, presumably because his captors shrewdly surmised that he would be a greater nuisance to the other side alive than dead. They were right. When he returned to the legations he admitted that he had told the enemy everything he knew. Loud were the demands for his execution but merciful voices, presumably those of the senior diplomats, prevailed and he was kept in close confinement for the remainder of the siege.

The loopholes in the barricades through which the defenders fired were a necessary hazard and as the sniping skills of the enemy seemed to improve, Sir Claude issued an instruction that they should never be left open except when in use. This was not always obeyed. Upham reckoned 'those Chinks have got it down pat. They can put five shots out of six through a loophole three inches square and don't need field-glasses to do it either.' On the 29th a Russian was killed in this way, while smoking a cigarette and foolishly puffing the smoke through the hole, and on the 30th the third American fatality, Private Tuchter, was shot in the eye while peering through another loophole.

These were days of severe casualties. As well as Tuchter and the Russian, four Germans were shot on the Wall and Private Phillips of the Royal Marines was killed by a ricochet in the British Legation compound. Those attending Tuchter's funeral were moved when a Russian jumped into the grave and smoothed the rough earth on which they were about to lay the corpse. 'He was my brother,' he explained, 'we fought together.'

116

# JULY

## 1st July

Taken by surprise the Germans were driven from their position on the Tartar Wall, thus exposing the Americans to an attack from the rear and forcing them to withdraw as well. Suddenly the Wall, the vital, commanding Wall, was there for the taking. But not for the first or last time the Chinese failed to seize the opportunity of occupying the vacated positions in sufficient strength to hold them against counterattack. In the course of the day the American commander, Captain Myers, with a mixed force of his own men, British and Russian, managed to retake the American position and set about building a new barricade to protect his rear from the Chinese-occupied German position. Corporal Gowney who, under Captain Wray, was a member of the British party assigned to this task, recalled crawling under fire over a number of rotting Chinese bodies which caused him 'to vomit somewhat violently'. Captain Myers handed round strong cigars which did something to quell the stench but Upham had a theory that 'a dead Chinaman has a peculiar odour all of his own', which even the pungent cigar smoke could not dispel.

This operation, though partially successful, was costly. An American, Private Kennedy, was killed and a number of others of various nationalities were wounded, including Captain Wray. According to Gowney, the wounding of Wray caused the Russians to bolt, spreading panic to the others. Gowney himself, it seems, was busy attending to Wray and a Royal Marine, confusingly called Myers, took charge and 'by persuasion and threats' forced the remainder to give covering fire while the wounded were evacuated. For this he received the Distinguished Conduct Medal.

While this was going on, word reached MacDonald that the French Legation, to the extreme east of the defended area, was also under severe pressure; a French civilian volunteer, Wagner, had been killed and the garrison had fallen back leaving the German Legation exposed on two sides, that is to say from the Tartar Wall where the former German position was still in Chinese hands and now from the French Legation as well. Herr von Below, the German Chargé d'Affaires, sent to MacDonald for reinforcements but by the time these, seven Royal Marines, arrived on the scene the French had managed to recover their legation and a perilous situation had been stabilized. Yet again the attackers had failed to follow up or consolidate a critical advantage.

But there was no easing of pressure elsewhere. Demands for reinforcements were coming from Colonel Shiba and the Italian commander, Lieutenant Paolini, in the Fu, which despite the dogged resistance of its defenders, was by now partially in Chinese hands. A Krupp gun which had been firing intermittently all day had been moved nearer the Allied line. Paolini thought he could take it and MacDonald and Shiba agreed that he should try. A captured gun and some ammunition would be of immense value.

But the ill-conceived and hastily mounted attempt was a disaster. Emerging from the Fu into a maze of streets, presumably with the intention of taking the gun position from the rear, Paolini's mixed force of about thirty men, including five British civilian volunteers, found itself trapped in a narrow alley, under fire from a barricade in front and from a high wall on one side. From eye-witness accounts (the whole operation was observed from a vantage point in the Han-lin, part of which was held by the British) it appears that, caught in a death-trap, some of the men tried desperately to crowd through a hole in the wall leading back into the Fu. Two Italian sailors were killed and Paolini and several others wounded. However, the leader of the volunteers, Russell, kept his head and he and his four companions gave covering fire while the regulars got through the hole. The volunteers then withdrew singly but one of them, Walter Townsend of the Consular Service, was severely wounded and died later.

Shiba, as senior officer on the spot, took full responsibility for this costly fiasco. The little garrison could not afford these adventures and it was agreed between MacDonald and the contingent commanders that such sorties in future would be permitted only in order to dislodge the enemy from positions which presented the defence with an unacceptable threat.

Fate decreed that just such a situation should arise on the following day, **2nd July**. MacDonald was obliged to authorize a similar operation when it was observed that the Chinese had considerably strengthened their position at the west end of the Tartar Wall and

118

had constructed a makeshift tower, already about fifteen feet high, from which they could fire down upon the defences in that sector overlooking the American Legation.

In the early hours of **3rd July**, while it was still dark, a force of about fifty Americans, British and Russians under Captain Myers was assembled at the American barricade within a few yards of the Chinese position. The British detachment of twenty-five marines was commanded by Nigel Oliphant, a civilian volunteer with some military experience (he had been a lance-corporal in the Argyll and Sutherland Highlanders), as no British officer was available. The fact that Sergeant Murphy, the senior Royal Marine NCO, was present and yet subordinated to Oliphant may seem curious to us but Oliphant was a 'gentleman', despite having served in the ranks, and therefore by the accepted practice of the time was, ipso facto, in command – probably to the relief of Sergeant Murphy.

Before launching his attack, the weary Myers, who had been on almost continuous duty since the beginning of the siege, made a depressing speech to his men to the effect that although he did not approve of the operation, orders were orders and must be carried out even if every man was lost in the attempt. The enemy must be expelled from this vital position. Anyone who didn't like the idea could stand down, he added. One man who claimed to have a sore arm did; that in itself must have taken a certain kind of courage but a disconcerted Oliphant was relieved that it was not one of the Royal Marines, most of whom had taken a dim view of Myers' speech and showed a marked reluctance to line up behind a commander who so obviously lacked faith in the outcome of the enterprise.

After some hesitation the Allies clambered over their barricade and advanced noisily towards their objective, with the Anglo-Americans on the left and the Russians on the right. The Chinese, alerted by the noise, opened a heavy fire and in the dark the two groups lost touch with each other. As the British and Americans pressed forward, Myers, victim of one of the absurdities of war, tripped over a spear which wounded him so badly in the leg that he was unable to continue. Oliphant, Murphy and several others soon covered the few yards to the enemy position and found themselves unobserved right up against the Chinese barricade and at the foot of the tower which appeared to be deserted. Dismissing the possibility of storming the barricade from the front, Oliphant attempted to work his way round to its rear but was checked by a warning shout from one of his men that they were about to collide with the Russians who, he thought, were coming round from the other side. Probably what the man saw in the confusion and darkness were Chinese retreating from the barricade, but Oliphant, nonplussed, stopped and 'squatted down to await developments'. The unfortunate civilian was completely out of his depth. He had no experience of this kind of thing, a commando operation for which nowadays men are trained for months or even years before being exposed to it, and, furthermore, was unfamiliar with this sector of the wall.

A nerve-racking wait it must have been, during which an American marine, Turner, was shot dead by a stray bullet and Oliphant killed a Chinese with his revolver, despite another shouted warning that the man might be a Russian. Eventually, and presumably realizing the futility of doing nothing, he ordered his men to keep up a covering fire on the barricade and made his way back to the wounded Myers for instructions. From him he learnt that the Russians had got no further than a few yards from their starting point before turning back with only one man wounded, so there were no Russians anywhere near the Chinese barricade. Better go back and finish the job, advised Myers. In the event this presented little difficulty as the only Chinese still there were dead!

MacDonald described this operation as 'brilliantly successful', as indeed, in a curiously unsatisfactory kind of way, it was. Had the Chinese remained in possession of this dominant position, the Germans having already lost their section of the Wall, the Americans might not have been able to retain theirs. This could have led to the evacuation of the American Legation and, in 'domino' sequence, the Russian and British Legations. Thus the Allies could have lost the whole of the defended area to the west of the canal. Next the virtually undefended Spanish and Japanese Legations could have fallen and Colonel Shiba in the Fu would have been completely surrounded. To the east the exposed French and German Legations could not have held out for long and that would have been that. The American missionary who regarded this action as 'the pivot of our destiny' did not exaggerate but nor were Myers' gloomy prognostications entirely unjustified. He himself had been put out of action and two of his men, Turner, his best sniper, and Thomas, were dead. Of the other contingents, Corporal Gregory of the Royal Marines and one Russian had been wounded. Later, in the clearing-up operation which followed the seizure of the Chinese position, another American marine was severely wounded.

There was in this action that element of grim farce which characterizes so many such operations – the confusion, the hesitation, the misunderstanding and the anti-climax. The wounding of Captain Myers was a severe blow to the morale and efficiency of the US Marine contingent. These men were, to say the least, rugged individualists. They were also much addicted to strong waters of which they seem to have acquired a considerable supply, probably from the three European-owned emporia situated in the legation quarter. They had little time for their other officer, the ineffectual Captain Hall, and paid scant regard to their NCOs, the senior of whom, Sergeant Fanning, had in any case been killed early in the siege. To make matters worse they distrusted Conger and, in particular, his First Secretary, Herbert Squiers, who, they believed, was helping himself to their rations. Furthermore, they suspected MacDonald of conniving at Squiers' alleged depredations and sometimes refused to accept his orders. But they seem to have had a reasonable working relationship with the other national contingents, although they disliked the British civilians who tended to address them, in the patronising fashion of the time, as 'my man', which they found extremely offensive. Nevertheless, as individuals they were useful fighting men and good shots and, bearing in mind that they were responsible for one of the most dangerous and vulnerable sectors of the defences, their contribution was probably of greater value than that of any other contingent except perhaps the Japanese.

Tiny both in numbers and stature, the Japanese contrasted sharply with their American and other Allies. There were only twenty-five of them, plus their commander, the Military Attaché, Colonel Goro Shiba, and in the course of the siege they suffered over 100% casualties since some of them were wounded more than once. Their musketry was not particularly good and they were prone to expose themselves unnecessarily to enemy fire, but their discipline was perfect, their stamina unflagging and their readiness to co-operate with the other contingents unfailing. Shiba, who later received a

British knighthood, emerged from the ordeal of defending the Fu as the most outstanding military figure of the siege.

Corporal Gowney has left a brisk, professional description of these men, representatives of a nation whose military ethic, so much feared by future generations, had, at the turn of the century, hardly been noticed in the west.

'These seemed to be all one size,' Gowney wrote, 'about five foot one or two in height, hardly an inch difference in them. They were very compactly built and sturdy with nine-shot magazine rifles, rather quaint weapons, bullet conical, bore almost square, bayonet smaller than ours, rifle name Murita. Uniform strong, serviceable leather boots, white spats, white trousers, black tunic, white cap. . . . They are splendidly disciplined, no fear . . . in our sorties and attacks they showed a tendency always to come to close quarters with the bayonet.' The Chinese, according to Gowney, had a particular dread of cold steel. 'I have known many instances of Chinese being dropped by dozens in their barricade-building by rifle fire, but no stoppage or delay: as soon as one was bowled over, another would take his place and so on until the barricade was built: but the moment the bayonet was brought into play, a different tale was told,' he concluded with relish.

## 5th July

Nigel Oliphant's brother David, also a civilian volunteer and a member of the legation staff, was shot and mortally wounded while felling a tree in front of the defences in the Han-lin. His was the 39th death among the defenders and 55 had been wounded. Deaths among the Chinese work-force, mostly Christian refugees, who toiled for long hours under heavy fire building barricades and repairing damage, were not recorded. They received smaller rations than the Europeans and were often roughly treated, preferring to work under the Japanese who, it is surprising to learn, did not kick them and knock them about as the European and American servicemen did.

## 6th July

On this day there was a curious incident. A Russian student, his mind presumably unhinged by the strain of the siege, left the French Legation and walked towards a Chinese barricade in Legation Street. When he got to within ten yards of it he was shot dead. As a large bounty was payable on European heads, several Chinese dashed from behind their barricade and one after the other were shot by the French sailors. But the Chinese won their prize in the end by dragging the Russian away in the night.

## 8th July

Captain Thomann, the commander of the Austrian contingent who was held responsible for the precipitate withdrawal from vital positions on the third day of the siege, was killed by a shell which fell on the German Legation. Also a bullet passed impertinently through the portrait of Queen Victoria which hung in the MacDonalds' dining-room.

The defenders' only artillery piece, the Italian one-pounder, was down to its last fourteen shells. However, the resourceful Armourer's Mate Thomas of the Royal Navy managed to refill the empty shell-cases with shot cast from such household items as metal tea-pots and candlesticks, charged with powder from the Russian shells (it will be recalled that the Russians forgot their gun but brought its shells) and percussion caps taken from .45 revolver ammunition. Some seventy of these missiles were used with apparent good effect and none misfired.

But Thomas's ingenuity and that of his American colleague, Mitchell, was put to an even sterner test when an old cannon, probably dating from the 1860 occupation of Peking by the Anglo-French, was discovered in a foundry by some Chinese Christians. By dint of much hammering, planing and filing, the two artificers managed to mount the cannon on a spare set of wheels belonging to the Italian gun. By the 8th the 'International Gun', more affectionately known as Betsy or the Empress Dowager, was ready for action. Her first shot, using the Russian ammunition modified to fit her bore, was fired at a Chinese battery at a range of some 300 yards

The International Gun, also known as Betsy or the Empress Dowager, with Royal Marines and others. Note the expensive materials used as sand-bags. (*National Army Museum*)

but, recorded MacDonald, 'the projectile went screaming over the battery into the Imperial City'. The second fell short and the third hit the battery – a classic artillery straddle. In the course of her career, Betsy probably did little damage to the enemy but much to boost the morale of the defenders who felt that at last they were getting their own back on the Chinese gunners.

## Tientsin

Eighty miles to the south-east at Tientsin, artillery was playing an even greater role. Since the middle of June it was estimated that some 40,000 shells had fallen on the Foreign Concessions in the course of a siege which, materially, was more devastating than that of the Peking legations. There were many human victims too, among

Midshipman Frank Esdaile, RN, aged 17. Perhaps the youngest Allied combat casualty of the Boxer campaign. (*Mrs E. Warmington*)

them perhaps the youngest Allied combatant casualty, 17-year-old Midshipman Frank Esdaile of HMS *Barfleur*, who died of his wounds on 7 July.

But there was a significant difference between the two sieges. The garrison at Tientsin was there because it wanted to be. It was not trapped. It could withdraw whenever it wished, and, indeed most of the non-combatant European population had been evacuated to Japan. Its problem hitherto had been that it had insufficient strength and, above all, inadequate organization, to move forward, to take the Walled City of Tientsin and to advance, with its rear secure, on Peking. This state of affairs was about to change.

Apart from artillery bombardments, which were by no means one-sided, particularly after the arrival of several 12-pounder guns in HMS *Terrible* from South Africa,* there was also intermittent and unco-ordinated infantry patrolling and skirmishing around the

---

* The ship's company of the *Terrible* were probably the only British servicemen to receive both the Queen's South Africa Medal and the China Medal.

Concessions, the city of Tientsin and its suburbs. As we have seen, General Dorward's lot was not a happy one. He never knew at any given time precisely how many troops and guns he had under his 'command'. To an extent this was unavoidable as men and weapons were arriving in dribs and drabs from Taku often without prior notice. But perhaps his greatest difficulty was mutual suspicion. The Russians, who were highly unpredictable, preferred to conceal their strength (or weakness) from the Japanese and vice versa. The French too were cagey. For example, after the campaign was over, a senior British officer, reporting to the War Office, had to admit that he had been unable to obtain accurate figures from the French command for fear that he might pass the information on to the Germans!

HMS *Terrible*. Apart from a very few individuals, her ship's company were the only British servicemen to participate in both the Boer War and the Boxer campaign. (*Illustrated London News*)

The day after Dorward's arrival at Tientsin, 27 June, the Russians decided, apparently without consultation with their Allies, to attack the East Arsenal which lay about two and a half miles to the east of the Concessions. They do not appear to have had much of a plan (they seldom had) and Captain Barnes of the (British) Chinese Regiment, watching from a tower in the British Concession, 'could see that the Russians were being worsted, for part of their line was

126

retiring at no mean speed'. Deciding that after all a little Allied support might be helpful, the Russian commander, General Stossel,* sent in haste to Dorward for reinforcements. Obligingly, Dorward produced three companies of the Chinese Regiment and a Royal Naval 'brigade'. With the Chinese companies covering the left flank, the Naval brigade under Major Johnstone (who had distinguished himself during the Seymour expedition) advanced on the arsenal, from which appeared to be coming an immense volume of small arms fire. In fact the defenders were letting off large numbers of fire-crackers, a habit which the Allies had encountered before and which was, presumably, intended to scare the wits out of your opponent without wasting any ammunition on him. In this instance, the ploy failed and the arsenal fell to the Allies without much further resistance.

Stossel's erratic behaviour remained a sore trial to Dorward and the other Allied commanders. Having defended since mid-June the railway station, which, even if no trains could pull in or out, was regarded as a vital asset against the day when the line to T'angku would be repaired and operational, Stossel announced suddenly on 2 July that he had had enough and was withdrawing his men. By the morning of the 4th Dorward had managed to collect a relief force consisting of the marines of HMS *Terrible*, fifty men of the Hong Kong Regiment, some French marines and sailors and a few Japanese, about three hundred in all. These took over the station and defended it for the remainder of the siege.

It may be of interest to dwell for a moment on two other British imperial curiosities, which, like the 1st Chinese Regiment, were involved in these events. These were the Hong Kong Regiment of Infantry and the Hong Kong and Singapore Artillery. Neither were recruited in the places which gave them their names, although they were based there. The men of both were Punjabi Moslems and Sikhs and the officers were seconded from the British or Indian Armies. About 400 men of these units took part in the Boxer campaign, which, in the case of the Hong Kong Regiment, was virtually its

---

* General Anatole Michailovich Stossel (1848–1915). This officer was sentenced to death for surrendering Port Arthur to the Japanese in January, 1905. The sentence was never carried out but he remained under its threat until 1909 when he was pardoned.

天津城埋伏地雷董軍大門勝西兵圖

天津北倉義和團民大破洋兵

Chinese versions of the Siege of Tientsin. The Chinese captions read: 1. 'The Chinese Army wins a great battle against the Western troops in the minefields near Tientsin.' No minefields are recorded in Allied accounts. 2. 'The Chinese Army conquers the Western Army during the Boxer Rebellion at Tientsin.' Of course, in reality no such victories were achieved. (*The late Mr Han Zhong Min/Research Centre of Inscriptions and Documents*) only taste of action (although earlier it had done a little skirmishing with dissident Chinese in the New Territories). But its life was short and in 1902, only ten years after its formation, it fell victim to government defence cuts. The officer commanding its two companies in the fighting around Tientsin and in the advance to Peking, Captain E. C. Rowcroft, was awarded the DSO and Subedar-Major Surdar Khan the Order of British India. Eleven of its men were killed, ten died of other causes and thirty-one were wounded.

The Hong Kong and Singapore Artillery had a longer existence and survived until the independence and partition of the Indian sub-continent in 1947. In China its two companies (or batteries) were equipped with four 2.5-inch mountain guns and four Maxim machine-guns. The commanding officer was Major St John and his adjutant, Captain Waymouth, was a veteran of Kitchener's recent campaign in the Sudan. Few casualties were suffered in China and Havildar Roshan Khan was awarded the DCM.

HMS *Terrible*'s 12 pounders and ammunition being landed at Taku. (*Illustrated London News*)

To return to Tientsin station, typically, the Chinese failed to exploit the moment of handover from the Russians to the relief force and waited for their fresh opponents to settle in before renewing their attack on the afternoon of the 4th. This consisted largely of shelling and several men were wounded in the station's engine-house, but by 7.30 pm it had petered out.

## 9th July

The Chinese attempted to move to the east and south of the Concessions whereby they hoped to cut the Allied lines of communication with Taku. This was foiled by a substantial mixed force under Dorward and a spectacular charge of Japanese cavalry (the only Allied cavalry in China at the time) scattered the Chinese. The Allies then took the Western Arsenal but heavy shelling and the fear of a massive explosion caused its evacuation by nightfall. General Nieh is believed to have been killed in this action.

## 10th July

The first major US unit, the 9th Infantry Regiment of three battalions, began to arrive in Tientsin having sailed from the Philippines

A Japanese cavalry trooper. The Japanese were poor horse-masters and their infantry was greatly superior to their cavalry. (*Institution of Royal Engineers*)

130

towards the end of June. A few days earlier, under increasing British diplomatic pressure, the Japanese Government had ordered the 5th Division under General Yamaguchi to Tientsin, the first elements of which increased the Allied force to a total of about 14,000 fighting men. Ponderously, the Allies were gearing themselves for the assault on the Walled City of Tientsin.

## Peking, 13th July

For Sir Claude MacDonald, and no doubt others, 'this was the most harassing day for the defence during the whole course of the siege'. In the Fu, Colonel Shiba and his Japanese-Italian group, despite resisting desperately, had had to fall back on their penultimate line of defence and three-quarters of its grounds were in enemy hands. Sir Claude sent him ten Russians as reinforcements but by the time they arrived the amazing little colonel was able to send them back with word that he had matters under control. He never hung on to men he did not need knowing they were almost certainly required elsewhere. Sure enough, no sooner had the Russians reported back to MacDonald when a messenger from von Below in the German Legation appeared begging for immediate help. The breathless Russians arrived just in time to join their German colleagues in a bayonet charge which drove the Chinese back.

The French too were in difficulties. Two mines had exploded under their Second Secretary's house, killing two French sailors and burying their commander, Lieutenant d'Arcy, who was dug out shaken and cut but not very seriously hurt. Apparently the mines had gone off prematurely, blowing up thirty of the Chinese sappers who had laid them. The Chinese could afford such losses but, by the end of the day, five irreplaceable legation guards had been killed and ten wounded.

## 15th July

A French and a British volunteer both died of wounds on this day. The Englishman, Henry Warren, was not seriously wounded but through exhaustion and debilitation lacked the strength to pull through.

In the Fu, Shiba's men too had reached a state of almost complete exhaustion. Since 20 June they had never had more than three or four hours sleep' consecutively and it was arranged, not without complicated re-scheduling of duties, that they should be replaced for a full 24 hours by Royal Marines and volunteers, as from 7 am the following morning.

## 16th July

A black day for the British contingent. Captain Strouts, its commander, accompanied by George Morrison, had taken the relief force to the Fu as arranged. After the handover, the two men, together with Colonel Shiba, had started to return to the British Legation when they were caught in a hail of bullets from a Chinese barricade into whose line of vision they had carelessly allowed themselves to stray. Morrison was hit in the thigh but not immediately disabled. Simultaneously, with a gasp of 'My God!', Strouts collapsed into Shiba's arms and was dragged under cover. Shiba ran

A group of Royal Marines who relieved the Japanese in the Han-lin on the day that their commander, Captain Strouts, was killed. (*Royal Marine Museum*)

132

for a Japanese surgeon who appeared within minutes and tried to staunch the flow of blood from Strouts' wound, a severed main artery in the thigh. By this time Morrison had fainted from his own wound but came to in the hospital in time to witness the last moments of his young comrade-in-arms. 'He said nothing but by and by gave a few sobs of pain, then his breath came quietly and he sank away into death.'

The loss of Strouts was a severe blow to the command structure, such as it was, of the defence. Not only was he one of the most efficient and energetic commanders but he had also acted as a kind of Chief of Staff to MacDonald, co-ordinating and organizing with skill and, above all, with tact. No bad word had been spoken of him in life and in death he was sorely missed. As Chief of Staff he was replaced by Herbert Squiers, the American First Secretary, a resourceful man with some previous military experience,* but as

Captain B. M. Strouts, the popular and respected commander of the Royal Marine legation guards, who was killed in action during the siege. (*Royal Marine Museum*)

* As a cavalry officer, Squiers had been at the Battle of Wounded Knee, which finally broke the resistance of the Sioux in 1890.

commander of the British contingent Strouts was irreplaceable. Halliday was, and would remain, out of action and Wray was a poor substitute. According to Poole who worked closely with Wray, 'he had not the confidence of the men' and it is noteworthy that at a time when honours and decorations were showered upon all ranks like confetti (they were regarded as compensation for low pay and poor conditions as well as rewards for gallantry and merit), Wray was not even Mentioned in Despatches.

The other contingents were in little better shape. Myers, though his bizarre wound was better, had developed typhoid. D'Arcy was wounded and so was Paolini. Thomann was dead. Many of the senior NCOs and Petty Officers had been killed or wounded and their remaining men were exhausted and undernourished. A number of the bravest and most capable volunteers had also been killed or wounded. Morrison, as good as any trained officer, would not be fit for duty for weeks.

Pichon burnt his files and even the phlegmatic MacDonald was at his wits' end. He revealed nothing of his despair at the time but later he said, 'The end, to those who knew, was clearly in sight . . . if our losses continued at the same daily rate, by the end of July, or even before then, there would be nobody left to oppose the entry of Tung Fu-hsiang's bloodthirsty ruffians but women and children and 120 grievously wounded men. But,' he concluded, 'the night is darkest before the dawn.'

Although there were still long hours of darkness ahead, events elsewhere in north China had brought that dawn a little closer. By 3.30 am *on 13 July* the assault on the *Walled City of Tientsin* was under way. It should have been impregnable to straight-forward storming tactics but, defended by the Chinese Army, it was not. There were gates at the four points of the compass but a resolute defence could have made them unapproachable. Elsewhere the massive walls could not be breached except by weeks of pounding with the heaviest artillery and the Allies had neither the weeks nor the artillery. They resolved therefore to take the city by storm and this, thanks largely to the determination and courage of the Japanese, they did.

But not without cost. Access to the gates was along raised causeways built across flat, marshy land easily dominated from the city

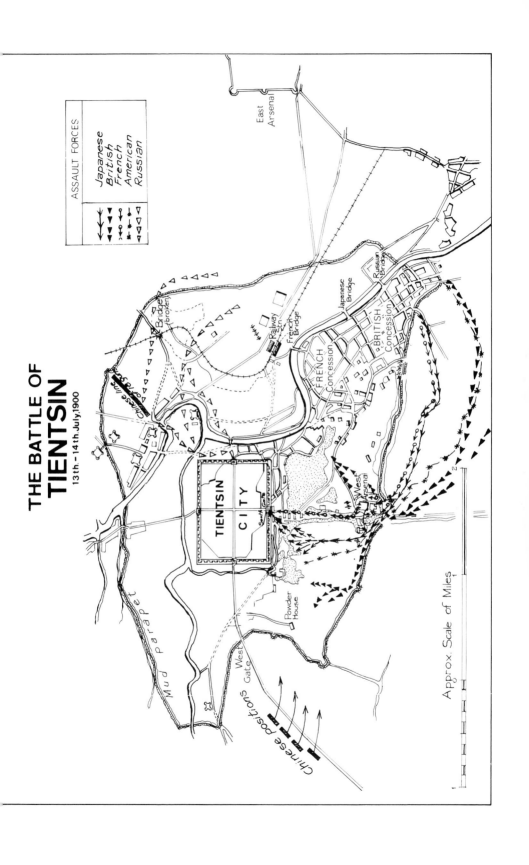

THE BATTLE OF
# TIENTSIN
13th – 14th July, 1900

ASSAULT FORCES

Japanese
British
French
American
Russian

East Arsenal

Bridge (broken)

Railway Stn

French Bridge

Japanese Bridge

Russian Bridge

FRENCH Concession

BRITISH Concession

TIENTSIN CITY

South Gate

West Arsenal

Powder House

West Gate

Chinese positions

Mud parapet

Approx. Scale of Miles

walls and swept with artillery and small arms fire. Moreover, the surrounding countryside was dotted with hamlets, isolated huts and criss-crossed with canals and waterways, ideal terrain over which well-trained infantry might have staged a fighting withdrawal into the city at great cost to the attackers. Although no such well-trained infantry existed in the Chinese Army (with the possible exception of Yuan Shih-k'ai's division which took no part in the conflict), nonetheless relatively heavy casualties were inflicted upon the assaulting troops.

There was no overall Allied commander and the precise numbers of men involved on both sides are unknown. Allied strengths, the individual national contributions and their casualties, vary from account to account. Commandant Vidal, for example, reported that some 8,000 men, including 1,400 French, took part, whereas the Regimental History of the US 9th Infantry gives a figure of 5,650 of whom only 600 were French. As for the Chinese, perhaps some 30,000 men, Imperial troops of the 1st and 2nd Divisions plus Greens and Boxers, were involved in the defence of the city.

The plan of attack worked out between the Allied commanders, with Dorward co-ordinating rather than commanding, was that the city would be stormed after the usual preliminary bombardment, in a two-pronged assault. The Japanese, British and Americans, and French, in three columns, would advance upon the southern entrance to the city while the Russians, with some German support (very few German troops had arrived) would circle round to the north-east and enter through the east gate.

The Russians, about 2,500 strong, who had the longer approach march, moved out of the Concessions at 5 pm on the 12th in order to deliver their attack at 10 am on the following day. At 3 am on the 13th the three 'southern' columns* set off 500 yards apart with the French under Colonel de Pelacot on the right, the Japanese under General Fukushima (Yamaguchi had not yet arrived) in the

* The strength of these columns given in Dorward's report are as follows:

| | |
|---|---|
| French | 900 |
| Japanese | 1,500 |
| American | 900 |
| British | 800 |
| Austrian | 30 |

136

centre and the Anglo-Americans under Dorward (Colonel Meade of the Marines was the senior American officer) on the left. The artillery bombardment of forty-two (Vidal's figure) guns, the heaviest being HMS *Terrible*'s three 12 pounders, opened up at 5.30 am.

At 6.30 the infantry attack went in with the South Gate of the city as its objective. The Japanese in the centre almost immediately began to forge ahead of the columns to their right and left, exposing their left to a powerful Chinese force including cavalry and causing Fukushima to ask Dorward for support on that flank. According to the British General, 'The 9th American Infantry was directed by me to give this support and also to support the attack of the [Royal Welsh] Fusiliers and [Royal] Marines.' But the history of the 9th tells a different story. According to its account, Dorward's instructions to Colonel Emerson H. Liscum, the 9th's elderly commanding officer, were vague. One officer overheard Dorward telling Liscum, 'Left or right, it makes no different but look smart!' Whatever the truth of the matter, the Americans moved up on the right rather than the left and found themselves out of position and uncertain of their role for the rest of the action. The Chinese threat on the left was held off by the Welsh under Captain Gwynne and the Royal Marines (Major Luke) supported by Maxims of the Hong Kong and Singapore Artillery.

By now the Japanese had re-taken the Western Arsenal in the vicinity of which Liscum met and endeavoured to consult with one of their senior officers, presumably with the intention of working

One of the 12-pounder guns, with gun carriage designed and built by the ship's artificers, landed from HMS *Terrible* suitably inscribed. (*Illustrated London News*)

out a joint plan of action. Unfortunately, in the absence of a common language 'the meeting only resulted in bowing and smiling and the pantomime introduction of two or three officers on each side all of which transpired under considerable fire'. Soon, these polite formalities completed, the Japanese pressed on, followed by the Americans but no one any the wiser or better informed.

Meanwhile the French on the right had been held up by heavy fire, were unable or unwilling to deploy into line and were bunched together on the road leading to the South Gate. The Japanese forward troops, on reaching the city wall, halted, presumably awaiting orders before attempting to blow open and storm through the South Gate. However, the fog of war was smothering even the efficient Japanese. At about 1 pm, Fukushima, assuming for some reason that his forward troops were already in the city, sent a note (in French) to Dorward informing him of this and asking for the artillery barrage to be lifted. Dorward obliged, with the result that the Chinese gunners and riflemen scrambled from their places of safety and opened a withering fire upon the assaulting infantry both from the city walls and the surrounding suburbs.

When the mistake was realized, the Allied bombardment was

An American infantryman of the 9th or 14th Infantry. (*National Army Museum*)

renewed but the 9th Infantry, many of whom were pinned down in open ground, had suffered severe casualties, including their Colonel. According to eye-witnesses, Liscum, mortally wounded, died clutching the Stars and Stripes which he had seized from a fallen colour-sergeant, and calling upon his men to keep up their fire. But their ammunition was running short and an appeal from Major Lee, now in command of the regiment, to Dorward brought Captain Ollivant of the Chinese Regiment with one of his men leading a laden mule forward with fresh supplies. They did not get far. When mule and muleteer were both killed, Ollivant loaded himself with some of the ammunition and staggered on. 'The Fates, however, were against him,' wrote one of his brother officers, 'and he had only gone a few steps when he was shot through the head.'

For the rest of the day there was little forward movement by the Allies, most of whom were stalled in the area between the Western Arsenal and the city. With great difficulty the Americans were withdrawn from their exposed position, most of their wounded being carried back by stretcher-bearers of the Chinese Regiment. Even the Japanese had run out of steam temporarily. From the Russians there was no news. Stalemate seemed to have been reached and ahead of the Allies was the daunting prospect of having to lay siege to the city and starve its defenders into submission while time ran out for the Peking Legations.

Fortunately, and perhaps on the advice of the experienced Fuku-shima, the city had not been surrounded and the north and west gates were safe exits for any who wished to depart. Many did and in the night much of the Chinese defence simply melted away. At 3 am on the 14th the tireless Japanese, at the cost of the lives of most of the sappers involved, blew the South Gate and entered the city. There was some desultory street fighting but most of the Chinese troops and Boxers had fled, leaving the civilian population to its fate – in many cases a grisly fate at that. Later in the morning, the Russians, 'delayed by unforeseen causes', to quote Dorward, entered through the East Gate and the city was given over to plunder, rape and murder of medieval proportions.

Relative to the rest of the campaign the Allied 'butcher's bill' had been heavy. Again the statistics vary but average around 800 killed and wounded, of whom about half were Japanese. The French, pinned down and huddled together on the causeway, had also suffered heavily, as had the US 9th Infantry, with their colonel and twenty-two men killed and three officers and seventy men wounded.

Dorward's report gives the following British casualties:

Royal Welsh Fusiliers: 5 men killed, 12 men wounded;
Hong Kong Regiment: 1 man killed, 7 men wounded;
Hong Kong and Singapore Artillery: 2 men killed and 5 men wounded;
Chinese Regiment: 1 officer and 6 men killed, 1 officer and 13 men (including 1 British NCO) wounded;
Royal Marines: 1 officer killed and 1 wounded, 16 men wounded;
Royal Navy: 1 officer wounded, 5 men killed and 19 men wounded.

Among those decorated for gallantry was Midshipman Basil Guy, aged eighteen of HMS *Barfleur*, who received the Victoria Cross for

Midshipman Guy, RN, the 18 year old who won the Victoria Cross for trying to save a wounded seaman under fire. (*Illustrated London News*)

trying to save the life of a wounded seaman under heavy fire. Colour-Sergeant Purdon, Coldstream Guards, and Sergeant Gi Dien Kwee,* both with the 1st Chinese Regiment, were awarded the Distinguished Conduct Medal.

As for the commanders of the various national contingents, all were soon to be superseded by more senior, but not necessarily more competent, officers. Dorward sent a somewhat ambiguous apology to Colonel Meade accepting the responsibility for placing the 9th Infantry in a dangerous position but suggesting that they had lost their way through inexperience. The Americans had much the same opinion of Dorward as he had of them. '[He] was only an engineer,' wrote one, 'and probably didn't know what he was doing anyway.' A few days later, he was replaced by a veteran Indian Army officer, Lieutenant-General Alfred Gaselee, and remained for the rest of the campaign as commandant of the Tientsin garrison.

Not a few descriptions have been left of the scenes at Tientsin on the morning of *14 July* – 'a picture of hell's delight,' wrote a US Marine officer, 'men shot, men bayoneted, men wounded, men who played dead as we neared them. Through the streets rushed Chinese, their shoulders bent beneath a burden of loot. Many commanders turned their men loose. Soldiers of all nations joined the orgy.'

Among other treasure, vast quantities of silver nuggets – 'sycee' – were found in the Tientsin Salt Commissioner's Yamen, most of which was 'liberated' by the Japanese. The Americans seized several hundred thousand dollars worth of gold from the provincial treasury but were convinced that the Japanese, and perhaps the British, had got there before them and taken the lion's share. Nor did Colonel Meade who, as senior US officer, had taken charge of this booty on behalf of Uncle Sam, trust the 9th Infantry to search for more gold in the vaults of the treasury, preferring to use his own marines, no doubt models of rectitude, for this tempting task. But for all Meade's conscientious devotion to its interests, the US Treasury was by no means the only beneficiary of the fall of Tientsin. Probably no single Allied officer or soldier left the city empty-handed. One group of young US Marine officers syndicated their spoils and eventually

---

* Sergeant Gi Dien Kwee is probably the only Chinese national ever to be awarded the DCM. Unfortunately, he was killed in an accident before he could receive it.

banked a tidy $8,000 worth of sycee, while some Welsh Fusiliers were so loaded with this weighty metal that later they had to discard much of it on the line of march.

Unfortunately looting, a traditional 'perk' for the soldiers after the horror and suffering of battle, was not the only activity in which the conquerors indulged. There seems little doubt that the behaviour of the Allied troops in the immediate aftermath of the battle was atrocious. On the basis of eye-witness recollections it is invidious to pick out individual national contingents for special condemnation as most of the observers directed their criticisms at nationalities other than their own, although there were exceptions. Lieutenant William Harllee of the US Marines declared that the Americans were the most drunken and indisciplined of all but added that the Russians were the most 'savage'.

Some men claimed to have tried to protect individual civilians. US Marine Private Adriance recorded coming upon a German raping a girl. 'When I spoke to him he reached for his gun but he was never able to reach a gun afterwards.' The girl in question was evidently a lucky exception to the rule that, according to Adriance, 'after they had ravished the girls and women they [the Germans and Russians] pierced them full of bayonet holes'.

'The United Nations' 1900-style. Allied troops and sailors perched on a heavy gun captured from the Chinese. At least five nationalities can be identified. (*Major A. P. B. Watkins*)

142

At Tientsin and elsewhere the Japanese won universal praise for their fighting performance, but, much more surprisingly, their behaviour towards the civilian population seems to have been superior to that of their allies. Certainly the battle for Tientsin and its aftermath reflected little credit on either Western arms or chivalry.

## Peking, 16th July

News of the fall of Tientsin soon reached the Forbidden City and fear gripped the hearts of the Manchus.

No sooner had the bodies of Strouts and Warren been laid in their shallow graves that afternoon when the first manifestations of these new doubts began to appear. The moderate Prince Ch'ing, who, it will be remembered, had been sacked from the Tsungli Yamen and replaced by the aggressive Tuan, was reactivated, at least in name. Conciliatory letters signed by him 'and others' began to arrive under flag of truce for the legates. It was not known if Ch'ing was truly the writer but it did not matter. MacDonald and his colleagues guessed that they were in correspondence with the Empress Dowager and some of her senior advisers, who were glimpsing the reality to which for so long she and they had been blind. The Boxers were phonies, good only for slaughtering unarmed missionaries and converts, the Imperial Army was a paper tiger and the barbarians were as irresistible as ever.

Up to a point it had always been possible to baffle the foreigner with a diplomatic cocktail of flattery mixed with oblique insult, expressions of concern for his safety mingled with threat, and sharp changes of direction. For the next fortnight or so this well-practised game was played with the legates as willing partners. They understood this sort of thing so much better than the vulgar brawl in which they had been involved since 20 June. Moreover, they too, through agents working for the Japanese, had heard about Tientsin. Surely rescue would arrive before the month was out, so the longer the game of diplomatic tennis could be prolonged the better.

## London

Meanwhile, although largely pre-occupied with events in South Africa, by the middle of July sections of the British press were

143

finding the silence from Peking intolerable. To the Fourth Estate no news is certainly not good news and sells no copy. On the evening of 15 July the *Daily Mail* received from its Special Correspondent in Shanghai a report which had travelled 'at the highest possible telegraphic cost' and which described in blood-curdling, and entirely fictitious, detail the fall of the Peking legations and the massacre of every European man, woman and child. There were, it seemed, no survivors and Alfred Harmsworth* and his editor spared their readers no clichés. Published the following morning, the 16th, under the headline THE PEKIN MASSACRE the sub-titles carried the reader along on a crescendo of fascinating horror.

All White Men and Women put to the Sword
Awful Story of 6th and 7th July
How Our People died fighting Prince Tuan's hordes
Death not Dishonour
With No Ammunition they died Sword in Hand
The climax was reached under the sub-heading
The Last Stand

'By this time (early morning 7th July), the walls of the Legation had been battered down, most of the buildings were in ruins from the Chinese artillery fire.

'Many of the allies had fallen at their posts, and the remaining small band who were still alive took refuge in the wrecked buildings which they endeavoured to hastily fortify.

'Upon them the fire of the Chinese artillery was now directed.

'Towards sunrise it was evident that the ammunition of the allies was running out, and at seven o'clock, as the advances of the Chinese in force failed to draw a response, it was at once clear that it was at length completely exhausted.

'A rush was determined upon.

'Thus standing together as the sun rose fully, the little remaining band, all Europeans, met death stubbornly.

'There was a desperate hand-to-hand encounter.

'The Chinese lost heavily and as one man fell others advanced, and finally, overcome by overwhelming odds, every one of the

---

* Later Viscount Northcliffe (1865–1922), one of Fleet Street's most ruthless giants and the father of modern 'tabloid' journalism.

144

Europeans remaining was put to the sword in the most atrocious manner.'

Thus, according to the *Daily Mail*, ended the Siege of the Legations. Some readers must have had difficulty deciding which was the more shocking – the report itself or its grammar.

In the days which followed, other newspapers embellished the story, adding a few juicy details of their own, while the stately *Times* was deceived into publishing obituaries* of its own correspondent in Peking, Dr George Morrison, and other leading figures such as Sir Claude MacDonald and Sir Robert Hart. A memorial service at St Paul's was arranged but, fortunately for the dignity of the Church, was cancelled when doubts as to the authenticity of the story began to creep in. Seldom, if ever, in the history of British journalism can so many have made such asses of themselves based on so little.

A few months later Morrison traced the authorship of the false report to an American gun-runner and forger called Sutterlee, alias Sylvester. In confirmation of his story, the *Daily Mail* cited an alleged cablegram to Reuter's in Shanghai from Yuan Shih-k'ai in Shantung Province. It is unclear if such a cablegram ever existed but the choice of a known crook like Sutterlee as its Special Correspondent may not have been one of the *Mail*'s more judicious appointments, although no doubt it temporarily increased its already legendary circulation. Morrison was half-amused and half-irritated by his glowing obituary and one of his friends suggested that after such a unique accolade *The Times* could hardly refuse to double his salary!

## Peking, 17th July

On the day of the publication of his obituary, Sir Claude MacDonald, still very much alive, held a strange conversation. While inspecting the defences on the Tartar Wall with his new Chief of Staff, Herbert Squiers, he was hailed by the commander of the enemy barricade some 60 yards distant. This officer asked to be allowed to bury his dead which had been lying and rotting for days within easy shot of both barricades and therefore immovable without mutual agreement. To the relief of the American marines who had been living

* See Appendix C.

with the stench in the airless heat of mid-summer, Sir Claude consented and, while the operation was in progress, called out through his interpreter to the Chinese officer suggesting that they should meet for a talk. After some hesitation, the Colonel (as MacDonald called him) agreed and for a while they sat chatting and smoking cigars. The Colonel, it turned out, was a Kansu Moslem, but under the direct orders of Jung Lu and not, as might have been expected, of the less amenable Tung. He told MacDonald that his chief wanted to stop the fighting, to which the British envoy replied that the foreigners had not started it in the first place and they too were anxious for peace. The Colonel offered to take a note to Jung Lu, an offer promptly accepted. A letter was quickly drafted to the effect that, in view of the 'negotiations' which the Tsungli Yamen had initiated on the previous day, the legation guards would not fire unless fired upon. In order to avoid misunderstanding it would be better if no more than two soldiers at a time should emerge from behind the Chinese barricades and that they should be unarmed. Furthermore, the construction of new barricades in advance of those

A view of the Tartar City of Peking as it was in 1900. (*Institution of Royal Engineers*)

146

already existing should be halted. This letter was duly conveyed to the Colonel and thence to Jung Lu. A line of communication had now been opened with the military as well as the Tsungli Yamen.

Private Upham and his fellow marines found it so quiet on the Wall that night that they could not sleep but in the morning they discovered the Chinese had started building a new barricade (as yet no reply had been received from Jung Lu to MacDonald's letter), so after a warning sign in Chinese had been displayed and ignored, the mighty 'Empress Dowager' cannon was brought into action blowing away part of the new barricade. 'They took the hint and quit,' Upham recorded with satisfaction.

The Japanese received a message from Tientsin, an edited version of which was posted on the Bell Tower of the British Legation. Although it confirmed the capture of Tientsin city and the preparation of a relief force, it also mentioned heavy Allied casualties and the shortage of transport. The bad bits were left out of the published notice and morale rose sharply.

Meanwhile Jung Lu's favourable reply to MacDonald's proposals was received, accepting the terms for a truce. For a few days this was almost totally effective, although it was clear from other messages received from the Chinese that, as ever, they were speaking with more than one voice. Some of these messages, calling for unconditional surrender, were conveyed by means of a trained dog which trotted happily to and fro between the Chinese and the Japanese barricades in the Fu, no doubt suitably rewarded at each end, with the messages and the strongly negative replies tied round its neck.

It was impossible for the foreigners to know what, if any, links there were between Prince Ch'ing's diplomatic initiative, MacDonald's parley with the Kansu colonel, Jung Lu's reply to the note, the dog-borne messages, a trade in eggs which sprang up between besiegers and besieged and the arrival at the legations of carts loaded with fruit, ostensibly the gift of the Old Buddha herself. A war of nerves was being played but by whom and to what end was unfathomable. The probability is that the game was three-cornered. Not only were the Chinese playing with the legates but with each other and when, within a few days, sporadic firing had broken out again, it was clear that the reactionaries still had the upper hand, a hand which was strengthened further by the arrival in Peking from the south of the arch-chauvinist and Imperial favourite, Li Ping-heng.

This lofty mandarin was, at least in his own estimation, a man of impeccable honesty and unswerving patriotism. He detested everything 'foreign', which meant everything modern – railways, telegraphs, mining, western-style education – as well as foreigners themselves. He had not been many days in the Forbidden City before his influence made itself felt. He breathed new life and confidence into the reactionary party by persuading the Empress Dowager that there was still a chance to exterminate the foreigners with impunity and, if in the end, there had to be negotiations, these could only be carried out successfully from a position of strength. Therefore the barbarians must be defeated or at least halted in their tracks. It is not clear how many, if any, troops he had brought with him from the south where he was Imperial Inspector of the Yangtze Naval Forces, a grandiose if largely meaningless title, but there is no doubt that he had the courage of his convictions. In due course he was to sally forth from Peking to challenge the approaching Allies. When he found that, through the incompetence of the generals and the cowardice of the troops and Boxers, they could not be checked, he committed suicide.

However, before leaving Peking he had seen to it that a number of the most senior and influential moderates at Court preceded him to the grave and with their demise the truce collapsed.

## 18th–28th July

As the Allies dithered at Tientsin so the self-confidence of the reactionary party began to return. Stiffened, as we have seen, by the presence of Li Ping-heng, the Old Buddha soon rounded on the moderates and heads began to roll. In all, five senior mandarins were executed before mid-August, including those who had called on the legates on 18 June. The degree of the Empress Dowager's stupidity, short-sightedness and/or lack of control over the reactionaries is emphasized by the fact that three of these men were put to death within a few days of the arrival at Peking of the Allied relief force; in other words at precisely the moment when they were most

148

likely to be of the greatest use to her. The only certainty is that total confusion and disarray, rather than the Empress Dowager, were ruling China during this period.

For the defenders of the legations this was a time of merciful rest, recuperation and repair. It also gave them the chance to pursue their little quarrels and vendettas with one another. Thanks partly to the foraging ability of their sixteen-year-old Etonian son, Fargo, the Squiers family had managed to keep an excellent table more or less throughout the siege. This was regarded with the gravest suspicion by the US Marines who, it will be recalled, were convinced that the 'Chief of Staff' was making free with their rations. One night, Private Upham tells us, Mr Squiers' turkey disappeared, a bird which 'he was saving for a rainy day' and 'he got out a search warrant for it'. Upham's account is circumspect but we are left in little doubt that he and his mates knew a good deal more about the disappearance of the turkey than he was prepared to admit. At all events, 'the Commander-in-Chief' seems to have become involved in the search for the missing bird. 'But,' continues Upham, 'whenever Sir Claude or Squiers comes on the (Tartar) wall they get a very chilly deal from the men. They are frequent visitors now that there is no danger.' As on the day following these entries in Upham's diary the more serious battle was renewed, we do not learn the fate of the turkey, although we can hazard a shrewd guess, nor do we know how the question of its disappearance was resolved.

Frequent rumours of relief were reaching the legations, mainly from Japanese sources. In reality there was no forward movement from Tientsin. Confused by conflicting reports and suspicious of each other, the home governments were uncertain as to the instructions they should give their commanders in China. Was there anyone still alive in the legations? Had they fallen or were they holding out? Had the foreign community, or at least the diplomats, already left Peking for Tientsin or elsewhere under escort? Had the Empress Dowager and the Emperor been poisoned, as one story had it? If so, then who was in power in the Forbidden City? On the one hand, the Press was insisting that the diplomats and other Europeans had all been butchered and, on the other, the Chinese envoys still en poste in the various capitals kept reiterating their assurances that the foreigners were being protected in the legation quarter by the

Imperial Government, although, of course, it would be better if they would agree to go to Tientsin under escort.

Militarily, too, there were serious problems facing the Allied commanders. Seymour, admittedly with a very small force, had received a bloody nose and had been fortunate to return at all. What was the enemy strength between Tientsin and Peking and how much opposition could be expected? Vidal estimated it at about 50,000, all of dubious quality. He did not include Yuan Shih-k'ai's 3rd Division, which, French consular intelligence sources believed, accurately as it turned out, would continue to sit on the fence. The cautious Dorward thought 60,000 Allied troops would be needed for a successful relief operation, whereas Fukushima felt 25,000 would be quite sufficient. The Americans, stronger now with the arrival of a second infantry regiment, the 14th, were still worried by the shortage of artillery and the Russians were convinced more cavalry was needed. The French were in no hurry to start as neither their commanders, nor anyone else, had much confidence in the Indo-Chinese infantry, which, together with a few marines and sailors, were about all they could muster before reinforcements

The Cossacks were better mounted policemen than operational cavalry.
(*National Army Museum*)

150

arrived from France. Most of the Germans, despatched by the Kaiser with such blood-thirsty instructions, were still on the high seas, as, blessed by the Pope, were the Italians. However, the Japanese had produced an entire division and, after the arrival of Gaselee with an Indian brigade, the British were rarin' to go.

That there was confusion and doubt in the minds of all concerned is not surprising since in Peking a kind of calculated lunacy had taken over. One minute the legates would receive a warning from the Tsungli Yamen that so great was the hatred of the Chinese people for all foreigners that nothing would satisfy them but the utter destruction of the legations and all their inmates, and the next carts loaded with fruit and vegetables would roll up to the gates of the British Legation accompanied by the visiting cards of a dozen or so senior officials, moderates and reactionaries alike. Sometimes these luminaries would appear in person for a ceremonious exchange of platitudes with one or more of the legates. The 'official' Chinese line was invariably to the effect that 'if you agree to leave for Tientsin we can guarantee your safety en route, but if you insist on staying in Peking an "accident" might occur for which we cannot be held responsible.' This, it will be recalled, had been the theme since before 20 June, the date on which the siege proper had started. It is possible that both moderates and reactionaries were peddling the same line for different motives. The moderates may have had reason to believe, perhaps through secret discussions with Jung Lu, that adequate and reliable protection could be afforded on the journey and that this was the only way to save the foreigners' lives and avoid catastrophe. The reactionaries, on the other hand, may have despaired of overwhelming the legations before the arrival of a relief force and may have seen a 'death march' to Tientsin as the only means of implementing their bloody plan.

During the truce, and even after the resumption of hostilities, the Tsungli Yamen took to relaying some telegrams to and from the legations, a slow process as the Peking telegraph office had been destroyed and the Yamen's couriers had to run or ride a considerable distance to find one in functional condition. At first the home governments regarded these messages with suspicion. Perhaps the Chinese, having stormed the legations and slain the inhabitants, had found the ciphers and were using them to mislead the Powers.

Nothing of any importance seems to have reached the legations from their foreign ministries, although M. Pichon was informed of his appointment as a Member of the *Legion d'Honneur* and Sir Claude of the death of the Duke of Edinburgh – valuable information to men within a hair's breadth of death. Mr Conger was able to send one message to the State Department (which did not arrive until 9 August) reading, 'Still besieged situation more precarious Chinese government insisting our leaving Peking which would be certain death rifle firing upon us daily by Imperial troops. Have abundant courage but little ammunition or provisions. Two progressive Yamen ministers beheaded. All connected with legation of USA well at present moment.'

But not all the legates in Peking agreed with Conger that 'leaving would be certain death'. De Giers, for example, who had favoured departure when it had been first mooted back in June was still tinkering with the idea in early August.

The Chinese 'authorities', whomsoever they may have been, were also busy on the wires. Apart from their repeated warnings, passed to the Chancelleries of the world through the various Chinese legations, that 'if they [the diplomats in Peking] delay leaving and an accident happens, who will take the responsibility?', they sought to sow dissention among the Powers with a little rumour-mongering; the British, they told the French, were about to seize Shanghai.

By 28 July Manchu confidence, largely through the pernicious influence of Li Ping-heng, had returned sufficiently for the reactionaries to initiate a renewal of general hostilities against the legations. At the same time the Allies at Tientsin were beginning to pull themselves together. More senior officers were arriving to take charge. On 27 July General Gaselee assumed command of the British contingent and General Yamaguchi of the Japanese. Soon all the major Allied contingents had new commanders. General Linievitch* had replaced Stossel, Major-General Henri Frey Colonel de Pelacot and Major-General Adna Romanza Chaffee Colonel Meade. Commissioned from the ranks of the 6th Cavalry (which, incidentally, had also arrived at Taku but without its horses) Chaffee was a grim

* General Nikolai Petrovitch Linievitch (1838–1908) was Commander-in-Chief of the Russian land forces in Manchuria towards the end of the Russo-Japanese War in 1905.

and forbidding veteran of many campaigns against the Red Indians, whom, it was said, he preferred to his bête noir, the United States Marine Corps.

## Peking, 29th July

In the afternoon the Chinese made their first overtly aggressive move against the legations since the truce began by starting to construct a barricade across the North Bridge of the canal. In fact, it was a matter of surprise to the defenders that this had not been done before, since a position there would command the whole length of the canal and the South Bridge, which was the only means of communication for wheeled vehicles between the western and eastern sectors of the defended area. This led to a sharp exchange of fire in which the former musketry instructor, Major Sir Claude MacDonald, happily joined with a borrowed rifle. The Italian one-pounder with its home-made ammunition was also brought into play but the gunner was soon wounded. Although his place was taken by a British sergeant, the Chinese rifle fire was so hot and accurate that the gun had to be taken out of action.

General Chaffee (seated centre) and staff at Peking. (*Institution of Royal Engineers*)

153

The following morning it was seen that a barricade six feet high covered the whole length of the bridge. Having failed to prevent its construction militarily, Sir Claude and his colleagues reverted to diplomacy. The barricade, they complained in a note to Prince Ch'ing, was a breach of the truce agreement and should be dismantled immediately. Have no fear, came the reply, what their Excellencies had mistaken for a barricade was in fact simply roadworks being undertaken by Tung-fu Hsiang's troops!

These Alice in Wonderland exchanges were to continue almost up to the end of the siege. The Chinese Government's letter of condolence addressed to Sir Claude on the occasion of the Duke of Edinburgh's death was quickly followed by a shell which landed in the British envoy's bedroom.

Meanwhile stories from the outside were pouring into the legations thick and fast. Allied armies were advancing at speed and in great numbers. No Allied troops had left Tientsin. They had won a significant victory over Imperial troops and Boxers. They had received a serious set-back at the hands of the Imperial troops and Boxers. Their arrival was imminent. They would not arrive for weeks. But these bewildering and contradictory reports were not only produced by rumour-mongers and spies earning a dishonest

The canal which ran through the Legation Quarter with the British First Secretary's house on the left. (*Illustrated London News*)

154

crust. On 28 July a Chinese lad of fifteen whom Sir Claude had despatched to Tientsin over three weeks before miraculously returned to Peking with a message dated 22 July from Mr W. R. Carles, the British Consul-General. This message, although some of its more absurd phrases were edited out before its gist was posted up on the Bell Tower notice board, caused outrage among the beleaguered but expectant community.

'Your letter of 4th July,' it read. 'There are now 24,000 troops landed and 19,000 here. General Gaselee is expected at Taku. When he comes I hope to see more activity. Tientsin city is under foreign government and the Boxers' power here is exploded. Do try and keep me informed of yourselves. There are plenty of troops on the way if you can keep yourselves in food for a time, all ought yet to come out well. The Consulate is mended to be ready for you when you come. Almost all the ladies have left Tientsin. Kindest remembrances to all in the Legation.'

As may be imagined the communication confirmed the worst suspicions of the pessimists, namely, that only six days earlier absolutely nothing had been done to set a rescue mission in motion. The sentence 'Gaselee is expected at Taku' and 'When he comes I hope to see more activity' must have been particularly infuriating. There was no indication as to when he might arrive or why, if 19,000 troops were already available, it was necessary to wait for him. The remark about food seems especially ludicrous and insensitive. How were they supposed 'to keep themselves in food' and for how long?

To give Mr Carles his due, perhaps he was being deliberately vague in case his message fell into enemy hands, but his circumspection must have done as little to advance his career in the *Corps Consulair* (the Foreign Office has always regarded the skilful drafting of telegrams and reports as of much greater importance than the actual achievement of foreign policy goals), as it did to boost the morale of the besieged, or even to convey to them any useful information.

## Tientsin, 30th July

But a good deal had happened at Tientsin since Mr Carles had taken up his pen to draft his maddening missive. All the new commanders

155

had assumed their duties and Gaselee, good-humoured, tactful and deceptively easy-going, was beginning to breathe some sense of urgency into his colleagues. Even the Russians and the Japanese were talking to each other and a dispute between Linievitch and Yamaguchi over seniority seems to have been resolved by arranging for Fukushima to deputise for Yamaguchi at commanders' conferences.

A Japanese patrol-in-strength (six battalions, an artillery battery and a squadron of cavalry) on this day discovered a large force of the enemy dug in at Peits'ang a few miles to the north of Tientsin. This might prove a serious obstacle and one which must be tackled, it was agreed, before the onset of the imminent rainy season made the movement of artillery and supply wagons immeasurably more difficult.

## AUGUST

### Peking, 1st–5th August

Time and again during the early days of this sweltering month the spirits of the hungry, weary defenders soared and plunged with each snippet of news, good or bad, true or false. After Mr Carles' sinister proviso 'if you can keep yourselves in food' a careful stock was taken which indicated that the lives of the Europeans could be supported for about another five weeks. Not so the Chinese Christians who do not seem to have been brought into these calculations. Their plight was already desperate. With their children dying, they scavenged for anything edible. Sometimes a legation guard, perhaps risking court-martial for wasting ammunition, would shoot a crow or a pi-dog for them, which they would stew with grass, weeds and the bark of the few remaining trees. The trade in eggs had dwindled to nothing after some of the vendors had been executed by Tung's troops and the spectre of mass starvation loomed larger by the day. What made the situation all the more unbearable was the inexplicable delay on the part of the Allies dawdling at Tientsin for who-knew-what reasons. 'It is marvellous to think,' wrote Nigel Oliphant bitterly, 'that the eight Great Powers cannot send an army eighty miles inland within seven or eight weeks!'

156

At enormous expense ($35 per day, it was said) the Japanese Legation had been retaining a spy, one of Tung's soldiers, who was a mine of false information. Uncharacteristically, his paymasters tended to be taken in by his imaginative yarns of great battles fought between the advancing Allies and Chinese forces with heavy casualties on both sides. Presumably the man was a double agent who fed whatever stories Tung felt were most likely to mislead and bemuse the defenders. However, on 2 August, a messenger arrived from Tientsin with genuine news from American sources. From this it became clear that the Allies were now aware that the legations were still holding out and that, albeit with ponderous deliberation, preparations were at last being made for the long-awaited rescue expedition to set forth. Just how long this would take was still uncertain but the message was less ambiguous than Carles's had been, although it contained the perhaps superfluous sentiment inserted by the American consul, Mr Ragsdale, 'It is my earnest wish that you may all be spared.' The Anglo-Saxon consuls at Tientsin seem to have had an awkward way with words.

## Tientsin

To be fair to the Allied commanders at Tientsin, they were faced with formidable logistical problems. Transport animals were virtually unobtainable locally, as was human labour. Large numbers of horses* were en route from Australia and the United States but would not arrive in time for the Peking expedition and hundreds of coolies had to be imported from Japan. The railway was unusable for its entire length and dozens of junks and other craft required for river transport on the Pei-ho had been destroyed in the weeks of fighting since mid-June or had been already expropriated by the Chinese troops fleeing northwards.

However, by the night of 3 August the strength and make-up of a relief force had finally been agreed. This would comprise the following elements which would move out of the Tientsin area on the 4th:

---

\* The enormous requirement for horses by the British Army in South Africa, where 350,000 perished during the War, had created a world-wide shortage and pushed up prices.

157

| British | Naval Brigade | 4 × 12-pounder guns |
|---|---|---|
| | | HMS *Terrible* 260 men |
| | | 300 Royal Marines |
| | 12th Battery Royal Field Artillery | 6 × 15-pounder guns |
| | Hong Kong and Singapore Artillery | 2 × 12-pounder guns |
| | | 4 × Maxims |
| | 2nd Battalion Royal Welsh Fusiliers | 300 men |
| | 1st Bengal Lancers | 400 men |
| | 1st Indian Brigade comprising: | |
| | 7th Bengal Infantry | 500 men |
| | 24th Punjab Infantry | 300 men |
| | 1st Sikh Infantry | 500 men |
| | Hong Kong Regiment | 100 men |
| | 1st Chinese Regiment | 100 men |
| | Some Royal Engineers and a number of signalmen and telegraphists of various British regiments were attached | |
| | Total | 2,900 men and 12 guns |
| **American** | 9th Infantry Regiment | |
| | 14th Infantry Regiment | |
| | One battalion US Marines | |
| | Light Battery F 5th Artillery with 6 × 3.2 inch guns (known as Reilly's Battery) | |
| | One troop 6th Cavalry | |
| | Total | 2,200 men and 6 guns |
| **Japanese** | 5th Division comprising: | |
| | Nine battalions of infantry | |
| | Six batteries of artillery | |
| | Four squadrons of cavalry | |
| | Total | 9,000 men and 24 guns |
| **Russian** | Three infantry battalions of the East Siberian Regiment | |
| | Two batteries of artillery | |
| | One squadron of cavalry | |
| | Total | 2,900 men and 16 guns |

158

| French | Two battalions of Infanterie de le Marine<br>A Naval Battalion<br>One artillery battery | |
|---|---|---|
| Total | | 1,200 men and 12 guns |

Small contingents of Germans, Italians and Austrians, mostly sailors, started with the expedition but, having no transport, returned to Tientsin on or about 7 August.

*Note:* The above information is compiled from various Allied Sources which do not tally. Their totals vary from 17,800 to 20,100 men.

A further 23,000 men, mostly Russian and Japanese, were left to garrison Tientsin, guard the T'angku–Tientsin railway line, T'angku railway station and the Taku forts.

Of the opposition, the Allies, their intelligence-gathering arrangements being virtually non-existent, knew little. There may have been as many as 80,000 Disciplined Troops, Braves, Greens and Bannermen in their path but the only real resistance en route to Peking was likely to come from the two regular divisions, the 1st and 2nd, one of which had already lost its commander, General Nieh. In and around Peking itself were Tung's 4th Division and Jung Lu's 5th or Headquarter Division, the former certainly hostile but the latter, controlling most of the artillery, an unknown quantity. No one seems to have hazarded a guess as to how many Boxers there were still upon the scene. As the story of their 'uprising' unfolds they recede further and further into the background and by the beginning of August they are seldom mentioned except as mere miscreants to be hunted down and killed on the spot or executed after a perfunctory trial.

There was excellent modern weaponry at the disposal of the Imperial Army but the will to use it, leadership and training were all lacking. The only man who might have provided this, Yuan Shih k'ai, remained firmly on the touch-line as a spectator.

159

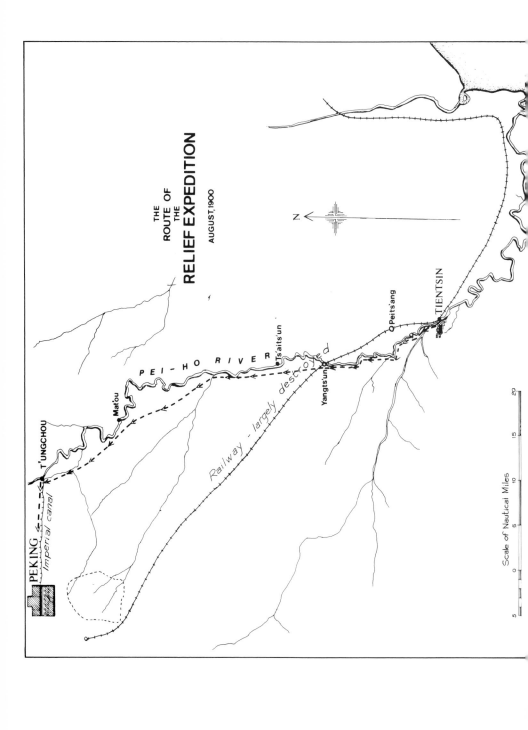

PEKING

Imperial canal

T'UNGCHOU

Ma'ou

PEI - HO RIVER

Tsaits'un

Yangts'un

Peits'ang

TIENTSIN

Railway - largely destroyed

THE
ROUTE OF
THE
RELIEF EXPEDITION
AUGUST, 1900

N

Scale of Nautical Miles

5    0    10    15    20

## 5th August

The campaign to relieve Peking, or rather the Peking legations, opened with a brisk action at Peits'ang where the Chinese were dug in on both sides of the Pei-ho to the south of the town in formidable positions.

British artillery en route to the relief of the Peking legations. The gun in the foreground may be one of HMS *Terrible*'s 12-pounders as the drivers appear to be sailors. The army personnel in the background are probably from 12th Battery Royal Field Artillery. (*The late Mr Han Zhong Min/Research Centre of Inscriptions and Documents*)

In the early hours of the morning the Japanese infantry seized the powder magazine to the south-west of Peits'ang in a swift and ferocious hand-to-hand fight. Moving up on both the left and right of the line of advance with the British and Americans in the centre, the Japanese were again sharply engaged in the approaches to the town where Chinese troops put up an unusually stiff resistance. However, well-supported by the combined artillery fire of the various Allied batteries, they had captured the suburb of Wang-chuang by 8.30 am and Peits'ang itself two hours later.

Floundering in the mud on the east bank of the Pei-ho where the fields had been flooded, the Russians and the French took no part

161

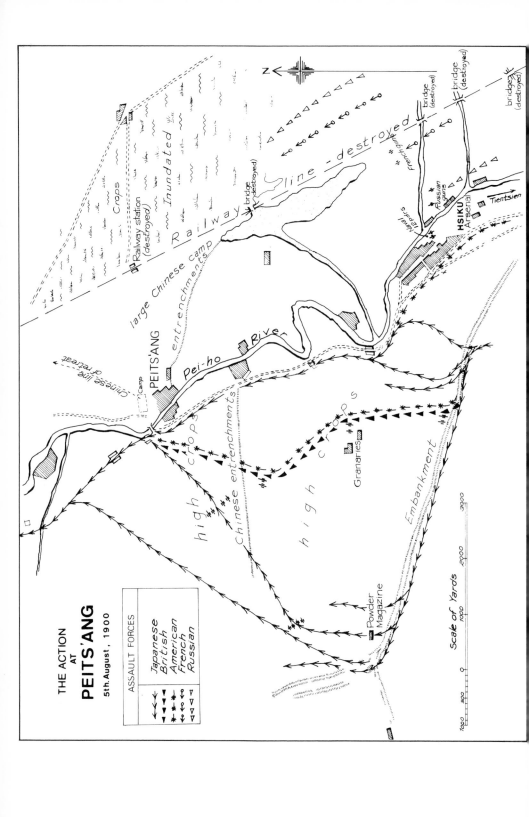

THE ACTION
AT
**PEITS'ANG**
5th. August, 1900

ASSAULT FORCES

Japanese
British
American
French
Russian

Scale of Yards

100 0    500    1000    2000    3000

Powder
Magazine

Granaries

Embankment

high crops

high crops

Chinese entrenchments

Camp

PEITS'ANG

Pei-ho River

Chinese line of retreat

large Chinese camp entrenchments

Railway "line - destroyed"

Inundated

Crops

Railway station
(destroyed)

bridge
(destroyed)

batteries

Russian
guns

HSIKU
Arsenal

Tientsien

bridge (destroyed)

bridge (destroyed)

bridge (destroyed)

French bund

N

in the infantry action, although their artillery had been used with good effect to bombard the Chinese entrenchments which stretched across both sides of the river, as a result of which those on the east bank seem to have been abandoned without a fight. Allied officers inspecting the defences after the battle were impressed by the skill and professionalism with which they had been prepared and were both amazed and relieved that better use had not been made of them. Even so, the Japanese had suffered three hundred casualties, including sixty dead. Other Allied losses were minimal.

It is tempting to speculate how the action at Peits'ang would have developed had the Japanese not been there. As in the case of the storming of Tientsin, the impression is left that the other Allies would have lacked the drive, ferocity and reckless courage to bring matters to such rapid conclusions. Peits'ang would probably have developed into an artillery slogging match and although no doubt the Chinese would have been dislodged eventually, it might well have taken several valuable days. Now heartened by this opening success and spurred on by international rivalry, the Allies drove northwards.

## 6th August

On the very next day the second action of the advance was fought at Yangts'un where, as was remembered by those who had been with Seymour, the railway crossed the Pei-ho just downstream of the town. The Anglo–Americans had crossed the river to join the Russians and French on the east bank, the Japanese remaining on the west bank where, for once, they took little part in the fighting.

Crushing heat and thirst proved to be greater adversaries than the enemy. Defeat on the previous day had broken Chinese morale and the Sikhs and US infantry, supported by Punjabis and Royal Welsh, encountered little resistance as they entered the town but came under shell-fire from Allied artillery, either Russian or British, the gunners having miscalculated the speed of the infantry advance. Casualties were suffered and would have been worse but for the swift action of Private Joseph Jackson, a signaller of F Coy, Royal Welsh, who, under fire from both sides, leapt onto the railway embankment signalling frantically to the Allied artillery to cease

163

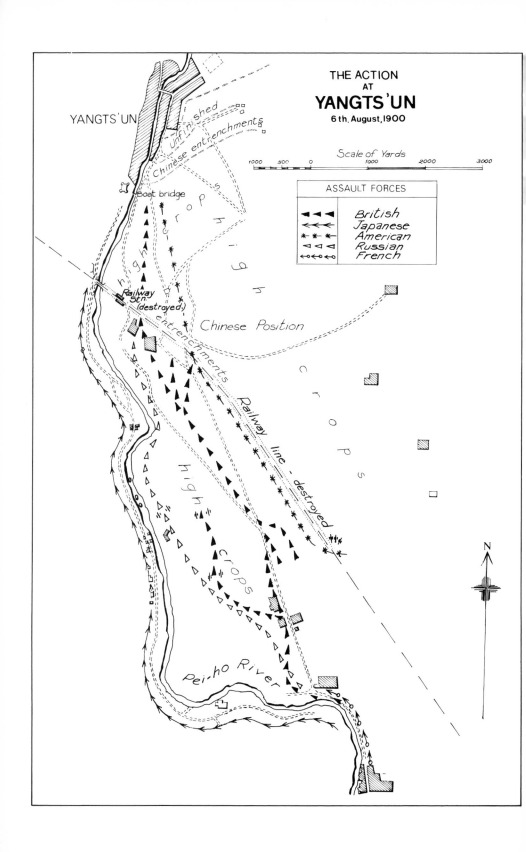

THE ACTION
AT
**YANGTS'UN**
6th. August, 1900

YANGTS'UN

Unfinished
Chinese entrenchments

Scale of Yards

1000    500    0        1000            2000            3000

Boat bridge

high crops

high

ASSAULT FORCES

◄ ◄ ◄   *British*
← ← ←   *Japanese*
✳ ✳ ✳   *American*
◁ ◁ ◁   *Russian*
↔ ↔ ↔   *French*

Railway Stn.
(destroyed)

entrenchments    Chinese Position

crops

Railway line - destroyed

high

crops

N

Pei-ho River

firing. For his courage and presence of mind he was awarded the Distinguished Conduct Medal.

It was as well that the Allies had not been faced with a stubborn defence as the attack was disorganized and hesitant. As well as coming under fire from their own side, the British and American troops, desperate for water, frequently halted the advance while they drank from wells or filthy puddles. '[The men] gathered in crowds and fairly fought for the water,' wrote the historian of the 9th Infantry. 'At last, however, they were brought under control and the regiment moved forward.' At least one man died from heat exhaustion and hundreds were temporarily missing when the rolls were called after the action. Colonel Bertie could muster only a hundred Welsh Fusiliers out of the two hundred with whom he had started the attack and had to cope with twenty-nine cases of sunstroke.

The most severe casualties had been suffered by the 14th Infantry, mostly inflicted by Allied guns, with eight dead and fifty-seven wounded of whom another fifteen died later. British and Indian casualties amounted to six killed and thirty-seven wounded.

Yangts'un was the last incidence of Chinese resistance to the advance before the Allies reached Peking itself. For the next week the troops had to cope with sun, dust, lack of water, exhaustion and the rivalry of their own generals rather than any warlike activities on the part of Imperial troops or Boxers.

## 8th August

After a day's rest at Yangts'un the march, described by Chaplain Leslie Groves of the 14th Infantry as 'beastly, brutal and foolish', continued through well-grown fields of maize and sorghum, stifling any breeze which might have cooled the sweating marchers. Even the Indian troops suffered, although the Japanese and Russians seemed impervious to the rigours of the climate. The French Colonial infantry, the lame ducks of the expedition, were left behind at Yangts'un, ostensibly through lack of transport, a severe blow to General Frey, for the honour of France was at stake. It was no longer only a question of who would reach the legations first but also of who could stay the course.

165

Sikh troops on the march to Peking. In reality they would have looked rather less warlike and rather more bedraggled. (*Illustrated London News*)

The order of march was the Japanese in the van (in case, presumably, there was any more fighting to be done), followed by the Russians and then the Americans with the British bringing up the rear. The Americans in particular complained that their position in the column forced them to march through the worst heat of the day as they had to start and finish later than the Japanese and Russians. As they slogged along in each other's dust the Allies took often unfriendly stock of one another. The Bengal Lancers, sneered Chaplain Groves, 'were only good for show', while the commanding officer of that once famous regiment, the blimpish Colonel R. F. Gartside-Tipping, pronounced the Americans 'like our Volunteers of the slackest and worst pattern'. The French he dismissed as simply 'beneath contempt'. General Gaselee, who was, incidentally, Gartside-Tipping's brother-in-law, tended to fume 'at the vacillation of these foreigners' and Groves blamed his own commander, General Chaffee, for the sufferings of the men on the march.

A Bengal Lancer with a 'Boxer' prisoner. Many such prisoners were not Boxers at all. (*Illustrated London News*)

The rank and file were perhaps more magnanimous in their view of each other. Private Sullivan of the US Marines wrote that 'a feeling of brotherhood has sprung up between the English and the Americans which is fine to see. They admire us as much as we admire them, one will give half his food or water to the other if it is his last on earth.'

There were differing opinions of the Indian troops. While Private Mitchell, a British Army telegraphist, thought 'the native infantry regiments did not come up to scratch', they were much admired by Lieutenant Harllee who believed that they were 'inferior in courage to no soldiers in the world'. He thought well of the 1st Chinese Regiment too – 'an intelligent-looking outfit'. But there was no good word for the French from anyone. Harllee found them 'the dirtiest and filthiest soldiers here. The only ones who have shirked.'

Only the Japanese were universally admired. Even Gartside-Tipping admitted that they were 'by far the best' and Harllee's opinion was that 'the world will always respect them'. Unfortunately this was not to be the case. Western, particularly British, admiration

167

for Japan reached its zenith a few years later during the Russo-Japanese War of 1904–5 (now strangely ignored or forgotten by military historians). In an article in *The Times* of 4th October 1904, the celebrated war correspondent Colonel Repington waxed lyrical on the subject of 'bushido', a philosophy which he likened to the ancient ideals of 'knightly chivalry and Spartan simplicity'. Indeed, during the early years of Japan's rise to equal status with the Great Powers, this assessment, if somewhat romantic, was by no means absurd. The speech chosen by Repington to illustrate his point might as well have been made by Leonidas to his men at Thermopylae as by an obscure Japanese naval commander about to embark upon a virtually suicidal mission against Port Arthur.

'Let every man set aside all thought of making a name for himself, but let us all work together for the attainment of our object. It is a mistaken idea of valour to court death needlessly. Death is not our object but success, and we die in vain if we do not attain success. If I die, Lieutenant Yamamoto will take the command, and if he is killed, you will take your orders from the chief warrant officer. Let us keep at it till the last man, until we have carried out our mission.'

However, thirty years later, the Japanese having long achieved the recognition and respect, which, up to then, they had deserved, allowed 'bushido' to degenerate into a kind of heroic barbarism. Although they retained their unequalled fighting qualities, the savagery typified by, for example, the so-called Rape of Nanking in 1937 and the appalling treatment of Allied POWs during the Second World War destroyed Japan's image in the West and led inevitably to the terrible denouements of Hiroshima and Nagasaki.

But we have wandered far enough from the line of march to Peking, the hardships and horrors of which Lieutenant Harllee has left a vivid description following the victories at Peits'ang and Yangts'un:

'We pulled out from our compound and had a succession of marches which are said to be as hard as any ever made. They were short, from ten to twelve miles a day, but our position in the column made it necessary for us to make them in the middle of the day and the dust of the wagon trains and light batteries ahead combined with the heat and alkali water and the treeless country made it severe.

'We marched through corn fields where the corn was higher than

168

a horseman's head and the heat was stifling. The halts for rest gave us no relief because the sunshine beat down upon us. The men cast away their rolls and some their haversacks and then lay down and died along the road. Both sides were lined with men in convulsions and foaming at the mouth and of all nationalities mixed up together. The Indian soldiers also died along the way. Then every short distance dead Chinamen with bayonet holes through them and all swollen up had to be stepped over. Some were beheaded and their heads suspended from corn stalks by their pigtails. All Chinese stragglers were killed, by the bayonet if practicable, and the Russians chopped their heads off. Some Russians fell into the hands of Chinese and were butchered.

'Burning villages lit up the skies at night all along the road. What couldn't be used by troops was destroyed. We did all our camping in corn fields and for over a week I was never under the shade of a tree.'

The harshness of the march and the fear of being left behind shortened tempers. An officer of the 9th Infantry witnessed the savage beating of a Russian wagon driver, who despite having rescued his horse and wagon from the river into which they had rolled, was battered about the head and face by his infuriated officer while the man himself stood rigidly to attention and at the salute. Despite such treatment, or perhaps because of it, these sturdy serf-soldiers, innured from earliest childhood to every hardship, seldom fell out on the line of march and suffered few casualties from heat exhaustion or dehydration.

On the evening of the 8th a despatch from Sir Claude MacDonald was received by General Gaselee at Ts'aits'un. It enclosed a plan of Peking drawn by MacDonald and Squiers showing the positions held by the legation guards marked with the flags of three nations, Britain, the United States and Russia. Unfortunately the accompanying directions as to the best means of entry were written in cypher, the key to which Gaselee's staff had contrived to leave behind at the British Consulate in Tientsin. An officer of the Bengal Lancers, Captain Griffin, with a small escort, was sent hurtling back to Tientsin to have it decoded. Returning on the 10th he caught up with Gaselee at Mat'ou. It is to be hoped, but not expected or recorded, that he brought the cypher key with him in case of further missives of the same nature. Whether he did or not, he was later decorated with the Distinguished Service Order.

In due course these directions were to enable the British to be the first to enter and relieve the legation quarter. Many years later, General Sir Edmund Barrow, who had been Gaselee's Chief of Staff at the time, admitted that 'we decided we would keep it strictly to ourselves until the last moment'. So much for co-operation between Allies!

General Gaselee (seated right) and staff at Peking. (*Institution of Royal Engineers*)

Crossing with MacDonald's message to Gaselee was one from Gaselee to MacDonald reading: 'Ts'aits'un; strong forces of Allies advancing; twice defeated enemy, keep up your spirits!' At about the same time Colonel Shiba received a similar message from General Fukushima, but in greater detail calculating the Allied arrival at Peking by the 13th or 14th. At last, and barring some unforeseen catastrophe, the exhausted defenders knew that they would be saved.

There was, however, to be no let-up in the attacks upon them; on the contrary, they intensified.

## Peking, 10th August

A tremendous fusillade and bombardment is unleashed against all sectors of the defence but, incredibly, no casualties are sustained.

## 11th August

The Chinese are still building towers and improving barricades on the Tartar Wall and the Americans and Russians are still trying to match them. Construction work goes on all night. 'When it comes to hard work the Ruskies are OK,' decides Upham, 'but cannot be depended on in an emergency although they would go any place with our men and have as much faith in us as they have in their officers.'

## 12th August

From the Tartar Wall large bodies of troops are seen leaving by the Ch'ien Men (Gate), but elsewhere the attacks continue. As usual

The Ch'ien Men. The main gate through the Tartar Wall. (*Institution of Royal Engineers*)

171

there is uncertainty among the Chinese, some still eager to press home the siege, others anxious to clear out while the going is still good. In the evening the defenders suffer their last officer casualty. Captain Labrousse of the French Army, one of several valuable officers who had found themselves in Peking by chance at the outbreak of hostilities, is killed. There are other casualties too. Sad little Chinese babies finally succumbing to starvation and two legation guards, one French and one Russian, to wounds received days before. Then yet another Frenchman is killed and an Austrian and a German hit. Now Shiba has information that there are only 2,500 Chinese troops left in Peking. Nobody mentions the Boxers any more. Already they are beginning to fade into history.

Rumours are rife. Thousands of Chinese have been slain in a great battle with the advancing Allies. Jung Lu has poisoned himself (perhaps a muddle over names here – Yu Lu, Viceroy of Chihli had committed suicide after the defeat at Yangts'un). An official market will be opened to trade with the legations, it is said. But, with grim absurdity, bullets continue to whistle and ping and shells crump here and there.

Among the defenders, hesitantly, a kind of 'end of term' atmosphere is developing, and spreading, perhaps, to their attackers. A request for a meeting with the legates is received from the Tsungli Yamen. But where to meet? Everywhere is under continuous fire. Anyway, the meeting is cancelled with a complaint that the foreigners 'have re-opened hostilities' and a Chinese general has been killed – 'this is not a friendly procedure'.

The sound and fury of battle seems to increase in inverse ratio to the diminishing number of attackers. Perhaps only the hard core remains. Perhaps someone is frenziedly trying to snatch a fatal victory from the jaws of a less fatal defeat.

But at Court confidence is rapidly evaporating, although the Old Buddha, her cypher of a nephew the Emperor and their entourage will tarry with indecision and fear in the Forbidden City for a few more days.

Meanwhile some advance Japanese patrols are now within five miles of the city and the main body has reached and taken unopposed T'ungchou, only twelve miles distant.

## 13th August

The day opens with a furious artillery and machine-gun exchange in the British Legation sector of the defence. Careful preservation of ammunition has meant that the defenders' few machine-guns have been used sparingly hitherto, but now the desperate necessity to hold out for a few more hours overrides the need to conserve ammunition and both the Austrian Maxim and the American Colt are brought into action, eventually silencing the Chinese artillery. Nevertheless, on this the penultimate day of the siege, MacDonald reckoned that the barrage did more damage to his quarters than they had suffered during the previous five weeks of bombardment.

As promised in MacDonald's despatch to Gaselee, the Union Jack, the Stars and Stripes and the Imperial Eagle of Russia are raised on the Tartar Wall, making excellent targets for Chinese marksmen. The Union flag is shot away but re-hoisted by Armourer's Mate Thomas and Leading Signalman Swannell. Casualties, almost the last, are suffered; a German and a Russian are killed, a French priest, two doctors and a Royal Marine wounded. Chinese officers can be heard vainly urging their men to a last desperate effort, but the soldiers content themselves with firing wild shots and throwing bricks. Most of them are ready, in Arthur Smith's words, 'to fold their tents and silently steal away'.

## With the Relief Force

At T'ungchou the Allied commanders had conferred and 'planned' the assault on Peking. On the grounds that his men were exhausted, not normally a priority on a Russian general's list, Linievitch suggested that this should be undertaken in three phases: the approach march to within two or three miles of the city; rest and reconnaissance; the final assault, with each national contingent being allocated a particular gate through the east wall (see map on p. 174) as its objective, this last phase to take place on the morning of 15 August.

Bearing in mind that the Allies were within earshot of the capital and could hear the tremendous bombardment to which the legations were still being subjected, it seems incredible that this slothful

# THE RELIEF

## OF

# THE LEGATIONS AND PEIT'ANG CATHEDRAL

14th.-16th. August, 1900

| THE ASSAULT FORCES | |
|---|---|
| ◄ ◄ ◄ ◄ | *British* |
| ← ← ← ← | *Japanese* |
| ○ ⟶ ◄○◄○ | *French* |
| – * * * | *American* |
| ◁ ◁ ◁ ◁ | *Russian* |

Hsi Chih Men

T A R T A R

Ti anan Men

I M P E R I A L

Peitang

Forbidden City

C I T Y

Tung Chih Men

*planned Russian route*

Ch'ao Yang Men

*actual Russian route*

Tsungli Yamen

LEGATIONS

C I T Y

Shun Chih Men

Ch'ien Men

Sluice Gate

Hata Men

Tung Pien Men

*Imperial canal*

Sha K'ou Men

C H I N E S E     C I T Y

Temple of Héaven

Scale of Yards

1000  500  0     1000     2000     3000     4000

time-table should have been agreed when up until then the commanders had been driving their men to the point of collapse. As they would have had little or no idea how long the legations could hold out, it meant, on the face of it, that they were prepared to risk the lives of the beleaguered foreigners being snatched from under their noses for the sake of a few hours' repose.

Of course the explanation is that nobody except the absurdly trusting British intended to adhere to the plan. However, as we shall see, this turned out to their advantage. Once the Allies had left the river at T'ungchou and had fanned out in the agreed formation with the Russians on the right flank, the Japanese, French (about four hundred French sailors and some of their guns had caught up with the other Allies) and Americans in the centre, and the British on the left, the race would be to the swift. The less the other fellows knew about your intentions the better chance you had of getting there first.

The front runners were the 'exhausted' Russians who, at about midnight on the 13th, launched a premature attack on the Tung Pien Men. This, as can be seen from the map, was not even their agreed objective, but that of the Americans. To achieve this, the Russians had cut right across the bows of their deadliest rivals, the Japanese.

Later numerous stories circulated to account for this premature and thoroughly unsporting manoeuvre. Perhaps the most picturesque of these was that the advancing Russians, originally bent on reconnaissance as agreed, came upon a body of some forty Royal Welsh Fusiliers heading purposefully in the direction of Peking. Furthermore, although under the command of two Irish colour-sergeants, Kelly and Murphy, these perfidious Britons were, it seems, conversing in their native tongue, Welsh. The suspicious Russians instantly concluded that a devious plan, incomprehensible to civilized listeners, was being hatched whereby the forty Fusiliers would enter Peking and relieve the legations without so much as a by-your-leave to anyone else! If the British were cheating then it was every Ally for himself! Let battle commence!

There seems little doubt that these forty men, under dauntless Hibernian leadership, were indeed wandering about well in front of the main body of the British contingent on the 13th, but the facts as to how they got there and what they may have intended to do are as lost now as the men themselves probably were then. That some of them were speaking Welsh is possible but improbable. It is unlikely that the two colour-sergeants knew the language and as at that time about 70% of the men of the battalion were English,* they were more likely to be conversing in the accents of Brummagum or London's East End. However, we cannot leave the matter without remarking that this may not have been the only occasion in Colour-Sergeant Murphy's military career when he was the first to arrive at an important destination. As Regimental Sergeant-Major of the battalion almost fourteen years later he is said to have been the first British soldier to set foot on French soil at the outbreak of the First World War.

But the origins of the Russian attack on the Tung Pien Men are probably more mundane. A patrol-in-strength under Linievitch's Chief of Staff, General Vassilievski, guided by Yuan Shih k'ai's former cavalry instructor, the Norwegian rough-rider Munthe, reached the Tung Pien Men without coming under fire. Whether or not they knew which gate they were at is immaterial. Vassilievski decided that the opportunity to exploit a weak spot was not to be missed and he took it. With Munthe and a few other men he crossed the moat and attacked the guard-room, killing the guards. A few shells smashed a hole in the outer gate and for the second time in forty years 'barbarian' invaders entered the capital city of the world's most populous nation.

## 14th August

But here Russian luck ran out. Finding themselves in a broad passageway between the outer and inner gates surrounded by towers, they soon lost the advantage of surprise and came under heavy fire as Chinese resistance built up. In this confined space, Vassilievski's force, consisting of an infantry battalion, a few guns and some Cossacks, was unable to deploy and break out of the bridgehead it had established. Soon the General was wounded and his men, now under Colonel Modl, remained locked in fierce but static fighting until mid-morning.

* See *Old Soldier Sahib* by Frank Richards. This unique account of the life and times of a private soldier in India during the early years of this century includes a chapter on the China campaign.

Who then came to the relief of the Russians? The historian of the US 14th Infantry records that at 6 am about two hundred French troops (presumably in fact sailors) overtook the Americans on the road to the Tung Pien Men. When asked by General Chaffee where they were bound their commander replied 'that he was going to join some Russians in front'. Chaffee's response was that the only troops ahead of him were a patrol of his own 6th Cavalry but the French marched on without further comment. When later it was revealed that the Russians were indeed 'in front' and had been engaged in heavy fighting since midnight it was naturally assumed that they had given prior warning of their intentions to their French friends (the only Ally whom they did not regard as a rival) and had asked them to come up in support in the morning.

An American cavalry trooper, probably of the 6th Cavalry, General Chaffee's old regiment. (*National Army Museum*)

On the other hand, if the premature attack had been premeditated, why was Linievitch with the Russian main body still immobile several miles from Peking throughout the night of the 13th and why did he

177

not arrive in support of his Chief of Staff until about twelve hours after the initial attack had been launched? Moreover, the two hundred Frenchmen do not appear to have reached the Tung Pien Men in time to join in the fighting as the 14th Infantry caught up with them and passed them, despite their objections, later in the morning.

Whatever the truth of the matter, somebody else had to extricate Vassilievsky's men. According to the official French report, the Russians suffered the indignity of being reinforced and, in effect, rescued by their main competitors, the Japanese. This, however, is not corroborated in Japanese reports which speak of their forces being engaged in heavy fighting around the Ch'ao Yang Men and the Tung Chih Men, the central and northern gates into the Tartar City, and simply add that 'the other Allied forces advanced through the Tung Pien Men'.

More probably it was the appearance of the Americans which relieved the pressure on the Russians. Again according to the History of the 14th Infantry, Companies E and H of that regiment crossed the moat at the same point as the Russians had on the previous night and found them still trapped between the outer and inner gates and still under heavy fire, some of which was now directed at the Americans. Unable to advance further by that route the American commander, Captain Learnard, decided the only way forward was over the wall. Volunteers were called for* and an agile young bandsman, Musician Calvin P. Titus† of Company E, was selected from these brave souls to make the first attempt to climb the wall. Only when he had succeeded without getting his head shot off did the officers see fit to follow. Eventually about twenty-five officers and men clambered up and, being now on level terms with the Chinese, were able to keep them pinned down so that the advance towards the inner gate below could continue and the Russians be released from their trap.

Meanwhile, the British, who were apparently the last to learn of the Russians' midnight adventure, hastened to their allotted gate,

---

* This seems to be a peculiarly American habit. In the British Army 'volunteers' are usually summoned on the basis of 'you, you and you'!
† Titus was one of no less than fifty-nine US servicemen to be awarded the Congressional Medal of Honour in the campaign.

178

the Sha K'ou Men, a gruelling nine miles march in stupefying heat in the course of which six horses of the 12th Field Battery died of exhaustion. The guns did not arrive until 4 pm and would not have arrived at all but for the tireless efforts of the men of the Chinese Regiment and the blaspheming matelots of HMS *Terrible*. In the event little artillery support was needed as most of the Chinese defence had been sucked into fighting around the gates in the Russian, Japanese and American sectors and the British were able to advance through the Sha K'ou Men unopposed.

When Private Upham heard disciplined bursts of Maxim fire coming from the east he was convinced that the Allies had arrived. 'Good news – the best we have heard yet. Sometimes we can hear volleys the Chinese cannot imitate no matter how hard they try,' he wrote. But others were less confident. Although the Chinese had used few machine-guns during the siege it was known that they had purchased large numbers of Maxims in recent years; it will be recalled that Seymour had found several in the Hsiku Arsenal. Now, Squiers reported to MacDonald, these deadly weapons were being brought

The Maxim machine-gun. Both sides possessed this deadly weapon but for unfathomable reasons the Chinese seldom, if ever, used theirs. (*Major A. P. B. Watkins*)

into action at last. However, by early afternoon this shadow of doubt had been dispelled when foreign troops were spotted from the Tartar Wall. The cry went up, 'They're coming! They're coming!', while grave diplomats and sober missionaries leapt for joy like children.

Eye-witness accounts of the Relief of the Legations vary in detail, as many accounts of many historic events do, but not in substance. Sir Claude MacDonald, speaking fourteen years later, believed that he had conducted the first British troops into the British Legation compound but General Barrow, Gaselee's Chief of Staff, told of the great moment thus: 'After bursting through the gate [the Sha K'ou Men] we pushed along the main road and then having crossed the road leading to the Hata Men, from which we were sniped, we diverged into the narrow lanes of the Chinese City towards the sluice gate* led by Mr Boyce Kup [nationality unknown], a China merchant who knew Peking well and whom we had attached to our head-quarters for this very purpose. The heat was stifling, the stinks were sickening and the progress was slow as the exhaustion was considerable. But at last at about 2.45 pm we struck the moat nearly opposite the water gate and there on the wall in front of us we saw the flags of England, America and Russia just as described in the cypher message. There was, however, an ominous silence and not a defender to be seen. For a moment we feared the worst had happened and that the flags were but a lure to draw us into the open between the Chien Men and Hata Men Gates. Suddenly we saw a flag waving, "Come in by the water gate", in the best English style of flag signalling. With a cheer we, some seventy officers and men, dashed across the moat under an ill-directed fire from the Hata Men and in a few moments were safe under cover of the vaulted arch of the water gate. It was barred against us but we quickly burst our way through, assisted by eager hands from inside, and then amidst the clapping of the Chinese Christians and the frantic cheering of the Europeans on the canal bank we struggled through the slime and mud and up the bank and found ourselves at 3 pm the first to achieve the rescue of the Legations, with Sir Claude waiting to welcome us, clad in immaculate tennis flannels.'

* This refers to the sluice gate of the canal, thereafter referred to as the water gate. It should be borne in mind that the canal served as a sewer.

Covered in mud and sewage and parched with thirst, the dishevelled and travel-strained appearance of the rescuers, led by Gaselee, his staff, Sikhs and Bengal Infantry (Rajputs), contrasted sharply with these 'immaculate tennis flannels' and the garden-party dresses and parasols of the ladies. Once the initial euphoria had died down and a certain anti-climax had set in, relievers and relieved began to take stock of one another. Had these civilians really had such a hard time of it, the soldiers began to wonder. Had it been so necessary to make such haste at the cost of the lives or health of so many men who had fallen on the line of march? And when the 14th Infantry arrived an hour or two later, the greeting they received from their compatriots, particularly the womenfolk, was far from what they had expected. Bearded, bronzed (19th century North Americans did not admire a sun-tan which might be mistaken for 'a touch of the tar-brush') and sweaty men who had hoped for at least a chaste kiss on the cheek or the soft touch of a feminine hand, found that the ladies recoiled from them, and one elegant creature

Indian troops, the first Allies to enter the Legation Quarter, coming through the water-gate.
(*Illustrated London News*)

181

was even heard to exclaim, 'Dirty!' But then, as now, Americans sought deeper meanings to human behaviour than did the inhabitants of the Old World and our friend the historian of the 14th Infantry generously explains this hurtful behaviour as a 'natural psychological phenomenon attributable to the sudden reaction'.

Meanwhile heavy and confused fighting continued. In the British compound, amidst all the excitement and celebration, a Belgian lady was wounded by a stray bullet (the only European female 'battle' casualty of the entire siege) and a Sikh sepoy on guard at the main gate was also hit. In the Fu, almost from force of habit, Colonel Shiba launched a final attack on the remaining Chinese barricades and drove the enemy helter-skelter from the place which he and his gallant band of Japanese and Italians had defended so stubbornly for so long.

However, his compatriots to the east were locked in battle with the most determined Chinese resistance they had encountered since Tientsin. It was not until after dark that General Yamaguchi's men finally smashed through the Ch'ao Yang and Tung Chih gates sustaining over one hundred casualties in the process. The Russians too had paid dearly for their precipitate and unsupported midnight

The survivors of the Japanese Legation guards and volunteers. Colonel Shiba is seated sixth from left with Baron Nishi, the Minister, to his left. Almost all these men had been wounded, some more than once. (*Ashahi Shimbun, Tokyo*)

attack on the Tung Pien Men with twenty-one killed and 109 wounded. In defence of their capital, and perhaps with a view to giving the Imperial family time to escape to the west, Chinese troops had shown for the first and last time in the campaign a dogged and resolute fighting spirit. The Boxers long gone, the men involved were almost certainly Tung's Braves of the 4th Division and estimates of their casualties vary, almost meaninglessly, from four hundred to four thousand. It seems unlikely that a count of Chinese dead was ever made and, in any case, it would have been difficult to separate military from civilian casualties. Harllee saw 'stacks of twenty or thirty of them [bodies] in the streets full of bayonet holes and the dogs chewing on them'.

The legations had been relieved but the Allies still had to consolidate their occupation of the capital – and no one seems to have thought about the Peit'ang Cathedral, not even the French.

## 15th August

Accounts of the flight and temporary exile of the Imperial family, described euphemistically in official documents as a Tour of Inspection, must be treated with a certain reserve and scepticism as they are based largely on vernacular newspaper reports and forged documents, such as the notorious diary of Ching Shan (see final chapter), but we must make the best of what we have.

For reasons which may be obscure to us but doubtless were clear to the Manchu Court, it was not until midnight on the 13th that flight was seriously considered. The thunder and roar of the Russian assault on the Tung Pien Men could be heard in the Forbidden City and panic set in, that peculiar kind of organized panic which exists only in the East and from which a semblance of order and concerted movement in a particular direction suddenly emerge from apparent chaos. Eventually by 3 am on the 15th, with the Allies already battering on the gates of the Forbidden City, sufficient carts had been assembled to convey the Imperial family with some officials and retainers through the North-West Gate (Shih Che Men)* to the Summer Palace.

* The names of the various gates of the Tartar City are by no means uniform on the maps and plans of that time.

183

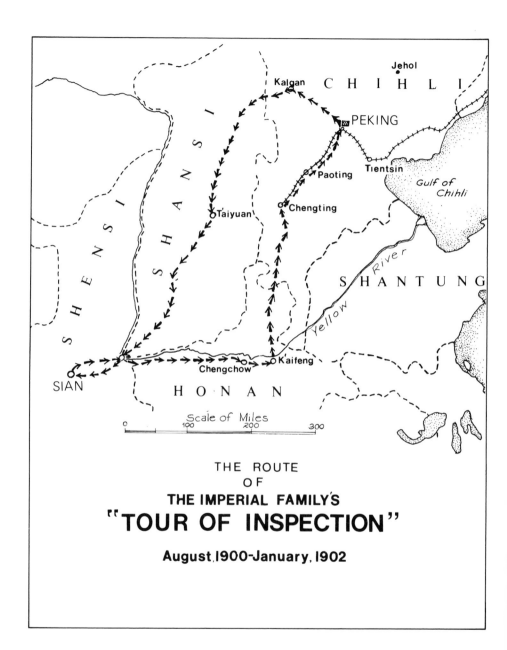

THE ROUTE
OF
THE IMPERIAL FAMILY'S
"TOUR OF INSPECTION"
August,1900-January,1902

Before leaving, a macabre scene is said to have taken place. The Empress Dowager had decreed that none of the Emperor's concubines were to accompany the Tour of Inspection, but one, known as the Pearl Concubine and the Emperor's favourite, made so bold as to suggest that the Emperor himself should remain. Infuriated by this insubordination, in an act of revolting cruelty, horrible even by the standards of her long and nasty reign, the 'Benign Mother' ordered the wretched women seized by eunuchs and flung down a well, which senseless crime was carried out despite the desperate pleadings of the Emperor himself.

Pausing at the Summer Palace long enough only to supervise the despatch of some valuables to Jehol in the north (there was plenty left to be plundered later by the Allies), the Imperial progress continued north-westwards to Kalgan and into the province of Shansi where the Empress Dowager was pleased to congratulate the Governor, Yu Hsien, on his splendid work in 'ridding Shansi of the whole brood of foreign devils', by which she meant the torture and murder of a number of missionaries and their families. Later, however, she advised the man to commit suicide as his continued existence might cause her embarrassment, but he did not take the hint and was eventually executed at the insistence of the Allies.

Having started their journey under conditions of extreme dis-comfort, travelling by Peking cart, one of the most agonizing forms of conveyance invented by man, dressed as peasants and with little food, the Imperial circumstances gradually improved. Litters were substituted for the carts and the further from Peking they travelled, the greater the respect and consideration they were shown by local officials.

As a young woman forty years earlier, the Empress Dowager had embarked upon a similar Tour of Inspection to escape the previous uninvited visit of foreign barbarians to Peking, but since then she had hardly left the capital and its environs. So, with her amazing resilience and reserves of mental and physical toughness, she began to relax and enjoy herself, rejuvenated by the new sights and sounds which surrounded her. She was soon to be joined by her favourite, Jung Lu, and together they would plan how best to pull the fat from the fire. Although, of course, for the sake of face, the hardest bargain must be driven with the Allies, everybody, with the possible exception of Jung Lu himself, was to be expendable in the struggle to rescue the Old Buddha and her dynasty from the consequences of her own stupidity.

The rest of her year in exile and her ministers' negotiations with the Allies will be dealt with later but now we must return to her capital where the conquerors were somewhat spasmodically consolidating their grip.

Early in the morning of the 15th the Americans, whether on their own initiative or with the agreement of the other Allies is unclear, advanced to attack and occupy the Imperial and Forbidden Cities. This, they hoped, would be their moment of glory. The entire American contingent was involved; the 9th and 14th Infantry, F (Reilly's) Battery of the 5th Artillery, a troop of the 6th Cavalry and the Marines.

The 14th and Reilly's Battery were to lead the assault on the south gates of the Imperial City. Captain Crozier of General Chaffee's staff conducted the commanding officer of the 14th, Colonel Daggett, to within sight of the first gate. Pointing to this massive obstruction, he delivered himself of as fine a piece of military pomposity and buck-passing as we are ever likely to encounter. 'Here,' he announced to Daggett, 'my duty ends and yours begins!' Perhaps for the sake of delicacy, the Colonel's reply is not recorded, but examining this formidable obstacle with a jaundiced eye he found it uninviting from an infantryman's point of view, summoned Reilly and requested that he knock it down. There were in fact three double gates made of strong timber eight inches thick. Reilly brought up two guns under Lieutenant Summerall and, at point blank range, blasted a hole through the centre gate. The infantry poured through but found themselves, rather as the Russians had at the Tung Pien Men, in an archway which opened into a courtyard dominated at its far end by a tower over another set of gates. Advancing cautiously into this potential trap, the leading platoon of Company M of the 14th came under heavy fire. In the brisk action which followed, Captain Reilly, a popular and capable officer, and half-a-dozen men were killed, but smashing their way through two more gates the Americans found themselves before the final entrance into the Forbidden City. But they were to be denied their crowning triumph and, at the moment of success, orders were received to halt the attack and withdraw.

The artillery had lost its commanding officer, the 14th four men killed and fourteen wounded and the 9th two killed and five wounded, all in vain. As the historian of the 14th indignantly recorded, politics had taken over. 'As the attack on the Imperial City commenced,' he wrote, 'the European Allies looked on incredulously, not believing that the Americans would make any substantial progress, but as the day wore on and gate after gate yielded . . . unbelief changed to admiring wonder. . . . The latter feeling quickly gave place to the jealous realization that it would never do for them to permit the Americans to reap all the glory of the campaign . . . No! They must stop the advance of these men in blue and khaki . . . so General Chaffee was reluctantly brought to see that it would be best to suspend operations and not enter the Forbidden City.'

We may accept this explanation from the pen of the chronicler of frustrated and disappointed men, or not. Doubtless international jealousies were involved. At one point some Russians had tried to join in the assault but had been more or less elbowed to one side by the Americans; and the French too, desperate to play some significant role in a victory which they had made hitherto no noticeable contribution, had opened fire from the Tartar Wall, but had endangered the Americans more than the Chinese and had been persuaded to desist. But of greater mutual concern to the Allied commanders and ministers must have been the whereabouts of the Manchus, the Imperial House of Ch'ing. Allied Intelligence (not to say intelligence) had been poor throughout the campaign and they had no means of knowing that the Imperial family had fled the Forbidden City several hours before the American attack and were well out of harm's way. Any injury to the Empress Dowager, the Emperor or the Heir Apparent, or even their capture, could cause grave embarrassment to the Allied governments and bring down their wrath upon the heads of their unfortunate military and diplomatic representatives on the spot. Better then to be sure that the Imperials had escaped before allowing the soldiers of any nationality into the Forbidden City.

In the 19th and early 20th centuries dynastic freemasonry was powerful and touchy. However wicked, corrupt and incompetent the Manchus might be, they were Royal and therefore, so far as the Romanovs, Habsburgs, Hohenzollerns and Saxe-Coburg-Gothas were concerned, untouchable. Perhaps these great imperial houses had some inkling of their own vulnerability. After all, only one of them was to survive the Manchus by more than a few years. Nor did western statesmen, even French and American republicans, desire the fall of the House of Ch'ing. They were aware that for the leading members of the dynasty to suffer in any way at the hands of foreign devils would entail unacceptable and irredeemable loss of face. Until the little local difficulty of the last few months, the Powers had done extremely well out of the Manchus so why upset the status quo? Give the old woman, her clan and toadies a chance to escape and then start the arm-twisting. The veteran professional Li Hung-chang was on his way to Peking (only two months late) and a satisfactory settlement could be the more easily reached with him while his Imperial mistress and her more obstructive hangers-on were out of the way. The fact of the matter was that in China the Powers' quarrels were with one another, not the Manchus, who just happened to be there.

A fortnight was to elapse before the Forbidden City was formally occupied with a great parade of Allied troops, by which time the Manchus were many li away.


## 16th August

Somebody remembered the Peit'ang.

## Royal Marines Legation Guard, Pekin.

| | | | | | | | | | |
|---|---|---|---|---|---|---|---|---|---|
| 1 | Ch. | 8273 | Pte. W. G. Angel (pro. corporal) | 30 | Capt. | | Wray, R.M.L.I. (brevet-maj.) | 53 | Po. | 7358 | Lc.-Sgt. J. E. Preston (pro. sgt., conspicuous gallantry medal, and medal for distinguished conduct on the field) |

1 Ch. 8273 Pte. W. G. Angel (pro. corporal)
2 Po. 4739 Pte. W. Betts
3 Ply. 8650 „ A. Alexander
4 Ply. 8669 „ G. Forrester
5 Po. 9286 „ J. Butler
6 Po. 5381 „ W. Cheshire
7 Ch. 9675 „ J. Greenfield
8 Ch. 9642 „ A. G. Mayo
9 Ply. 8623 „ W. R. Harding
10 Po. 9255 „ G. Goddard
11 Po. 9251 „ J. W. Walker
12 Ply. 8602 „ A. Jones (pro. cpl.)
13 Po. 9243 „ J. Marriott
14 Ch. 8798 „ G. T. Jones
15 Po. 9008 „ J. Rumble
16 Ch. 6471 „ H. Sands
17 Ply. 8333 „ K. King
18 Po. 8926 „ W. T. Woodward
19 Po. 9226 „ C. Baker
20 Po. 8924 „ J. R. Pitts (since transferred to Ch.)
21 Ply. 8698 „ J. R. Myers
22 Ply. 8677 „ C. Johnson
23 Ply. 8630 „ S. W. Haden
24 Po. 9258 „ W. Smith
25 Po. 9331 „ W. R. R. Edney
26 Po. 8604 „ W. J. Sparkes (pro. corporal)
27 Capt. Poole, W.R.R.
28 „ Halliday, R.M.L.I. (V.C. brevet-major)
29 Sir Claude Macdonald

30 Capt. Wray, R.M.L.I. (brevet-maj.)
31 Po. 5082 Cpl. D. J. Gowney (pro. sergeant, distinguished conduct medal)
32 Ch. 4982 Sgt. A. E. Saunders (pro. colour-sergeant)
33 Ch. 9451 Pte. J. G Howard
34 Po. 9344 „ J. D. Newland
35 Po. 5308 „ E. Webb
36 Po. 8879 „ W. J. Hunt
37 Ch. 5376 Sgt. J. Murphy (pro. clr.-sergt., distinguished conduct medal)
38 Ply. 6529 Cpl. W. Gregory (pro. sergt.)
39 Ply. 8611 Pte. W. Viney
40 Po. 8816 „ W. Horne
41 Ch. 11033 „ H. A. Webster
42 Ply. 8684 „ D. Hill
43 Po. 8912 „ F. Tanner
44 Ch. 9635 „ E. G. O'Neill
45 Po. 8932 „ E. E. Powell
46 Po. 9195 „ W. A. Taylor
47 Po. 9239 „ T. G. Smith
48 Ply. 8649 „ A. S. Roberts
49 Po. 8603 „ J. Mears
50 Ply. 8654 „ A. Dunkley
51 Po. 6830 Cpl. G. Sheppard (pro. sergt.)
52 S. B. A. Fuller

53 Po. 7358 Lc.-Sgt. J. E. Preston (pro. sgt., conspicuous gallantry medal, and medal for distinguished conduct on the field)
54 Ch. 9640 Pte. A. T. Layton
55 Ch. 9672 „ A. J. Tickner
56 Ch. 8579 „ H. Grainger
57 Po. 8927 „ R. Hendicott
58 Po. 8935 „ W. Rowe
59 Po. 8605 „ J. W. Heap
60 Po. 9113 „ A. E. Westbrook
61 Po. 9277 „ H. J. Green
62 Ldg.-Signalman H. Swannell
63 Ch. 7695 Pte. W. Turner
64 Ply. 8687 „ T. R. Allin (pro. corpl.)
65 Ply. 8665 „ J. Dean
66 Po. 7036 „ W. Ford
67 Po. 5186 „ H. J. Salvin (pro. corporal)
68 Ch. 9676 „ W. J. Masters
69 Po. 8959 „ G. Davis
70 Po. 9346 „ J. Ormiston
71 Po. 3155 Bugler A. E. Webb
72 Ply. 8617 Pte. F. J. Cresswell
73 Po. 8885 „ A Jones
74 Armourers Mate Thomas
75 Po. 9081 Pte. G. Lister
76 Ply. 8653 „ J. Murray
77 Po. 5819 Cpl. J. Johnson (pro. sgt distingd conduct medal)
78 Ply. 8622 Pte. S. Mellows

NOTE.—We have endeavoured to give the correct names in the above key block, but considering the time that has elapsed since the photo was taken, we cannot vouch for its entire accuracy.—Editor G. & I.

The surviving British Legation guards with Sir Claude MacDonald photographed immediately after the relief. Also Key. (*Royal Marines Museum*)

189

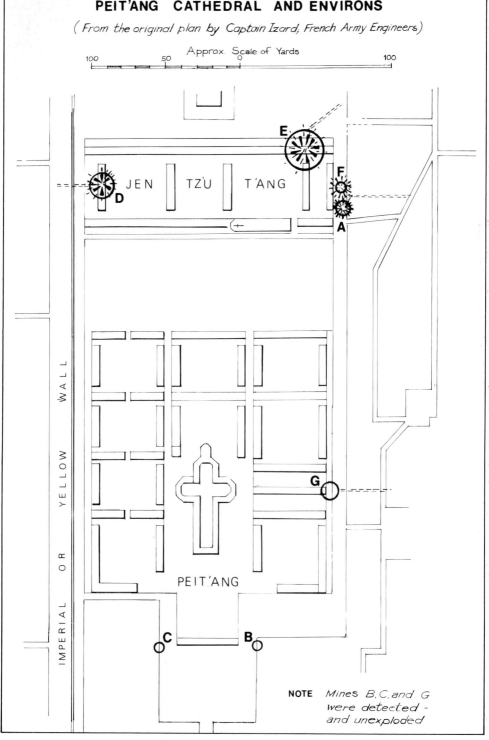

PLAN OF
# PEIT'ANG  CATHEDRAL  AND  ENVIRONS

*( From the original plan by Captain Izard, French Army Engineers).*

Approx. Scale of Yards

100          50          0                    100

JEN     TZ'U     T'ANG

E

D

F

A

IMPERIAL  OR  YELLOW  WALL

G

PEIT'ANG

C          B

**NOTE**   *Mines B, C, and G*
*were detected -*
*and unexploded*

# 7

# The Other Siege

And how can man die better
   Than facing fearful odds
For the ashes of his fathers
   And the temples of his Gods . . .

*Horatius*, Lord Macaulay


The Peit'ang or North Cathedral lay within earshot of the Legation Quarter and within the walls of the Imperial City. This considerable complex of buildings, surrounded by a perimeter wall twelve to fifteen feet high and about a mile in circumference, had been constructed some years earlier at considerable expense to the Imperial Treasury as a gift and a compliment to the Roman Catholic Church and therefore, indirectly, to France, long regarded as the secular protector of Roman Catholicism in China.

The cathedral itself, an imposing if somewhat garish edifice, towered above a number of other ecclesiastical buildings; the palace of Bishop Favier, France's answer to Sir Robert Hart in the hierarchy of Old China Hands; a hall of residence for his priests; a rest-house for missionaries in transit; two convents; several schools; a printing press and a number of shops.

To its north and across a broad street lay another group of buildings known as the Jen Tz'u T'ang. This included a refuge for the destitute, an orphanage for some five hundred children, a residence for twenty-two French, Italian and Chinese nuns and a dispensary.

This more or less self-contained Christian enclave came under the firm but benign management of Bishop Favier, his right-hand man Monseigneur Jarlin and an aged Mother Superior.

As we have seen, Favier, with his ear closer to the ground than

191

any of the diplomats (and most of the other Old China Hands, including Hart), had been urging since the early months of 1900 that the Boxer movement be taken seriously. Many Chinese Christians had sought refuge in and around his cathedral and by the beginning of June he was faced with protecting and feeding some 3,400 souls, rather more than there were in the British Legation compound and the Fu combined during the siege. He had done his best to stock up with food and his stables were full of edible draught animals: horses, mules and donkeys. But apart from a few obsolete rifles which he had managed to collect together, he had nothing with which to protect his see and nobody to do the protecting. So, when the legation guards arrived from Taku on 31 May, he prevailed upon M. Pichon to provide him with a detachment of thirty sailors from the *D'Entrecasteaux* under Enseigne de Vaisseau (Sub-Lieutenant) Paul Henry, a 23-year-old Breton.

In this random choice Favier and the other inhabitants of the Peit'ang complex were extremely fortunate since, even allowing for the hagiographical exaggerations of his admirers, here was a very

The Peit'ang Cathedral in 1989. (*Zhang Shui Cheng*)

192

exceptional young man. Deeply religious and fervently patriotic, Henry might have been born specifically for the role he was about to play, namely to defend to the death the sanctity of his religion and the honour of his country. It is a cliché to say of a man that others 'will follow him anywhere', but this was surely true of Henry. From the beginning to the end of his brief career, and especially in the unique circumstances which ended it, he seems to have inspired a rare devotion and confidence, not only in the rough seamen under his command, but in all those with whom he came into contact, including the elderly cleric Favier and his flock.

Led, incongruously, by that ultimate civilian, M. Pichon, on a white horse, Henry's detachment marched from the French Legation to the Peit'ang on the morning of 1 June. On arrival the young officer took immediate stock of the position and, despite coming to the initial and theoretically correct conclusion that the place was indefensible, immediately put in hand measures to defend it. There was no lack of willing hands to assist. Monseigneur Jarlin took charge of the civilian work-force and, as a former soldier, added a certain snap to his spiritual exhortations. In addition to his three senior Petty Officers, Jouannic, Mingam and Elias, Henry enlisted the services of a young Austrian theological student of unusually martial disposition for a man of his calling named Gartner, who acted throughout the siege as a kind of supernumerary officer – a similar role, perhaps, to that of Nigel Oliphant and some of the other volunteers with the British contingent.

By 5 June the French detachment had been reinforced by ten Italian sailors under Midshipman Olivieri sent by their minister for the specific, but not exclusive, task of protecting the Italian nuns resident in the Jen Tz'u T'ang. They were to be under Henry's overall command. Additionally, about a hundred of the most stalwart of the Chinese Christians were given pikes and a few ancient rifles which the bishop had acquired and formed into a mobile auxiliary force.

In the early days of June, the days, as it were, of the 'phoney war', Henry made the best use of a time of relative tranquillity. It seemed to him that the main south entrance to the cathedral precincts was particularly vulnerable to attack. He was right, for it was at this point that the Chinese were to concentrate much of their aggressive effort. Here he dug three lines of communicating trenches and threw up parapets with the spoil. The perimeter wall was strengthened and loop-holed and the road separating the Jen Tz'u T'ang from the Peit'ang was barricaded at both ends so that the previously divided groups of buildings were made one. Finally, around the whole defended area a trench was dug inside the wall.

As all this hard work had been virtually completed before communication with the legations had been finally severed on 18 June, we must conclude that the likelihood of a fierce and protracted siege was much more firmly fixed in the mind of Bishop Favier than it was in the minds of the diplomats and military commanders at the legations, and that this feeling had communicated itself with some force to Henry. We do not know what instructions he had received from his superior officer, Lieutenant d'Arcy, before leaving the French Legation on 1 June, but the urgency and meticulousness of his preparations compare most favourably with those undertaken during the same period in the legation quarter. Bearing in mind that the Franco–Italian detachment and their auxiliaries had to defend a perimeter roughly half the length of that around the legations with about a tenth of the number of men, it will be appreciated just how vital these precautions were. Notwithstanding these efforts, the problems of defence remained enormous. Only to the north did the defenders have a reasonable field of fire over a large area of waste land. From the west, the Cathedral complex was dominated by the mighty wall of the Imperial City, about double the height of the wall of the Peit'ang, and to the east and south Chinese houses, ideal firing positions for the attackers, encroached right up to the perimeter.

On 9 June watchers on the Cathedral roof saw the first of the fires which were to consume large areas of the city blazing around them. On the 11th, in answer to a pre-arranged bugle call from the roof, Henry's men 'stood-to' in earnest for the first time, but it proved to be a false alarm.

On the evening of the 15th, a day which brought news of the murders of dozens of Christians in Peking, including the French Fathers Dore and Garregue, the first red-clad Boxers were sighted forming up outside the main south entrance. Armed only with swords and torches they advanced slowly with strange posturings and ritualistic movements. Within 300 yards of the entrance they knelt and appeared to pray, whereupon the French, taking no chances, opened fire. Presumably this particular band of Boxers had not taken the precaution of testing the validity of its claim to invulnerability, for many fell dead or wounded and the rest bolted. Reporting to d'Arcy, Henry claimed fifteen dead and double that number wounded for the expenditure of only fifty-five rounds. Later, on receipt of information from outside, he amended this to forty-seven dead. The standard of French musketry may have been high, although this is by no means confirmed by other sources, but it seems rather improbable that they would have scored eighty-five per cent fatal hits at 300 yards! Nevertheless, these splendid figures doubtless boosted morale, a great deal more important to a beleaguered garrison than mere factual accuracy.

For a few more days there was to be little indication that the Chinese army was involved, or was about to become involved, in hostilities against the foreigners. However, on the 18th all communication between the Peit'ang and the outside world, including the legations, was cut and, despite repeated attempts to get messages through, would not be renewed until the siege was lifted nearly two months later. On the 22nd the first major bombardment was opened up on the Cathedral.

A gun placed opposite the south entrance opened fire in the early morning and by 9.30 am had pumped 186 shells into and around the cathedral complex. Accurate rifle fire by the defenders eventually forced the gun's crew to seek cover, leaving the gun itself exposed and unprotected. Henry wasted no time. Within minutes a squad of twenty Chinese under Jarlin and escorted by a few sailors was organized to dash out, seize the gun and its ammunition and drag it back into the defended area. Some initial hesitancy on the part of the 'snatch' squad was quickly overcome by the forceful and persuasive Jarlin and the weapon was hauled, under fire, into the cathedral precincts. But as we hear little of the use of this prize by the defenders during the siege it may well be that few of its shells were recovered with it.

In the course of the bombardment a Chinese Christian woman had been killed, the first fatal casualty of the Siege of the Peit'ang.

On the 27th an act of individual courage led to a serious loss. Jouannic, Henry's second-in-command, noticing a number of abandoned rifles within a few yards of the south entrance, ran out to collect them but was shot and mortally wounded. He died three days later.

The following day, the 28th, the attackers, using makeshift flame-throwers, two water pumps squirting lighted petrol (devices, one suspects, as dangerous to the user as to the target), tried to set fire to the main gate. Somehow the flames reached the Cathedral roof which caught fire and, although this was extinguished, it was decided that a sortie must be mounted to burn down the houses from which the attacks were being launched. This counter-attack, again led by the intrepid Jarlin, not only succeeded in setting fire to the houses but also recovered the two pumps the enemy had been using.

On the 29th the beleaguered garrison realized that an internal and potentially even more deadly danger than the Boxers had to be faced. Smallpox had broken out among the orphans and refugees who were dying at the rate of fifteen a day. The heat was intense, up to 100°F, food was poor and strictly rationed and medical facilities primitive. Despite all this the devoted nuns and brothers managed to keep the epidemic under control and, miraculously, the death rate appears to have fallen rather than risen as the siege progressed.

The sorties undertaken in the early days of the siege were not to be the last, but thereafter a largely defensive posture was maintained. The risks of such acts of derring-do were too great and the rewards too small. As we have seen, they had seized a gun but without its ammunition it was of little value and, unlike their colleagues at the legations, they lacked the wherewithal to make any. Nonetheless morale was high and Henry told his men proudly, although not without a certain bravado, 'Had I fifty of you instead of thirty, I would march on the Imperial Palace!'

The fighting throughout July was continuous but largely one-sided in that Henry exercised such strict fire-control that seldom were more than a hundred cartridges used in a day by the defenders. Even while the periods of truce were being observed at the legations, there was no let-up at the Peit'ang. Afterwards the theory was developed that the Old Buddha had decided to throw the Cathedral as a kind of compensatory bone to the Boxers and their supporters as it became clear to her that it was both too difficult and too dangerous to overwhelm and destroy the legations. There may or may not be some substance in this. Certainly the Peit'ang should have been even easier to take than the legations and the consequences of the massacre of its inmates might have been less serious for China and the dynasty than the slaughter of the diplomats, whose security during the last century and for most of this one was internationally regarded as inviolable, indeed almost sacred.

Day and night bullets, rockets and shells rained upon the cathedral and its precincts. Many of these missiles, however, whistled over their targets to crash into Chinese dwellings on the other side, some of which were inhabited by Boxers and troops, thus inadvertently aiding the defenders. Until 18 July casualties were light. Up to that date only three sailors, two French and one Italian, and a few civilians had been killed, but on that day a major success was scored by the attackers.

Henry and the others had long suspected that tunnelling and mining operations were going on around and under the perimeter wall but although counter-tunnelling gangs of Chinese Christians had been set to work, the exact locations of any mines which may have been laid had not been pin-pointed. On the 11th a mine (see A on the plan on p. 190) had exploded at the south-east corner of the Jen Tz'u T'ang killing one man and causing a certain amount of material damage, but early in the morning of the 18th the entire garrison was awakened by a huge detonation. Rushing to the west end of the Jen (D), a hideous sight met their eyes. Before them was an enormous crater with bits and pieces of the bodies of one of the counter-tunnelling gangs scattered in and around it, while from the commanding heights of the Imperial (Yellow) Wall, enemy troops kept up a withering fire upon those trying to rescue and succour the wounded. Many people were buried alive – and dead – and it was not until the sailors' heavy return fire drove the enemy from the wall that the full extent of casualties was revealed; twenty-eight dead, including the French brother, Joseph-Félicité, who had been in charge of the gang, and as many wounded. The survivors were badly shaken and Henry, who from the beginning seems to have believed that he would be required to give his life to save his companions, made his Will and wrote his last letter to his family.

It is impossible, even in this age of scepticism, to be unmoved by his words, words which a young man of his profession today would probably regard as sentimental and, even if they came to his mind, would find difficult to commit to paper.

'My well-beloved parents,' wrote the young Breton, 'my dear brothers and sisters.

'If I am killed these final words will convey to you my last farewell. Do not feel too much sadness. I have died for the most beautiful of causes. I have done, I hope, all my duty. I leave to you the little that I have and I ask you to set aside from the money which I leave the sum of two hundred francs for the Missions in China, so hard pressed at this moment.

'I embrace you with all the tenderness of my heart, as I have always loved you. I send my last farewell to you, my dear parents and friends. Ask my uncle* to offer God his communion for the repose of my soul.

'Once again, a last farewell, my dear ones, pray for me. In the name of the Father, the Son and the Holy Ghost, Amen.'

The next day, the Feast of St Vincent, following the death of one of their comrades, Stoker Frank, Henry's men revealed their stress and frustration by breaking discipline for the first and only time

Enseigne de Vaisseau Paul Henry, the tragic hero of the Siege of the Peit'ang. (*René Bazin*)

* A priest.

198

while under his command. After celebrating the Feast, perhaps with stronger waters than those of which the saint himself would have approved, a group of French and Italian sailors decided, on their own initiative, to attack and destroy the enemy positions on the Imperial Wall. Swarming up ladders and followed by crowds of Chinese Christians intent upon avenging the victims of the previous day, they proceeded to lay about them vigorously, hurling down sandbags, tiles and bricks. The enemy, taken aback by the fury and unexpectedness of the assault, contented themselves with cries of 'Kill! Kill! Kill!' from a safe distance. When word of this reckless escapade reached the French commander he dashed to the scene with Olivieri and subjected his crest-fallen men to a rare tongue-lashing, foreign to his firm but gentle nature. 'What are you men doing here? Who gave you permission to leave your posts? If you do it again you will be court-martialled!' he shouted. But, never one to miss an opportunity of inflicting damage on the enemy, he sent for petrol and set fire to the scaffolding which the Chinese used for access to the top of the wall on their side.

It is worth recording that throughout this terrifying and tumultuous ordeal the inmates of the Peit'ang received no word of any kind from without their walls – not even from the legations. Usually, during the brief lulls in their own fighting, they could hear the gunfire coming from the legation quarter and when this from time to time fell silent, they had every reason to assume that their compatriots there had been overwhelmed and slaughtered. They knew nothing of truces or parleys. They lived minute by minute, hour by hour, preserving their priceless ammunition, firing only 33 shots one day, 55 the next, 27 the next and so on, chewing on a bit of horsemeat if they were lucky, deafened by the roar of continuous bombardment.

Sleepless, selfless, their youthful leader, sparing himself nothing, led by example. It is hard to find one to compare with him at the legations. Halliday, bold but too impetuous; Shiba, hard, professional, fearless; the unlucky Strouts, competent and steady but perhaps less imaginative; Myers trying to lead tough unruly men by persuasion; MacDonald, much older, cool but remote. Somehow Paul Henry stands out alone. Perhaps it is invidious to select a special Hero of the Sieges, but, if we must, then surely he is our choice.

From time to time, with almost suicidal courage, a Chinese Christian messenger would attempt to get through to the legations. None ever made it – even one way. Only their heads would return, festooned with their own intestines and displayed gleefully on pikes by their killers to the horror of their watching friends. Although there were more people at the Peit'ang, the siege there had an isolation and a dreadful loneliness which the legations somehow escaped. At the Legations there was some occasional contact with the outside world, even some dialogue with the enemy. At the Peit'ang there was neither.

However, despite the risks, occasional armed sorties were made with the objective of obtaining some information, some hint of what was happening elsewhere, by capturing a prisoner. One such patrol of Chinese Christians, under the Austrian novice Gartner, on 20 July found three Boxers asleep in one of the few houses still standing near the main entrance. Either badly briefed, undisciplined or both, in a frenzy of hatred against their tormentors, the Christians slew the Boxers with their own weapons before setting fire to the house. Jarlin, whose task it would have been to interrogate the prisoners, was not best pleased.

By this time food stocks were running seriously low and on the 21st it was estimated that, at 1 lb of rice, beans or millet per head per day, only fifteen days' rations remained. The daily allowance was progressively reduced, until, on 10 August, only 400 lbs of rice and one mule were left. Thereafter no rations whatsoever were issued to any but the fighting men. The non-combatant population was obliged to subsist as best it could; leaves, grass and bark were gathered and occasionally a pi-dog, bloated on the corpses of Chinese soldiers and Boxers, would be shot and hoisted over the wall on a hook. Searing heat and the constant wailing of sick and starving children, 170 of whom died, took a greater toll on the nerves of the defenders than even the continuous thunder of the artillery and the rattle of musketry. Only their ammunition stocks, thanks to the strictest discipline, were holding out well. By the end of July they still had over 6,000 rounds, enough to last several months at the current rate of expenditure.

But as the seemingly endless days wore on even Henry's morale began to slump. When time allowed, cheering conversations with

200

the fatherly Favier, whose faith that rescue would ultimately arrive never faltered, refreshed the young Breton's tired spirit. Despite severe casualties to the enemy, 23 and 29 July were days of particularly savage and unremitting bombardment, serious damage being done to the walls, especially of the Jen Tz'u T'ang.

Early on the morning of the 30th it was reported to Henry that a large breach had been blown in the east wall of the Jen by shellfire. The sailors had opened a heavy return fire through the breach, forcing the Chinese gunners to withdraw, once again leaving their gun vulnerable to a sortie. Henry decided that if the gun were to be brought back into action then his position, indeed the whole of the Jen, might become untenable and therefore it had to be seized or put out of action. So critical did the situation seem to him that he called upon over half his remaining regulars, led by himself, to undertake this desperate venture.

Just as the raiding party was about to dash from cover, word reached Henry that an even more perilous situation was developing on the north wall and that a major infantry attack was under way. Ordering the others to wait where they were and accompanied by only two seamen, Delmas and Callac, he hurried to the new danger point. On arrival he could see what appeared to be enemy infantry deploying for an assault. Delmas, a crack rifle shot, immediately opened fire, later claiming 28 hits with 29 cartridges. However, he was firing from an exposed position and, after a few minutes, was wounded in the right arm. Callac took his place, but the Chinese rifleman who had hit Delmas must have kept his eye fixed on the same spot for he immediately fired another shot which passed through Callac's shoulder and into Henry's throat, severing his vocal chords. As Callac staggered back so the enemy marksman fired again, hitting Henry in the left side and penetrating his body. In a daze and already dying, he turned and started to walk away, followed by his horrified men, their own wounds forgotten. Somehow he walked for over fifty yards before collapsing. No word could he speak but his face was calm and there was a slight smile on his lips. He did not linger. Receiving the Last Rites from a Chinese priest, he slipped quietly away, apparently without pain.

With the defenders numb from shock and disbelief, discipline and all sense of self-preservation temporarily disappeared. Men milled around weeping and cursing. The undefended Jen was exposed to attack from both north and east but no advantage was taken by the enemy. Granted they were unaware of the extent and importance of the drama taking place behind the hated walls to their front but, incredibly, neither the assault from the north nor the bombardment from the east was resumed, at least not until Olivieri and Quartermaster Elias had brought the men back to their senses and reorganized the defence.

Equally inexplicably, from the moment of Henry's death, the vehemence of the assault upon the Peit'ang complex began to abate. Although one last hideous catastrophe was to overtake the inmates, from 30 July onwards Favier and his colleagues began to feel that, militarily, the worst was over and that the main threat was now from disease and starvation.

They buried Paul Henry in the Cathedral garden beneath a statue of Notre Dame de Lourdes. Perhaps he lies there to this day, surrounded by nine of his men, French and Italian, all oblivious to the sound and fury of the tempestuous century at the dawn of which they fell in a better cause than many.

The defenders allowed themselves no further breakdowns of discipline or vigilance. However, they could not safeguard against the enemy's mining operations. In the course of the siege, seven mines were laid (see plan) of which four exploded. As we have seen, the first did little damage and the second a great deal. The worst was left to the end. At 6.30 on the morning of 12 August a huge explosion drowned the rumble of the distant guns of the relief force. A mine (E), afterwards estimated as having contained some 1,800 lbs of explosive, had blown up the north-east corner of the Jen, demolishing 100 yards of wall and killing 136 people: 80 adult civilians, 51 children and five Italian seamen. Olivieri, who was completely buried under a huge mound of earth and rubble, was miraculously dug out alive eleven hours later. In terms of loss of life it was the worst single episode of the siege, either at the Peit'ang or at the legations, and, although another mine (F) exploded the following day without doing any damage, it was one of the last major acts of hostility on the part of the Chinese.

It will be remembered that, after making good progress on 15 August, the Americans were ordered to cease their operation to

The crater caused by Mine E at the Peit'ang. The explosion killed 136 people and wounded many others. (*Institution of Royal Engineers*)

enter the Forbidden City. However, this did not prevent the other Allies, spearheaded as usual by the Japanese, from advancing steadily through the remainder of the Tartar City. At about 8 o'clock on the morning of the 16th the Japanese arrived at the foot of the wall of the Peit'ang. Half an hour later the grinning face of a Japanese captain peered over the coping. Clambering up the last few rungs of his ladder, the officer advanced, hand outstretched, towards Monseigneur Jarlin who was speechless with mixed emotions. Even Jarlin and his devout master Favier must have reflected at that moment upon the capriciousness of the Almighty. Not only had He snatched from them the gallant young officer to whom they owed their salvation from a revolting and agonizing death and whom they had grown to love like a son, but He had allowed large numbers of children and other innocents to be blown up almost on the eve of rescue and, to cap it all, He had arranged for the only 'heathens' in the entire relief force to perform that rescue! Verily the ways of the Lord are mysterious, the worthy clerics must have sighed.

Soon, as a belated compensation, the French arrived. A few shots were fired, almost ceremonially, at a long-departed enemy. There were embraces, tears and cheers. Doubtless the Marseillaise was sung. It was a pity about the Japanese but *tant pis*. What matter who had got there first? The siege had been raised. Good had prevailed over Evil.

Four hundred had died in the Peit'ang and Jen, over half of them children. Of the fighting men, six Italians, five Frenchmen and thirty-eight Chinese auxiliaries had lost their lives and many of the rest had been wounded.* The defenders had spared themselves nothing. Their courage, endurance and fortitude had been little short of superhuman. The Siege of the Peit'ang will remain for all time an outstanding example of the triumph of the human spirit over the seemingly inevitable.

---

* Also two French priests were killed and six wounded.

# 8

# The Occupation

A Chino's life isn't worth a nickel.

Lieutenant William Harllee,
US Marine Corps

For a while after the arrival of the Allies looting was the most popular, indeed almost the only, activity in Peking. Everyone, soldiers, diplomats, foreign civilians and Chinese alike, looted everything they could lay their hands on. Sir Claude and Lady MacDonald were, reputedly, great plunderers* as was Herbert Squiers who later boasted to Morrison that he had amassed $200,000 worth of art treasures. William Harllee had so many trunks packed full of furs, silks and crockery that, just for fun, he decked out some coolies in the finest clothes he could find and sent them on their way rejoicing. However, whereas the Allies looted more or less with impunity, although there was trouble if one Ally looted on another's patch (Peking was divided into national zones like Berlin after the Second World War), the Chinese were shot for it. 'We have orders to kill them if we catch them,' wrote Harllee, 'and as they are all at it all the time you see what a small chance a Chink has for his life.'

General Gaselee endeavoured to organize British looting in accordance with Good Order and Military Discipline. He issued orders to the effect that all loot must be pooled and equitably divided under the supervision of the Commander Royal Engineers. It is not clear how well this worked or how much notice was taken of the order.

---

* In later years this imputation was deeply resented by the MacDonalds' daughters. Certainly no great wealth is reflected in the Will of Lady MacDonald who died in comfortable but modest circumstances in 1941.

A British officer displays loot after the relief of the Legations. One item, not visible on the table, purchased from an American soldier for $20, was sold at auction in London three-quarters of a century later for over £6000.

Field Marshal Graf von Waldersee reviewing Allied troops in the Imperial City at Peking. Japanese, French, German and British officers can be seen to his right and rear. (*National Army Museum*)

The Russians stripped the Summer Palace bare and many 'punitive expeditions' were mounted almost entirely for the sake of pillage, although the troops sometimes indulged in a little extraneous killing at the same time, especially if, by some stretch of the imagination, a man could be taken for a Boxer. One Welsh Fusilier later admitted shooting a harmless civilian for no better reason than to test the effect of a dum-dum bullet. The result apparently exceeded his expectations.

The Germans and the French stole some priceless astronomical instruments which had been erected two hundred years before by the Jesuit fathers and, after quarrelling over them, divided them into two, half going to Berlin and half to Paris. The Japanese made away with £62,000 worth of silver, a commodity for which they seemed to have a particular taste and an unerring eye for its whereabouts. As the Prussian Field-Marshal Graf von Waldersee, himself an expert looter, pointed out, 'every nationality accords the palm to some other in respect to the act of plundering.' Much the same applied to unauthorized killing; the other fellows did that sort of thing, but never your own men.

Von Waldersee, by a surprising mutual agreement reached between the Allied governments several weeks before the relief, had been appointed Commander-in-Chief of the Allied forces in north China. He had appeared on the scene too late to take any part in the fighting but he installed himself in the Winter Palace with a glittering staff, a sergeant-major as a personal bodyguard and a Chinese courtesan to warm his bed. Determined to obey the Kaiser's order that his men should behave 'just as the Huns a thousand years ago', he set about pillaging and terrorizing his temporary fief with methodical gusto. Only one untoward incident disturbed the even tenure of his office. His Chief of Staff accidentally set fire to his own quarters and burnt himself to death.

However, von Waldersee's appointment was by no means popular with all the Allied commanders in north China. The French particularly resented a German generalissimo and the Japanese commander Yamaguchi was of the opinion that the main object having been achieved, namely the relief of the Peking legations, there was no need to place Japanese troops under foreign command. He was over-ruled by Tokyo, but the German's appointment was in any case

207

cosmetic rather than practical and most of the Allied commanders went their own ways and followed their own governments' instructions.

George Morrison reported unfavourably to *The Times* on von Waldersee's behaviour and that of the German troops but awarded the 'palm' for looting to the French. They, he claimed, added insult to injury by making the Chinese whose property they had looted 'carry the spoils down to the French camp'. One way and another, Morrison managed to infuriate nearly everyone and within a few days of the relief none of the foreign diplomats, who had received advice by telegraph of his reports in *The Times* of their behaviour during and after the siege, would speak to him. However, he seems to have got on well enough with MacDonald, although the British legate accused Morrison's servant of stealing a piece of legation silver while his master was in the hospital there.

For all this, much wealth was simply redistributed within Chinese society. Most of the rich and official classes had managed to flee Peking before the arrival of the barbarian, but the poor had nowhere

Boxers executed by the Japanese. Chinese Imperial troops are also present so this must have been official! (*Institution of Royal Engineers*)

208

to go and, even if they had, nothing to sustain them on the way; so they stayed and, if they survived, they looted. It's an ill wind. . . .

Curiously enough, the only item of loot, if a document may be so described, which has any historical significance, did not actually exist at the time it was reputedly looted! The story of the so-called Ching-shan diary is as remarkable as the circumstances which led to its being 'found' and the character of its 'finder'. It deserves, therefore, to be told in full.

The China Medal is no great rarity but those with the bar 'Defence of Legations' are coveted treasures. Apart from those received by the marines and sailors of the British Legation guard, about fifty-five were awarded to civilians (and to Captain Francis Poole who, although a serving officer, was not formally attached to the guard) who had played an active part in the defence. Thus only about 135 were issued.*

On the roll of those civilians who received this honour is the name

German troops, regarded as the most brutal of the Allies, arresting 'Boxers' during the Allied occupation of north China. (*Illustrated London News*)

---

* See Appendix A.

Backhouse. Until a few years ago the eye of the keenest collector would not have rested for longer on this name than on any other. Today, however, if that medal with that bar and with that name engraved around the rim were to appear on the market it would fetch a tidy sum indeed, for Edmund Backhouse, later the second baronet, was one of the great cheats of history. He was also, in his way, a genius and his genius lay in two directions, linguistics and lies, the former enabling him in many instances to produce and to perfect the latter.

The life of this extraordinary creature (1873–1944) was passed largely in obscurity, although his name was known in certain scholastic circles and he enjoyed brief prominence as the co-author of two modestly successful books on China. However, beneath this tranquil surface was a treacherous whirlpool of fantasy, forgery, trickery, theft, betrayal and perversion, little of which came to light until the 1970s when an eminent historian decided to research and reveal Backhouse's astonishing career.*

Here we can deal with it only briefly and to the extent that it impinges upon the subject of this book. The eldest son and heir of a prominent banker, Backhouse arrived in China in 1898 in the hope of obtaining a position under Sir Robert Hart in the Imperial Chinese Customs, which, perhaps surprisingly, was regarded as a respectable career for a young gentleman. He had been a scholar at Winchester and went up to Oxford in 1892 to read classics, but, despite his academic brilliance, did not complete the course. As an undergraduate he liked to cut a dash, mixed with 'aesthetic' company and bankrupted himself. To the relief of his family, who had to pay off his debts, he left England in about 1895 but it is uncertain what he did, where he went or what he lived on between his departure and his arrival in China. Whatever the truth may be, according to his own (unpublished) pornographic memoirs, he spent his time in riotous living and sexual adventures of an ambidextrous nature. He also acquired, with amazing speed, fluent knowledge of a number of languages including modern Greek, Russian and Japanese.

Arriving in Peking he did not take up a post in the Customs but, having set about learning Chinese, which he seems to have mastered

* *Hermit of Peking* by Hugh Trevor-Roper.

210

in record time, he attached himself to George Morrison for whom he acted as interpreter and translator. As we have seen, Morrison himself had little or no knowledge of Chinese.

Trapped in the British Legation during the siege and being of military age, although certainly not of martial inclination, he was obliged to volunteer for active duty – hence the medal with bar. As a fighting man he does not seem to have distinguished himself and his name does not appear in any of the contemporary accounts of the siege.

After the relief, finding himself in trouble with the Russians for looting in their sector of the city, he obtained the permission of the British authorities to move into the house of a former Imperial official called Ching-shan who had been murdered, apparently by his own son. Backhouse has left more than one account of his first inspection of his new abode on 18 August, 1900, but the most detailed was composed nearly thirty-seven years after the event and the narrative goes something like this.

On the instructions of Sir Claude MacDonald Backhouse is escorted to Ching-shan's house in the British sector by a detail of Royal Welsh Fusiliers under Sergeant Burke (a Sergeant Burke does

The main entrance to the British Legation immediately after the siege. The soldiers are probably Royal Welsh Fusiliers. (*National Army Museum*)

211

appear on the medal roll of the battalion). On arrival at the house an altercation ensues between Burke, on behalf of Backhouse, and an Indian native officer whose Sikh sepoys are already in the process of ransacking the house. Clearly the Indian resents the intrusion of this civilian and his British Army escort. However, the appearance of a British officer of Baluchis (not Sikhs) settles the argument in Backhouse's favour. This is a questionable point, for what it is worth, as there is some doubt if a Baluchi battalion had arrived in Peking by 18 August.

Be that as it may, upon entering Ching-shan's study, no doubt closely attended by Burke, Backhouse finds the Sikhs using what he recognizes instantly as a valuable document, for 'base purposes'. This document, Ching-shan's diary of course, he is able to wrest from the bearded warriors before it is too much damaged, but he keeps the find to himself.

Perhaps it is understandable that he does not immediately display his prize to Burke, to whom it would mean nothing anyway, or even to the various British officers who crop up in his narrative, until he has had time to examine it more thoroughly. What is much more surprising is that, having examined it, he does not mention it to his friend and mentor, Morrison, to whom, as *Times* correspondent, the diary's revelations would have been an invaluable scoop. For it purported to explain the burning question of the hour. Why had the Chinese failed either to obliterate the legations by concentrated shell-fire or take them by storm? According to the diary, the Empress Dowager's favourite and Commander-in-Chief of the Imperial forces at Peking, Jung Lu, realizing the appalling implications for the dynasty and for China should the legates and other foreigners be slaughtered, had consistently opposed the Boxers and the siege. Furthermore, he had refused to hand over his artillery to the blood-thirsty Tung Fu-hsiang and had frequently intervened with the Old Buddha to restrain the excesses of the reactionary party at Court. In short, he had played no small role in saving the legations and the foreigners.

Opinions along these lines were already held by some diplomats and Old China Hands like Sir Robert Hart and, it need hardly be added, Jung Lu and his friends did nothing to dispel this version of events, which, in any case, may have been at least partially true.

Why then did Backhouse conceal this highly topical and valuable diary? Probably because it was yet to be written. No doubt something he found in Ching-shan's house sowed a seed in his fertile and corrupt imagination. Here, by using his masterly linguistic talents, was the opportunity to turn a dishonest penny. But the work was hard and laborious and by the time it was completed Jung Lu was dead (he died in 1903) so there was no 'squeeze' to be obtained from that source. However, the chance to profit from his toil came nine years after his great 'find' when he proposed to a British writer resident in Shanghai, J. O. P. Bland, that they should collaborate on a book entitled *China under the Empress Dowager*. As Backhouse's biographer has put it, '. . . a practised journalist and author Bland would organize the book, while Backhouse, as a scholar, would supply the documentary material.' The documentary material was of course, inter alia, the diary of Ching-shan, now at last to be revealed in all its fascination.

We cannot here go into the controversy about the authenticity of the diary which has simmered over the years but it is now accepted by the experts as a forgery, albeit one of the most brilliant forgeries in history. Indeed, it deceived many accomplished sinologues for many years and raised doubts in the minds of others as to whether it could possibly have been written by a foreigner. Perhaps Backhouse was helped by a Chinese collaborator but that is by the way and beyond proof.

Ironically, in the end Backhouse gained little from this masterly deception. Despite the impeccable behaviour of his long-suffering and entirely unsuspecting co-author Bland, he managed to deprive himself of part of his share of the royalties arising from the book. But this was the story of his life. So many of his elaborate and minutely detailed trickeries and frauds, involving governments, private enterprises, academic institutions and individuals alike, came to nought through some basic weakness in his character, even as a con man. He died in poverty taking most of his weird secrets with him to the grave.

The Allies remained in occupation of Peking for barely thirteen months during which time they did not endear themselves to the local population nor did they enhance the reputation of western civilization. The bulk of the Allied forces were withdrawn from the capital on 17 September, 1901, only ten days after the signature of the settlement document known as the Boxer Protocol. However, before turning to diplomatic issues, we must deal with some outstanding military and religious matters.

Although both the Chinese Army, or rather that part of it which had been engaged in the conflict with the Allies, and the Boxers had been broken and scattered, casualties, at least by Chinese standards, had been small. No figures are available but they probably amounted to no more than a few thousand. As we have seen, there had been few pitched battles and the sieges both at Peking and the Tientsin Concessions had been characterized by an immense volume of largely inaccurate fire-power rather than assaulting troops. Therefore bodies of soldiers and Boxers, often leaderless and starving, roamed the countryside living off the land and the peasantry as best they could.

Various Allied expeditions were mounted to deal with these bands and to pacify the areas in which they operated. Unfortunately, the pacifiers were often, perhaps usually, as terrifying to the local populace as were the bandits. 'It is certain,' wrote the Reverend Arthur Smith, 'that the three shortest of the Ten Commandments were constantly violated, with no redress for "the heathen Chinese".' The excesses of the foreign soldiery were motivated largely by the desire for loot but also for revenge. About 240 missionaries of various denominations (mostly Protestant) and nationalities had been murdered in north China in the years 1899–1900, many of them, men, women and children, in circumstances of unspeakable horror. Countless Chinese Christians had suffered a similar fate.

It would be morbid to dwell upon these atrocities at great length, but Smith gives some examples which will serve to illustrate the nature of these revolting crimes.

One Catholic bishop had his hands cut off and, after lingering in agony for three days, was doused with petrol and burnt alive. In his diocese alone some five thousand Chinese Christians were murdered. Another Catholic priest, after being carried some distance with hands and feet lashed to a pole, was buried alive. When, in his frenzied struggle for air, he managed to force his head through the covering of earth, he was battered to death. But on the whole the Catholics fared better than the Protestants. There were many more of them, about one million as compared with less than one hundred

214

thousand Protestants, and safety lay in numbers. Also, thanks largely perhaps to the far-sighted Bishop Favier, many Catholic missions were well-prepared for the uprising, had built fortifications and acquired weapons.

The Protestant missionaries and their families (of which, of course, the Catholic clergy had none), were more isolated and surrounded by fewer adherents. But one of the worst atrocities, carried out under the direction of the Governor of Shansi Province, Yu Hsien, involved both denominations, forty-five foreigners and a number of Chinese Christians being murdered on one day. Two of the Protestant ladies had their heads hacked off while their children clung to them. Nor were these spared, being despatched immediately after their mothers. This was the sadistic orgy which was to excite the admiration of the Empress Dowager, and cause her to congratulate its perpetrator.

Many missionaries, in various parts of north China, who escaped with their lives, suffered incredible hardships and privations before eventually reaching safety. Others died in the attempt.

Much of the killing of Christians and the plundering of their property was not done by Boxers but by ordinary Chinese, including officials and so-called gentry, who hated and resented both the foreign missionaries and their converts for a variety of reasons which we have discussed in an earlier chapter. These feelings were reciprocated by the Occupation forces, who, as soon as and as long as the opportunities arose, gave free physical expression to them.

Nor was much restraint exercised upon them by their commanders. Lieutenant J. R. Gaussen of the Bengal Lancers, operating in the Tientsin area in co-operation with the US 6th Cavalry, captured a Boxer and brought him into headquarters. The next day the man was shot, whether with or without trial is unclear, and Gaussen was reprimanded for bringing him in alive in the first place!

This officer, who had been very disappointed at being left behind with his squadron when the rest of the regiment marched for Peking with the relief force, was involved in a number of brisk, if rather one-sided, actions. On one occasion he rescued an American corporal, whose horse had been shot, under heavy fire. On another he took part in a cavalry charge which resulted in large numbers of fleeing Boxers and Imperial troops being 'stuck' by his Indian sowars (troopers) like so many wild boar. Gaussen regarded this as poor sport and succeeded in stopping what he described as 'horrid slaughter' by ordering his men to go and burn some villages instead.

Gaussen, who was awarded the DSO for his work around Tientsin, shared the general opinion of the local commander, Dorward – 'very nice, but fearfully slow'. He got on well with his American colleagues and was deeply impressed by their horses, equipment and rations, though slightly disconcerted to be addressed as 'Cap' by the troopers.

Indeed, it seems that the only national contingents which reached a reasonable working relationship with one another were the British and the Americans. The generally tense situation was aggravated by the low quality of some of the troops making up the Occupation force. The French, for whom only the glorious defence of the Peit'ang raised their contribution to the Boxer campaign above the level of a national disgrace, sent some of their worst units to China, including a penal battalion of the Foreign Legion. The British, with most of their army bogged down in South Africa, were reliant mainly on Indian troops. The calibre of the regiments of the Indian Army

Lt J. R. Gaussen of the Bengal Lancers. Annoyed at being left behind at Tientsin, in the event he saw more action than his brother officers who went to Peking. (*Major A. P. B. Watkins*)

had, since the earliest days of the Raj, varied from excellent to abysmal. There were probably some of both in China. At any rate, they did not hit it off with the other nationalities, quarrelling in particular with the French and the Russians, many of the latter being recruited from primitive Asiatic tribes.

The Royal Welsh Fusiliers were withdrawn back to Hong Kong in October, 1900, and ex-Private Frank Richards, who joined the battalion in India shortly thereafter, recounts in his memoirs stories told him by China veterans. No doubt these tales lost nothing in the telling but it seems that brawls between 'Allies' in Peking often led to bloodshed and sometimes death. On one occasion, he was told, a group of Fusiliers clashed with some Germans in a Chinese dive. In the ensuing fracas, for which the Welsh had armed themselves with young fruit trees uprooted from a nearby orchard (the improbability of such weapons lends a certain credence to the story), four Germans were killed and two injured. Some of the Fusiliers were carted off to hospital but most escaped with cuts and bruises. Brought before a sympathetic senior British officer, they were sentenced to only 48 hours in the cells and were told they were being punished not for fighting but for failing to kill all the Germans! An unlikely yarn but one reflecting the attitudes of the time and place. As one observer put it, what was remarkable about the Occupation was not that it succeeded in imposing peace upon north China but that it did not lead to war among the Allies.

Morrison, who had as little time for 'foreigners' as the Chinese did, was full of stories about Allied relationships, some in better taste than others. An example: 'I sent my servant on a message. He was robbed by a Russian, buggered by a Frenchman, killed by a German. In my dismay I made complaint to a British officer. He looked at me, put his eye-glass into his eye and said, "Was he really? What a bore!"'

Later, Edmund Backhouse was to write to Morrison complaining of the behaviour of the guards at the Italian Legation. Since he had a taste for that sort of thing himself, he probably wrote with his tongue in his cheek.

'The Italian soldiers,' he informed the journalist, 'are making the Hata Men vicinity intolerable by constant acts of indecency with the donkey boys there plying for hire. They pay a dollar or two to their

217

victim and then after assaulting him take the dollar back. A few days ago a man I know heard shrieks proceeding from the German cemetery and learned on enquiry that an unfortunate donkey boy had been decoyed there by two Italian soldiers. It is a terrible blow at foreign prestige with the Chinese.'

Whatever the troops may have got up to in their spare time, militarily speaking the mopping-up operations around Peking, Tientsin and further afield were pretty futile. Many of those denounced as Boxers and executed were probably the victims of personal enemies paying off old scores, while most of the Boxers themselves just melted away whence they had come, blending in with the teeming millions of the Chinese peasantry. Strangely enough, they seem to have belonged to a single generation and, to the best of Western knowledge, have never re-emerged in any recognizable shape or form. Bishop Favier believed that many of the eight hundred workers who toiled at the repair and reconstruction of the Peit'ang were ex-Boxers. He bore no grudge and, so far as we know, took no steps to confirm his suspicions. But for him China would never be quite the same again. For the few years which

The Allied occupation of Peking. German and Indian troops pose together but in fact they were at daggers drawn. (*Institution of Royal Engineers*)

218

General Frey (seated) and staff at Peking. Second from right may be Bishop Favier. (*Institution of Royal Engineers*)

remained to him he appeared only in the robes of a Catholic bishop and never resumed the Chinese garb it had been his practice to wear for forty years. As for the pig-tail he had snipped off at the beginning of the siege, it was probably too late to grow that again anyway.

# 9

# The Negotiations

After the sack of the City,
when Rome was sunk to a name . . .

Rudyard Kipling

Corrupt and shrewd, but in his way patriotic, Li Hung-chang, China's
Grand Old Man of international double-dealing, had been summoned to Peking from Canton by the Empress Dowager in June
but, using various excuses, he had wisely failed to comply. Sir Robert
Hart's appeal to him had been similarly ignored. He did not believe
that the Boxer disease could be cured before it had run its course
and had no intention of becoming one of its victims. He knew that
sooner or later he would have to pick up the pieces, but it would
have been pointless and dangerous to get involved while fighting
continued.

Moving north cautiously and by stages he arrived at Tientsin on
18 September, more or less under Russian protection. This did not
enhance his suitability as the chief negotiator of a peace settlement
in the eyes of the other Powers. He was regarded as a creature of
the Russians, having accepted, it was said, a few years earlier, a
huge bribe from the Tzarist government in return for railway and
other concessions. It was not that he liked the Russians – in common
with most high-ranking mandarins he disliked all foreigners – but
they paid better. However, the Court having fled, taking most of its
senior advisers with it, the Powers were faced with little choice but
to deal with Li and, when all was said and done, he was at least a
man with whom one could do business.

Bearing in mind that Li and his co-negotiators had to conclude a

many-faceted settlement with eleven Powers, who also had to negotiate with one another, and that parallel discussions between China
and Russia on the separate issue of Manchuria,* which was under
virtual Russian occupation, were carried on simultaneously, it is
astonishing that a settlement was reached within twelve months of
the commencement of negotiations. To add to the complications,
most of the Powers changed their leading representatives in mid-
stream. For example, MacDonald was replaced by Sir Ernest Satow
and Conger by a Mr Rockhill. The main points to be agreed were
the punishment of the princes and high officials who had supported
the Boxers; the indemnity to be paid by China to the various Powers
and compensation to individuals; the future role and stationing of
foreign troops in north China.

On the first point, the Powers demanded the death penalty for a
dozen or so high officials and generals including two princes of
the blood, Tuan and Chuang, General Tung and the murderous
Governor Yu Hsien.

On the second point, there was much squabbling among the
Powers themselves, each accusing the others of greed. Also numerous personal claims had to be considered, some large, some small,

Representatives of the Allied and Chinese governments negotiating the Boxer
Protocol. Li Hung Chang is seated first right. (*The late Mr Han Zhong Min/
Research Centre of Inscriptions and Documents*)

* Whereas by the end of October 1900 there were a total of about 90,000
Allied troops in Chihli Province, in Manchuria there were over 200,000
Russians.

221

many frivolous or fraudulent. Morrison banged in a demand for £5,804 10s 3d, including £2,625 for being wounded during the siege. It is not clear if he was paid out in full.

But it is worth dwelling for a moment on the theory of Chinese War indemnities. Throughout the 19th century, the Powers had held to the principle that whenever they subjected China to one of their periodical thrashings, such as the Opium Wars or the Sino-Japanese War, the victim must be further punished by the exaction of huge indemnities. Happily the practice was not translated to the domestic penal codes of the respective Powers, since it would have meant that a householder, having been beaten and robbed by a burglar, would have been ordered by the courts to pay his assailant a substantial sum of money in addition to that of which he had been robbed! No one protested the system, as, in the final analysis, only the silent, suffering Chinese peasantry paid through the levying of higher taxes, increased customs tariffs and tribute. Seldom was the amount of the indemnity immediately available for payment, or even if it was, the treasury mandarins were unlikely to hand it over. Therefore loans had to be negotiated on the world money market at high rates of interest, thus pleasing the bankers. The recipient governments were gratified that their military expenses had been defrayed by the indemnities and, finally, the mandarins who negotiated them were content since the higher the settlement the fatter the commissions they would receive from the lending banks. Thus everyone was happy bar those who had actually to pay.

For once, however, in the case of the Boxer indemnity, China probably got off more lightly than she deserved. After all, the whole episode was a self-inflicted wound, handled from start to finish with incredible stupidity and ineptitude. But fortunately for China the Powers were more concerned with jockeying for position than exacting retribution.

At first the Germans were bombastic, demanding that the guilty men in high places be handed over to the Allies for condign punishment before even opening negotiations for a settlement, but the others recognized this demand as an unnecessarily insulting potential breach of China's sovereignty and accepted some preliminary dismissals of senior officials as a compromise. In any case, the Germans, despite the appointment of von Waldersee, had little authority in

222

China. The people who counted were the British, Russians and Japanese. Lord Salisbury and the Foreign and War Offices wanted no trouble. A nice quiet settlement maintaining the status quo was what they sought and more or less what they obtained. Their five and a half thousand British businessmen, a third of the total European population of China, must be allowed to continue to trade happily and profitably as though nothing had happened. Furthermore, there must be no great commitment of British troops, who, thanks to the stubborn Boers, were in very short supply.

The Russians, anxious to consolidate their position in Manchuria permanently, posed as China's friend and protector, presenting themselves as honest brokers seeking to mitigate the rapacious demands of the other Powers.

The Japanese played a similar game. Their thoughts were already on an anti-Russian alliance with Britain whose mighty Far East fleet, coupled with their own splendid army, they saw as an immovable barrier to Russian ambitions in the area. They too offered themselves as China's friend, urging her not to meet Russian demands in Manchuria.

Remarkably, although the final document was not signed until 7 September, 1901, the main points of the Boxer Protocol had been agreed by the end of 1900. These were based on a French list of proposals, which, to all intents and purposes, had been accepted in outline by the other Powers, Li Hung-chang and the Empress Dowager, now established temporarily with her Court at Sian.

It is important to note that among those who approved the Protocol in embryo was Yuan Shih k'ai, virtually the only military commander in north China to maintain any credibility after the shameful débâcles of the last few months. This he had achieved by doing absolutely nothing; a masterly feat of fence-sitting, preserving his well-trained division, and thus his power-base, intact. His approval had a decisive influence on the opinion of the Old Buddha without whose sanction no agreement could be signed.

The final provisions of the Protocol boiled down to the following:

Of those for whom the death penalty had been demanded, Yu Hsien was to be executed, Prince Chuang was to commit suicide (a subtle difference perhaps), Prince Tuan was to be banished to a remote region for the rest of his life and General Tung was to be removed from his command. Several others, already dead, were to be posthumously degraded. One hundred and nineteen provincial officials were to be executed or to receive milder punishments. The likes of Tuan and Tung probably counted themselves lucky and Yu Hsien undoubtedly received his just desserts, but most of the others were nothing but scapegoats for the vicious old hag who continued to preside over the Court and dynasty.

An indemnity of £67.5 million was to be paid over 39 years at 4% annual interest. The largest beneficiary, who was to receive 29% of

Boxers on trial . . . (*Library of Congress*)

the total, was Russia. Next came Germany with 20%, followed by France with 15.75%, Great Britain 11.25% and so on, dwindling down to 0.30% for 'Others'.

The methods of calculations of the total sum and the national shares are impenetrable – at least to the present writer – but it has been estimated that only about 20% of the amount payable (£150,000,000 including interest by 1939) was received, or at any rate retained, by the beneficiaries. Having settled the claims of their individual nationals, in 1908 the Americans 're-scheduled' their

. . . and the inevitable verdict (*René Dazy*)

share so that it could be devoted to the education of Chinese students at home and abroad and most of the other creditors followed suit in due course. But we do not know what became of Colonel Meade's crock of gold!

Special missions were to be sent to Germany and Japan to apologize for the murders of von Ketteler and Sugiyama.

The Legation Quarter of Peking was to be extended, fortified and permanently guarded by troops of the various nationalities. No Chinese, except legation staff and servants, might reside therein.

Foreign troops were to be stationed at twelve strategic points between Peking and Taku, including Tientsin.

The Taku forts and other forts regarded as an impediment to military movement between the coast and Peking were to be razed.

There was to be an embargo on the importation of arms into China for two years. (It is highly unlikely that the contracting parties insisted on the observation of this clause as the trade was much too remunerative to the armaments industries of the West for it to be discontinued.)

The Protocol signed, the bulk of the remaining foreign troops (the

A group of Chinese ambassadors sent abroad to apologise to the Allies for the Boxer uprising. (*The late Mr Han Zhong Min/ Research Centre of Inscriptions and Documents*)

Russians and the Americans had already withdrawn) marched, or rather railed, out of Peking on 17 September, 1901. They left behind them about 1,500 legation guards and another 4–5,000 men at the twelve garrisons en route to the coast.

The way was open for the return of the Court from its Tour of Inspection.

But the aged Li Hung-chang could not yet lay down the heavy burden of diplomacy. The Manchurian question proved far more difficult to solve. Basically, what the Russians were seeking was little short of annexation. Li, exhausted and perhaps tempted by fresh bribes, was inclined to give in to their demands, but the other Powers, notably Japan and Britain, the Court and many powerful mandarins including the pre-eminent Viceroy of Hankow, Chang Chih-tung, urged resistance. In November, 1901, Li died at the age of seventy-eight, worn out by over a year of ceaseless struggle on behalf of his country and its worthless ruling dynasty. The

'Lest we forget.' A ruined corner of the British Legation inscribed with the above legend. The stout gentlemen in rickshaws on either side of the British NCO are probably Chinese officials assessing the damage for reparations. (*Institution of Royal Engineers*)

227

negotiations, now directed by Prince Ch'ing, dragged on for several months, until eventually, daunted by international pressure, Russia agreed to evacuate Manchuria in three stages over eighteen months, a pledge which she failed to honour. China herself was powerless to react to Russia's bad faith but Japan, backed by Britain, was not. This, in due course, was to lead to the Russo–Japanese War of 1904/5, which ended in a decisive victory for Japan. More important, perhaps, was the effect this costly and disastrous war was to have within Russia herself; a wave of discontent which led slowly but inexorably to the Great Revolution of 1917. But that is another story.

One of the consequences of the Boxer uprising which should not be overlooked was the revamping, strengthening and renaming of the Tsungli Yamen.

In the past, few high mandarins had wished to waste their talents on dealings with barbarians, thus the Tsungli Yamen had tended to be staffed by nonentities and junior officials; an ad hoc affair with no permanent senior members and regarded as the least important of all the Boards, as the departments of state were known. The new, if less euphoniously named Wai-Wu-pu, under the presidency of the respected Prince Ch'ing, was a more influential and prestigious entity.

Thus did the Chinese ostrich begin gingerly to remove its head from the sand and take the outside world more seriously. Perhaps it was through the good offices of a newly confident Prince Ch'ing that a number of Manchu and Chinese dignitaries, including Li Hung-chang, were persuaded to attend a glittering banquet given by the French commander, General Voyron (who had succeeded Frey), in honour of his Allied colleagues. At this remarkable function, which was held during the final stages of the Boxer Protocol negotiations, Voyron, in his welcoming speech, confirmed to the guests the good intentions of the Allies, who, he said, had come to China, not to impose themselves upon the Chinese government and people, but simply and solely to deal with one pernicious and abominable sect, the Boxers.

In his graceful reply, the high representative of Her Imperial Majesty, the Empress Dowager, thanked the Powers on her behalf for coming to the aid of the Government of China in its hour of need. According to our witness, the famous French author Pierre Loti,* his remarks were greeted with *'un silence de stupeur'* and the embarrassed emptying of glasses.

---

* Pierre Loti was a nom de plume. His real name was Captain Louis Viaud (1850–1923) and at that time he was serving with the French squadron off Taku.

# 10

# The Return of the Old Buddha

All the world's a stage and all
the men and women merely players

William Shakespeare

Theatricals, in which she herself would often take part, were the
Empress Dowager's abiding passion throughout her life. No sooner
had she left Peking than she began to write and rehearse her greatest
role. She was to play the lead in a production designed to soothe
the 'strong and savage barbarian'. In the first act, by a series of
edicts and decrees, written of course in her nephew the Emperor's
name, all responsibility and blame for the Boxer catastrophe was
neatly shifted from her on to him, his ministers, advisers and relatives.

We left Our Divine Mother bumping through Shansi Province
in considerable discomfort and arriving in the provincial capital,
T'aiyuan, where she installed herself in the Governor's Yamen.
Here, as we have already recorded, she had the opportunity to
congratulate the butcher Yu Hsien for slaying with great courage
and determination a large number of Christians, foreign and native,
men, women and children.

Soon she was joined by Jung Lu, who, from that moment, did not
cease to urge her to return to Peking. He was already convinced
that the Allies did not see their interests in exacting direct retribution
upon the true culprit and that they would be satisfied with scapegoats.
Moreover, he was equally sure that a Sovereign absent too long in
the remote provinces was in danger of losing her hold, whatever
remained of it, upon the rest of the country. But his mistress (some

230

The locomotive which brought the Imperial Family back to Peking in January 1902. (*Institution of Royal Engineers*)

said in both senses of the word) was not persuaded. She required more definite assurance that the Powers would not insist upon the reinstatement of the Emperor to full authority and her own retirement. She wanted a settlement with the barbarians signed and sealed before delivering herself into their de facto jurisdiction. Indeed, within a few weeks, she had moved even further south-west to Sian, capital of the neighbouring province of Shensi, where, an edict announced, 'our needs' could be better provided for (there was famine in Shansi) and telegraphic communications were better. Here magnificent arrangements had been made for her reception and the Governor's Yamen specially converted for Imperial use.

This move probably had more to do with a rumour that the Allies were about to send an expedition to T'aiyuan to avenge the massacre of the Christians than with the quality of the telegraph lines, although these did bring her regular news from Peking and the progress of the negotiations. Some telegrams were more welcome than others. One, informing her that the coarse foreign soldiery had vandalized the Summer Palace, chucking her throne into the lake and covering

231

the walls with 'lewd and ribald drawings and writings' filled her with understandable 'wrath and distress'. Nevertheless, her year at Sian was not an unhappy one and there was plenty of time to plan her come-back.

The ground work had already been done. Ultimate blame was to lie with the helpless Emperor. 'We, the Lord of this Empire,' he had been forced to write in a decree, 'have failed utterly in warding off calamities from our people and we should not hesitate for one moment to commit suicide in order to placate our tutelary deities and the gods of the soil, but we cannot forget that duty of filial piety and service which we owe our sacred and aged mother, the Empress Dowager.' Clearly the art of the false confession and the retrospective re-arrangement of embarrassing events predated the advent of Communism in China by many decades.

By the summer of 1901 the Old Buddha was satisfied that within a few months it would be safe for her to return, with suitable pomp and dignity, to her capital. She must have been amazed by the leniency of the Protocol conditions. The indemnity meant nothing to her; that could be flogged out of the peasantry. In the matter of individual punishment, she was well-prepared to sacrifice even her most loyal courtiers and followers, with the possible exception of Jung Lu, but was perhaps mildly relieved that so few of them were to be obliged to meet their ancestors in the immediate future. Old Li had done a good job. It seemed that the barbarian was already partially soothed. All that remained was for the Emperor to receive their uncouth representatives in audience and for her to entertain with flattery and giggles their hideous, big-nosed, giant-footed wives. As another sop to the Powers she took the precaution of disinheriting the Heir Apparent, by all accounts a mannerless lout, of whom they had always disapproved and who had the misfortune to be the son of the discredited Prince Tuan. Later, in another public relations gesture, she was to rehabilitate and honour posthumously the murdered Pearl Concubine.

The stage was set for a triumphal home-coming from her Tour of Inspection, but there was to be no unseemly rush. Dates for departure and arrival (which tend to vary from one account to another) at various stages of the journey must be carefully fixed in consultation with soothsayers. In any case, it was announced, 'Our Sacred

232

Mother's advanced age renders it necessary that we should take the greatest care of her health . . . a long journey in the heat being evidently undesirable, we have fixed on the 19th day of the 7th moon (1 September) to commence our return journey.'

In fact bad weather delayed the long-awaited departure until 24 October and what a huge sigh of relief the provincial authorities of Shensi must have heaved on that day!

It was seven hundred miles back to Peking and four hundred and fifty to the railway terminus at Chengting. The convoy required for the journey included the yellow sedan chairs of the Imperial family and no less than three thousand baggage carts, escorted by a host of cavalry. George Morrison described this splendid, medieval progress in a report to *The Times*:

'Along the frost-bound uneven tracks which serve for roads in northern China, an unending stream of laden wagons croaked and groaned through the short winter's day and on, guided by soldier torch-bearers through bitter nights to the appointed stopping places. But for the Empress Dowager and the Emperor, with the Chief Eunuch and the ladies of the Court, there was easy journeying and a way literally made smooth. Throughout its entire distance the road over which the Imperial palanquins were borne had been converted into a smooth, even surface of shining clay, soft and noiseless under foot; not only had every stone been removed but as the procession approached gangs of men were employed in brushing the surface with feather brooms. At intervals of about ten miles, well-appointed rest-houses had been built, where all manner of food was prepared. The cost of this King's highway, quite useless of course for the ordinary traffic of the country, was stated by a native contractor to amount to fifty Mexican dollars for every eight yards – say, £1,000 per mile – the clay having to be carried in some places from a great distance. As an example of the lavish expenditure of the Court and its officials in a land where squalor is a pervading feature, this is typical.'

The principal traveller spent her 66th birthday and a long rest at K'aifeng in Honan Province as the homeward route was a circuitous one. Here elaborate theatricals were performed in her honour. These included a well-publicized piece off stage designed to impress the foreign legates whom she would soon be facing in Peking. The local Prefect, in what was doubtless a carefully scripted scene, warned her against returning to the capital lest she be arrested and humiliated by the foreign devils. Her Majesty was then able to rebuke the well-meaning fellow publicly, thus demonstrating her faith in the good-will of the Allies.

Crossing the mighty Yellow River in a magnificent dragon-shaped barge, she began to issue pro-foreign decrees, always, of course, in the Emperor's name. Hitherto foreigners had never been allowed to witness a royal procession through the capital. Now this was to be permitted. Furthermore, the venue for the Emperor's audiences with the legates was to be upgraded to his central Throne Hall and their means of conveyance to and from these august ceremonies were to be of a standard accorded only to the highest dignitaries.

The entraining of the Imperial party, for the first time ever, called for nice timing. The departure and arrival schedules had not only to be agreed with the British and Belgian railway officials but, not so easily, by the Imperial soothsayers and astrologers in accordance with the most auspicious portents. Unfortunately historians have not reached similar unanimity, even as to the day upon which this

Imperial chairs hurrying through the streets of Peking on the return of Their Majesties in January 1902. (*National Army Museum*)

historic home-coming was accomplished. We will rely on a mixture of Morrison and, with some trepidation, Backhouse.

The royal train, itself twenty-one carriages long and preceded by four freight trains bearing the vast tribute with which the Imperial family had been loaded along the way, stopped for the night of 6 January at Paoting. In order to arrive at the appointed hour, some say noon, others 2 pm, at the new and specially constructed Peking Railway Station near the Chien Men, an early start had to be made. Nothing daunted, the Old Buddha was slap on time, arriving to board the train in the dark and in the middle of a freezing sand storm, led by torch-bearers to her luxuriously appointed compartments, upholstered in yellow silk and complete with throne. At 7 am sharp on 7 January, 1902, the train pulled out on the last stage of this memorable Tour of Inspection.

The arrival, precisely on schedule, combined a strange dignity with the inevitable chaos with which such oriental occasions are conducted. Even the sardonic Morrison was impressed. Backhouse was there too, and for once had no need to invent anything. The

The return of the Emperor to the Forbidden City in January 1902. (*National Army Museum*)

235

first to emerge from the train was the Chief Eunuch checking baggage lists and Bills of Lading, the accuracy of which were of paramount importance to his Sacred Mother, who seldom got her priorities wrong. The Emperor left his aunt, upon whom all eyes were fixed, to play her great role. 'Then standing out enshrined stood alone and looked at us,' noted Morrison in his diary. 'Curious sight. Well dressed Manchu head-dress. Uncoloured with missing teeth. Brave and undeterred. Unprepossessing face. Could not but admire courage.'

All the Chinese spectators were on their knees and an officious chamberlain shouted for the foreigners to remove their hats, which they already had. From them, incredibly, spontaneous clapping broke out as Her Majesty the Empress Dowager turned and bowed and smiled at those whom so recently she had tried to kill.

The barbarian had been successfully soothed once again.

# 11

# The Whys and Wherefores

Not Heaven itself upon the past has power
But what has been, has been, and I have had my hour

John Dryden translating Horace

All events are, in a sense, unique, but some, to adapt a famous phrase, are more unique than others. There was nothing particularly unusual about the Boxer uprising itself. Various groups of people with special interests and grievances have revolted, and are still revolting, in various parts of the world since the dawn of history. But the events which flowed from this particular uprising have a unique uniqueness.

In the first place there is the purely practical consideration that the Peking Legations were so placed in relation to one another as to make the diplomatic quarter as a whole, or nearly as a whole (the Peit'ang was 'non-diplomatic' and outside the quarter), defensible. Were such a siege to have been laid in any other capital city the legations could have been picked off piecemeal – although the failure to overwhelm the isolated Peit'ang raises doubts even on this point.

Secondly, we have to try to account for the astounding Imperial decision to back the Boxers. That the ramshackle, badly officered and unco-ordinated Chinese Army was incapable of suppressing the Boxers need not surprise us. Guerrilla and terrorist movements of all kinds everywhere are, and always have been, notorious for their apparent immunity to the counter-insurgency efforts of even the best-trained security forces with the full backing of their governments, which the Chinese military and provincial authorities did not have. But that a decision should have been taken at the highest

237

level to assist a terrorist movement, indeed to take over from that movement at a fairly early stage, in an armed aggression against the diplomatic representatives of all the strongest Powers on earth, defies logical explanation. Indeed, it can only be explained by ascribing to the Empress Dowager and the pro-Boxer party at Court entirely illogical reasons. At this point the east–west incomprehension gap intervenes. We have to accept, against all our instincts, that those who supported the Boxers, that is to say a powerful section of the central government of an ancient civilization, including the de facto Head of State, actually believed in the supernatural powers of their protegés. They must have persuaded themselves that not only could the Boxers take the legations and kill the foreigners and native Christians, but, above all, that they would be able to annihilate, or hurl back into the sea, the inevitable invading army which the Powers would send to avenge their nationals. No doubt this belief was to be bolstered by the failure of the Seymour expedition.

Today, Third World countries may, and do, gamble successfully on the reluctance of the leading nations of the world to punish such misdemeanours. Not so ninety years ago. Many of the Powers were in those days only too pleased and eager to demonstrate their military and naval muscle and to vie with one another in displays of strength and virility. The Manchu Court must have known this and could not for one moment have imagined that the Allies (as they, the Manchus, had succeeded in making them) would forbear to invade.

Presumably the anti-foreign party and the Empress Dowager believed in the Boxers because they wanted desperately to believe in them. Was not here the chance to be rid of the arrogant foreign devils and their ceaseless demands for more, more, more? And who else could purge the land and the people of the pervasive evil of Christianity – that barbaric superstition so utterly inimitable to all Chinese traditions and which had given rise to the longest and bloodiest civil war in her history, the Taiping rebellion?

Interestingly, the Old China Hands did not go out of their way to seek explanations as to why the Boxer movement had received Imperial support. They were more concerned to speculate, as foreigners and survivors of the siege, on another question. Why were they still alive? Why had not even the Peit'ang, let alone the legations, fallen? Why had the Chinese military performance been

238

even more dismally lacklustre and incompetent than the most cynical of them could have expected?

Backhouse has provided us with Jung Lu as an explanation. But that is not quite enough. What about the reputedly rabid Tung and his ferocious Kansu Braves? What were they doing slopping about behind barricades, vaguely firing off their (modern) rifles, then sitting on the wall chatting and smoking with Sir Claude MacDonald? Jung Lu would not let them have any artillery, it was said. But the defenders had no artillery worth the name either. There were a hundred opportunities for a dozen simultaneous infantry assaults on different sectors of the defence. None was taken. Captain Izard of the French Army Engineers, in a technical appraisal of the siege of the Peit'ang written shortly after the relief, found that no serious attempt had been made to exploit the breaches in the walls created by the mines, not even Mine E which had destroyed 80 metres of wall, a gap quite indefensible by the remaining handful of sailors and auxiliaries. One British survivor gave it as his opinion that had the legation guards been faced with Zulus or Sudanese dervishes, also without artillery and few effective fire arms, they could not have held out for a day. A mild exaggeration perhaps but not more than that.

Sherlock Holmes, in reflective mood, once pronounced to Dr Watson that, having discarded all the impossibilities in a case, the solution was to be found in whatever remained, however improbable (or words to that effect). Unfortunately, so far as we know, the Great Detective did not at any time concentrate his mighty powers of deduction upon the Mystery of the Peking Legations. Had he done so, having eliminated all other explanations for the failure of the siege, he might have concluded that *nobody*, including the reactionary party and the Old Buddha, wanted to destroy the legations and the diplomats once they had been disillusioned as to the capabilities and magical powers of the Boxers, and once the terrible dangers of the path they had taken dawned upon them.

Further, he might have deduced that the deadly power struggle which raged behind the walls of the Forbidden City between the moderates and the reactionaries in July and August, 1900, was no longer about whether the legations and their inmates were to be destroyed but about how *not* to destroy them *without losing face*. This

239

would account for the continuing efforts to persuade the diplomats to leave their legations. The early offers of safe-conduct to Tientsin may have been made with murderous intent but the later ones may have been genuine, however incapable of fulfilment.

Certainly with the fall of Tientsin, even the most bigoted of the reactionaries (with the possible exception of Li Ping-heng) must have realized that they had steered their country and its sacred dynasty towards the abyss, and that the fall of the legations could mean the fall of that dynasty and the slaughter of the foreigners the dismemberment of China.

The reader may be unconvinced by this Holmesian explanation but he will be hard put to produce a better one!

On the other side, much criticism has been directed at the Old China Hands of the day for their failure to appreciate the significance of the rise of the Boxers and the time it took them to realize the extent of the support these fanatics enjoyed in high places. Perhaps we should exempt Bishop Favier from a generalization, but it seems that however long a European spent in China he learnt little of the country and less of its people. If we are to judge them by modern standards then we must excuse them, for nothing has changed. During the 1989 student demonstrations in Peking and the other great cities of China, and in their bloody suppression, television viewers and newspaper readers around the world were treated night after night and day after day to the opinions of the modern equivalents of George Morrison, Sir Robert Hart and Professor Huberty James. None had the slightest idea what he was talking about; none failed to get everything absolutely wrong. Goggle-eyed and breathless with anticipation, we listened to reports of fighting between various army units; the opposition of the generals to the policies of the Old Guard; the deaths and the topplings of the Hard Liners; the refusal of the troops to fire on the students and the dawn of yet another new era in China. Just possibly, some of this may have been true but it amounted to nothing. The comprehension gap is as wide as ever and likely to remain so. Writing sixty years ago, Somerset Maugham has one of his Chinese characters say of English sinologues, 'Those who know most about China know nothing.'*

* The Philosopher in *On a Chinese Screen*.

This was true at the time of the Boxers, true when Maugham wrote it and true now.

But perhaps the whys and wherefores are not as important as the outcome. On the Sunday after the relief of the legations, the Reverend Arthur Smith preached a sermon to the survivors. In it he said, 'We honour the living for their heroism in defending us, we cherish the memory of the brave dead but most of all we thank the Lord who has brought us through fire and water into a safer place.' Perhaps we should leave the explanations at that.

The Boxer uprising, although in itself a tiny bubble at the source of the most turbulent and bloody century in human history, had a profound effect upon the future of China and her neighbour Japan. Despite the Old Buddha's play-acting and the apparent indulgence and complacency of the Powers after their initial outburst of indignation, China's last great imperial dynasty was in terminal decline and its lunatic behaviour during the crisis accelerated its demise. When the Emperor Kuang-Hsu and his aunt the Empress Dowager

George Morrison, the self-appointed and disappointed champion of both China and the British Empire. (*Mitchell Library*)

died in suspicious and unexplained circumstances on consecutive days (14 and 15 November, 1908), the late Emperor's nephew, the two-year-old P'u-I, came to the throne as Emperor Hsuan-t'ung. His actual reign was almost non-existent as he was made to abdicate, before reaching the age of comprehension, after the 1911 republican revolution; but, thanks to cinema,* in the west he is perhaps the best known today of all China's emperors, as well as the last.

For some years, under a remarkable arrangement called the Articles of Favourable Treatment, P'u-I was allowed to remain in the Forbidden City with his titles, his eunuchs, a generous pension and all the trappings of monarchy. In 1917 there was an abortive attempt at restoration but in 1924 he was forced to take refuge with the Japanese, who, in due course, set him up as their puppet head of state in Manchuria. In 1945 he was captured by the Russians and eventually deported to China. After years in prison, and perhaps working as a gardener, he is thought to have died in 1967.

Ironically, P'u-I's successor as China's head of state was his uncle's,

'The Last Emperor'
(*Backhouse and Bland*)

* Bertolucci's *The Last Emperor*.

242

the late Emperor Kuang-Hsu's most bitter enemy, Yuan Shih-k'ai, who had betrayed him in 1898. Yuan's period in power was marked by quarrels with his fellow, and perhaps better known, revolutionary, Dr Sun Yat Sen. But Yuan was not a republican at heart and in 1916 he tried to set up a new dynasty with himself as its founder and first emperor. The attempt failed and he died a few months later. Although an unscrupulous double-dealer, Yuan had rendered a great, if negative, service to his country in 1900 by refusing to bring his troops into action against the legations or the relieving force.

Of the leading 'moderates', Prince Ch'ing prospered until the fall of the Manchu dynasty when he was accused of corruption and sent into retirement at Tientsin. He too died in 1916. But apart from the Old Buddha, who has stamped her mark in history as one of its minor monsters, few, if any, 'immortals' have survived. With the possible exception of some of the Japanese officers, Fukushima and Shiba for example, most of the Allied military commanders were second-class and are forgotten. The same may be said of the diplomats, although the despised Pichon did achieve high office in later life.

As for the nations concerned, although China had been saved from dismemberment by the skin of her teeth, it would be nearly half a century before she rid herself of all forms of foreign military occupation and to this day she is still chained by the influence of an alien political philosophy.

Perhaps the greatest beneficiary was Japan. Although her victory over China a few years earlier had aroused some interest in the West it was not until the summer of 1900 that the true quality of her fighting men was brought sharply and dramatically to the attention of the Powers. It was demonstrated that not since the Spartans of old had there been trained infantry like the Japanese. None with courage so irresistible in attack nor so stubborn in defence. For them no strong point was too strong to take, no last ditch too indefensible to defend. The Russians had not the sense to be warned, but, for the time being at least, the British had. Russia challenged Japan for supremacy in Manchuria and Korea and received a severe drubbing both on land and at sea, whereas Britain sought, and temporarily achieved, alliance with her.

We cannot deal here with the history of China and the Far East in the first half of the 20th century but it may be briefly summarized, if over-simplified, by noting that as the power and influence of the European nations waned in the area, that of Japan and the United States increased. Despite Japan's over-confidence, misjudgements and inhuman behaviour in the Second World War and the consequent devastation of 1945, in the closing decade of the century she stands poised to assume, for better or for worse, Super-Power status.

China herself has taken no such strides forward. Since 1900 one horror has succeeded another. Although the Communist victory of 1949 brought to an end four decades of war and civil strife on Chinese soil, the new government immediately involved its army in the Korean conflict and ushered in an era of almost continuous terror for its people until, or so it seemed, the death of Chairman Mao in 1976. To the astonishment of the ever-gullible West, the great 'reforms' and 're-opened door' policies of the post-Mao period have proved to be largely cosmetic. There should be no surprises left for the so-called experts, but there will be.

The Alliance which defended and relieved the legations barely out-lived the emergency. Some of those who took part would serve again in greater and more momentous conflicts. Some former Allies would, within a few years, be shooting at each other. Those who survived the siege were perhaps fortunate to be living at the time they did. Were a similar state of affairs to arise today the reaction of the Powers is unlikely to be so robust and positive. The probability is that while their diplomats, nationals and local dependants were being slaughtered, their governments would be locked in debate at the Security Council, issuing statements deploring the behaviour of the offending régime and calling for economic sanctions.

Few embassies today have properly trained and equipped guards; the US Marines, for example, attached to American diplomatic missions are there largely for ceremonial and administrative purposes, without realistic defensive capability. In the case of the seizure of the US Embassy in Tehran, no resistance to the intruders was offered and the single feeble and ill-conceived attempt to rescue the hostages ended in total and ignominious failure. Despite (or perhaps because of) huge defence budgets and colossal arsenals of massively destructive weapons, the Western Powers have proved themselves incapable of defending their citizens at home and abroad from all

244

the various forms of both sponsored and free-lance terrorism which blight the world today. In that sense we have regressed since the turn of the century.

In the case of the siege of the Peking legations, all the senior diplomats with the exception of von Ketteler and Sugiyama, who were assassinated before it started, survived. Indeed, one of the many remarkable aspects of that siege (in contrast to the Peit'ang) was the very small number of non-combatant casualties from enemy action. Of the eighty or so foreigners who were killed or died of wounds, nearly all were either servicemen or armed volunteers, and, with very few exceptions, were killed by rifle fire while manning the walls and barricades. Only one European woman (a Belgian, on the day of the relief) was wounded and not a single European child was hurt, although six died from disease or malnutrition, out of the 223 present. One, called Siege Moore, was born! According to Smith, on the whole the children rather enjoyed it all, playing Boxers and Soldiers while the grown-ups fought grimly for their survival. No complete record was kept of 'friendly' Chinese casualties. Many, especially children, must have died of privation and sickness, a number were killed while working on the defences and about 400 at the Peit'ang.

Finally, we must take a last glance at some of the individuals whose fate it was to endure this bizarre ordeal. Few of the senior diplomats lingered long in Peking after the relief. Perhaps in the opinions of some of their governments, their traumatic experience had rendered them unsuitable as peace negotiators. MacDonald swopped posts with Sir Ernest Satow in Tokyo* where he played an important role in the formation of the Anglo-Japanese Alliance. Edwin Conger filled various other diplomatic positions, mostly in the Americas, and died in 1907. Herbert Squiers, though barely in his fifties, died in 1911.

Of the legation guards, Halliday VC survived the First World War to become a full general. Several others of his contingent stayed on in the Royal Marines for many years, including Corporal Gowney who, by the outbreak of the war in 1914, had risen to the rank of

---

* MacDonald remained in Tokyo, where he became the first British Ambassador, as opposed to Minister, until 1912. He died in 1915.

Quartermaster-Sergeant. In 1912 his fellow holder of the DCM, Sergeant Murphy, time-expired and bored with his job as an Admiralty messenger, applied to Morrison for employment in that strange and distant land where he had spent the most extraordinary summer of his life. As for those who had fought with him and who will remain in Peking for all eternity, in a pleasant corner of the garden of the British Ambassador's Residence there is to be found a memorial plaque in their honour. The inscription reads thus:

IN MEMORY OF
CAPTAIN B M STROUTS, AGED 30
Royal Marine Light Infantry

DAVID OLIPHANT, AGED 24     J GEORGE HANCOCK, AGED 24
HENRY WARREN, AGED 21   WALTER E TOWNSEND, AGED 21
ROGER D DRURY, AGED 22
Her Britannic Majesty's Consular Service

R B DECOURCY          Imperial Maritime Customs
F HUBERTY JAMES       Professor at the Imperial University of Peking

Private D W PHILLIPS                    Private A W SCADDING
Private G SAWYER                          Private W HORNE
Royal Marine Light Infantry

WHO GAVE THEIR LIVES IN DEFENCE OF
THIS LEGATION
June 20 – August 14 1900

ALSO OF

MURRAY KER, AGED ONE YEAR AND TEN MONTHS, WHO
DIED SIX DAYS AFTER THE SIEGE, SON OF W P KER
Assistant Chinese Secretary   HBM Legation

THEREFORE IS IT AS GREATE FOLLIE TO WEEPE
DEATH IS THE BEGINNING OF ANOTHER LIFE

*'Neither Men nor Their Lives are Measured by an Ell'*

THIS TABLET IS PLACED HERE BY SOME OF THOSE
FOR WHOM THEY DIED AND OTHERS
TO WHOM THEIR MEMORY IS DEAR

The unfortunate Captain Hall, second-in-command of the American contingent, did not emerge from the experience with such flying colours as some of his colleagues. Indeed, he appears to have been the only serviceman of any rank or nationality accused of cowardice, an accusation against which he was vigorously defended by his commander in the USS *Newark*, Captain Bowman McCalla, who was not, of course, present during the siege.

The story is a curious one and Hall seems, at least to some extent, to have been the victim of inter-service and departmental rivalry. Following accusations made to General Chaffee immediately after the relief that Hall had abandoned his position on the Tartar Wall on 28 June without orders from his superior officer, Captain Myers, Chaffee ordered a 'secret enquiry' to be held. The outcome of this investigation and the form it took is far from clear, and, in any case, McCalla held that it was outside Chaffee's jurisdiction to order it. Hall, who was not informed, at that stage, of the identity of his accusers, repeatedly demanded and was eventually granted, an

The Garden of Remembrance at the British ambassador's residence in Peking in 1989. The memorial plaque to the British who fell in action or died during the siege may be seen in the far corner. (*Commander M. H. Farr, RN*)

247

official Court of Enquiry. This was held at Cavite in the Philippines and was something of a farce as only one of Hall's accusers, the Marine contingent's medical officer, Dr Lippett, gave evidence and he denied making the statements attributed to him at the previous enquiry. His other three accusers, Captain Myers, Herbert Squiers and an American civilian called Pethick, who had been for many years private secretary to Li Hung-chang, failed to put in an appearance. Myers was refused permission to travel to the Philippines by the Navy Department and the other two, who, we must assume, could not be subpoenaed, pleaded pressure of work and ill-health. Hall was honourably acquitted of the charge of cowardice.

The episode is a murky one and it is impossible at this distance in time to come to any definite conclusions as to its rights and wrongs. As McCalla has pointed out in his unpublished memoirs, positions on the Tartar Wall, where the fighting was heavy, confused and often in the dark, were frequently abandoned and re-taken by elements of various national contingents. Hall does seem to have been rather an ineffective officer and there is every reason to believe that the discipline of the US Marines left something to be desired, but that does not make him a coward. On the other hand, although we know that the Marines disliked Squiers and that Chaffee disliked the Marines, we cannot ignore the fact that one of his accusers was his commanding officer, Myers.

McCalla was inclined to blame Myers for placing himself and his men under the command of the diplomats MacDonald, Conger and Squiers, and noted that Hall, on assuming command of the American contingent when Myers was wounded, had refused to accept orders or 'threats from Diplomatic sources'. Clearly McCalla believed that herein lay the roots of the accusations against Hall. Perhaps with wisdom in hindsight, he felt that overall command of the legation guards should have been entrusted to Colonel Shiba. The old sailor regarded war as too serious a business for diplomats to meddle in.

We have left until last the Old China Hands. As a breed these survived until the Communists seized power in 1949. They were the personification of western capitalist influence in China and disappeared with the eradication of both capitalism and that influence. But those with whom we are concerned were, of course, long gone before then. Bishop Favier died in Peking, the scene of his most testing and triumphant experience, in 1905. Sir Robert Hart, Favier's oldest contemporary, was never in his lifetime officially removed from his position as Inspector-General of the Imperial Chinese Customs, although he had retired to England three years before his death in 1911. His half-century of service to China co-incided with, and was indeed a strong element in the maintenance of, the protracted zenith of British power and influence in that country.

Although many years younger, George Morrison outlived Hart by less than a decade. Never completely at ease with *The Times* management in London (and vice versa), he left journalism in 1912 to become political adviser to President Yuan Shih-k'ai, an appointment which inspired some ill-disposed person to remark upon the difficulty of two people giving and receiving advice without the advantage of a common language. However, he continued to advise the Chinese Government after Yuan's death and took part, on China's behalf, in the Paris Peace Conference after the Great War. But by then his health was deteriorating rapidly and he died in England, the country he loved so much and knew so little, in 1920 aged 58. His services and loyalty to the British Empire had received no recognition whatsoever and he had been denied the knighthood and other honours which he believed were his due. In one of his last diary entries he left a note of the haunting lines which head this chapter. His biographer suggests that he may have intended them for his epitaph, but they may serve equally well as the epitaph for a Boxer, a beleaguered diplomat, an heroic young naval officer, a patriarchal bishop, the Old Buddha, or even for Imperial China herself.

# Appendix A

## Some Nominal Rolls of Legation Guards and Volunteers with Casualty Figures

**Royal Marines**

| | |
|---|---|
| Captain B. M. Strouts, commanding | Killed |
| Captain L. S. D. Halliday | Wounded and awarded Victoria Cross |
| Captain E. Wray | Wounded |
| Sergeant J. Murphy | Awarded Distinguished Conduct Medal |
| Sergeant J. E. Preston | Wounded and awarded Distinguished Conduct Medal and Conspicuous Gallantry Medal |
| Sergeant A. E. Saunders | |
| Corporal D. J. Gowney | Wounded and warded Distinguished Conduct Medal |
| Corporal W. Gregory | Wounded |
| Corporal J. Johnson | Awarded Distinguished Conduct Medal |
| Corporal G. Sheppard | |
| Lance Corporal A. Jones | |
| Lance Corporal H. J. Salvin | |
| Lance Corporal W. J. Sparkes | Wounded |
| Bugler A. F. Webb | |
| Private T. R. Allin | Wounded |
| Private A. Alexander | |
| Private J. Buckler | Wounded |
| Private W. Betts | |
| Private C. Baker | |
| Private F. J. Cresswell | |
| Private W. Cheshire | |
| Private G. Davis | |
| Private J. Dean | Wounded |
| Private A. Dunkley | |
| Private W. Edney | |

| | |
|---|---|
| Private G. Forester | |
| Private W. Ford | |
| Private H. J. Green | |
| Private J. Greenfield | |
| Private H. Grainger | |
| Private G. Goddard | Wounded |
| Private J. G. Howard | |
| Private S. W. Haden | Wounded |
| Private D. Hill | |
| Private W. J. Hunt | |
| Private R. Hendicott | |
| Private W. Horne | Died of wounds complicated by typhoid |
| Private W. R. Harding | |
| Private J. W. Heap | Wounded |
| Private G. Jones | |
| Private J. Jones | |
| Private C. Johnson | |
| Private K. King | Wounded |
| Private A. J. Layton | Wounded |
| Private G. Lister | |
| Private J. Masters | |
| Private J. A. Myers | Awarded Distinguished Conduct Medal |
| Private A. G. Mayo | |
| Private J. Murray | |
| Private S. Mellors | |
| Private J. Mears | |
| Private J. Marriott | |
| Private J. D. Newton | |
| Private E. G. O'Neil | |
| Private J. Ormiston | |
| Private C. W. Phillips | Killed |
| Private J. F. Pitts | |
| Private E. E. Powell | |
| Private A. S. Roberts | |
| Private J. Rumble | |
| Private P. A. Rose | |
| Private W. G. Roe | Wounded |
| Private H. Sands | |
| Private A. W. Scadding | Killed |
| Private G. Shilliam | |
| Private F. Smith | |
| Private W. Smith | |

252

| | |
|---|---|
| Private A. G. Sawyer | Died of wounds |
| Private A. J. Tickner | Wounded |
| Private W. Turner | |
| Private F. Tanner | |
| Private W. A. Taylor | |
| Private W. Viney | |
| Private H. A. Webster | |
| Private W. T. Woodward | Wounded |
| Private E. Webb | |
| Private J. W. Walker | |
| Private A. E. Westbrook | Wounded |

**Royal Navy**

| | |
|---|---|
| Sickberth Steward R. G. Fuller | |
| Leading Signalman H. Swannell | Awarded Conspicuous Gallantry Medal |
| Armourer's Mate J. T. Thomas | |

**British Volunteers entitled to China Medal
with bar Defence of Legations**

| | |
|---|---|
| Sir Claude MacDonald, British Minister | |
| R. E. Bredon, Deputy Inspector General Customs | |
| E. Wyon, Superintendent Chinese Mint | |
| Captain F. G. Poole, East Yorkshire Regiment (language student) | Awarded Distinguished Service Order |
| Dr W. Poole, British Legation Medical Officer | |
| H. G. M. Dening, 2nd Secretary, British Legation | |
| H. Cockburn, Chinese Secretary, British Legation | |
| W. P. Ker, Chinese Secretary, British Legation | |
| B. G. Towers, Assistant Consular Service | |
| D. Oliphant, Assistant Consular Service | Killed |

253

W. P. M. Russell, Student,
Consular Service

J. G. Hancock, Student                    Killed
Consular Service

A. J. Flaherty, Student
Consular Service

H. G. Bristow, Student
Consular Service

C. C. A. Kirke, Student
Consular Service

H. Porter, Student Consular
Service

W. N. Hewlett, Student
Consular Service

C. A. W. Rose, Student
Consular Service

R. D. Drury, Student Consular             Killed
Service

L. H. R. Brown, Student
Consular Service

L. Giles, Student Consular
Service

W. E. Townsend, Student                   Killed
Consular Service

Sergeant R. D. Herring, British
Legation Staff

I. R. Brazier, Chinese Customs

C. H. Brewitt Taylor, Chinese
Customs

I. H. Macoum, Chinese
Customs

B. L. Simpson (alias Putnam
Weale), Chinese Customs

A. G. Bethill, Chinese Customs

L. Sandercock, Chinese
Customs

I. H. Smyth, Chinese Customs

C. Mears, Chinese Customs

A. F. Wintour, Chinese
Customs

R. B. De Courcy, Chinese                  Killed
Customs

I. H. Richardson, Chinese
Customs

254

W. S. Dupree, Chinese Customs

M. Honiton, Imperial Chinese
   Bank

N. Oliphant, Chinese Postal        Wounded
   Service

I. K. Tweed

A. W. Brent

H. B. Bristow

Dr G. E. Morrison, *Times*        Wounded
   Correspondent

Captain P. Smith, Royal
   Marines retired

Rev. F. Norris, British Legation
   Chaplain

Rev. R. Allen

Rev. T. Biggin

Rev. J. Stonehouse

A. Peel

G. B. Peachey

E. Backhouse

H. Warren        Died of wounds

Lt. Col. A. G. Churchill

I. Allardyce

S. M. Russell

J. Baillie

## Total Recorded British Casualties

| | |
|---|---|
| Killed and died of wounds | 11 |
| Wounded | 20 |
| Assassinated before siege (Prof. James) | 1 |
| Died of disease after siege (Murray Ker) | 1 |

## United States Marines

Those marked with an asterisk were awarded the Congressional Medal of Honor.

Captain J. T. Myers, command-        Wounded
ing

Captain N. T. Hall

Sergeant Walker*

Sergeant Fanning        Killed

Corporal Dahlgren*
Corporal Hunt*
Private Ammann
Private Brosi
Private Butts
Private Boydston*
Private Barrett
Private Carr*
Private Davis
Private Daly*
Private Donovan, E. J.
Private Donovan, W. F.
Private Fischer*                    Killed
Private Greer
Private Galligher
Private Gainnie*
Private Gold                        Wounded
Private Hobbs
Private Herter
Private Horton*
Private Hall                        Wounded
Private Kehm                        Wounded
Private King                        Killed
Private Kuhn
Private Kennedy                     Killed
Private Lavin
Private Mullen
Private Mueller                     Wounded
Private Moody                       Wounded
Private Moore*
Private Martin
Private O'Leary
Private Preston*
Private Quinn
Private Schroeder                   Died of wounds
Private Silvia*                     Wounded
Private Scannell*
Private Turner                      Killed
Private Tinkler
Private Tuchter                     Killed
Private Thomas                      Killed
Private Upham*
Private White
Private Young*

Private Zion*
Musician Murphy*                     Wounded


**United States Navy**

Dr Lippett                           Wounded
Chief Machinist Peterson*
Gunner's Mate 1st Class Mitch-       Wounded
ell*
Seaman Sjogren
Seaman Westermark*
Hosp. App. Stanley*


**Total Recorded American Casualties**

Killed or died of wounds             8
Wounded                             10


**French Naval Detachment at the Peit'ang**

Sub-Lieutenant P. Henry, com-        Killed
manding
Second Master Joannic                Killed
Quartermaster Elias
Quartermaster Mingam
Leading Fusilier Prigent
Leading Fusilier Queffurus
Leading Fusilier Le Goff             Wounded
Leading Fusilier Ruello
Leading Helmsman Delmas              Wounded
Leading Signalman Stephany
Gunner Urcourt
Gunner Callac                        Wounded
Gunner Le Sech                       Wounded
Gunner Costanza                      Wounded
Stoker Souve
Stoker David                         Killed
Stoker Louarn
Stoker Seneghal
Stoker Frank                         Killed
Stoker Guezennec
Stoker Cambiaggi
Stoker Le Coz
Ordinary Seaman Fay

Ordinary Seaman Le Quere
Ordinary Seaman Lales
Fusilier Derrien
Fusilier Peuziat
Fusilier Le Ray
Fusilier Rebour                          Killed
Fusilier Lehoux

N.B. No nominal roll of the Italian naval detachment can be found.

**Total Recorded Combat Casualties at the Peit'ang including Volunteer Priests but excluding Chinese Christian Auxiliaries\***

| | |
|---|---|
| Killed or died of wounds | 13 |
| Wounded | 15 |

**Total Recorded Combat Casualties to all Nationalities, excluding Chinese,† at the Legations and the Peit'ang**

| | Killed and Died of Wounds | Wounded |
|---|---|---|
| American | 8 | 11 |
| Austrian | 4 | 11 |
| British | 11 | 20 |
| French | 17 | 45 |
| German | 12 | 15 |
| Japanese | 10 | 29 |
| Italian | 13 | 15 |
| Russian | 5 | 20 |
| Total | 80 | 166 |

\* About forty Chinese Christian auxiliaries were killed or died of wounds but there is no figure for wounded.

† Including about four hundred at the Peit'ang, perhaps as many as a thousand Chinese Christians died from various causes during the siege.

# Appendix B

## Some of the Small Arms used by Allied and Chinese Forces during the Boxer Campaign

**American**
Lee Straight-Pull 6mm made by Winchester (Marines and Navy)
Krag Jorgensen .30 (Army)

**Austrian**
Model 1890 Mannlicher 8mm

**British**
Lee Metford and Lee Enfield .303
Martini Henry .45

**Chinese**
Mauser 11mm
Hanyang 8mm

**French**
Lebel Model 1886 M93
Lebel Model 1890 or 92 8mm

**German**
Mauser 11mm
Commission 8mm

**Italian**
Mannlicher Carcano 11mm
Commission 8mm

**Japanese**
Murata 8mm type 30
Arisaka 6.5mm

**Russian**
Moisin Nagant Model 1891 7.62mm

# Appendix C

Extracts from *The Times* 'Obituaries' of
Sir Claude MacDonald and Dr G. E. Morrison
published on 17 July, 1900

### Sir Claude MacDonald

The obituary opens with a resumé of Sir Claude's military and diplomatic career and continues . . .

'No diplomatic representative of the Queen has come to so tragic and untimely an end as that, which there is only too much reason to fear, has overtaken Sir Claude MacDonald. Sir Louis Cavagnari, it is true, was murdered with all his staff at Kabul in September, 1879. But treacherous as was that outrage, it cannot even bear comparison with the appalling catastrophe which has overwhelmed the whole of the unfortunate European community within the blood-stained walls of the Chinese capital.'

After referring to Sir Claude's successes and failures in China, the latter often due to the 'vacillating counsels of Downing Street', the obituary goes on to say . . .

'If Chinese obstruction has been allowed in many cases to render these successes nugatory, the blame cannot in fairness be imputed to Sir Claude MacDonald alone, though ill-health would seem to have materially weakened after a time his original grip of his work.

'How the British Minister and his colleagues together, it must be added, with Sir Robert Hart and all the leading members of the foreign community in Peking failed altogether to see any signs of the coming storm is a mystery which will probably now remain forever unsolved. . . . Sir Claude MacDonald, there can be little doubt, was in great measure misled by the extraordinary confidence he had been induced to repose in the ability and loyalty of the Empress Dowager.'

The obituary concludes with a reference to Lady MacDonald and their daughters:

'[Lady MacDonald was] universally popular and beloved of the staff. [Her] pride and happiness in the important position to which her husband had attained were marred only by her growing apprehensions of his health, which was ill-fitted to bear the prolonged strain of anxious and sedentary occupation. . . . Two little daughters, the younger one born in China, perfected the happiness of a union which was truly a union of hearts and when one thinks of the cruel death in which they were still to be united it would seem as if the prophetic vision of some such a fate as theirs must have inspired Browning to write the noble lines in "Prospice":

"For sudden the worst turns the best to the brave
   The black minute's at end,
And the element's rage, the fiend-voices that rave,
   Shall dwindle, shall blend,
Shall change, shall become first a peace out of pain,
   Then a light, then thy breast,
O thou soul of my soul! I shall clasp thee again,
   And with God be the rest!"'

*Author's Note*

This obituary must have caused considerable annoyance to the MacDonalds when they read it a few weeks later. In the first place, there is no indication from any other source that Sir Claude was in poor health at the time. Had he been, it seems extremely unlikely that his diplomatic colleagues would have appointed him 'Commander-in-Chief'. Not only that, but he was to continue his 'anxious and sedentary occupation' for another dozen years. Nor is there any evidence that his grip was weakening, whatever his shortcomings as a diplomat may have been, nor that his successes, which included the leasing of the New Territories and Wei-hai-wei, were in any way 'nugatory'.

The *Times* obituarist was justified in drawing attention to Sir Claude's (and everyone else's) extraordinary misjudgement of the situation in north China in the first half of 1900 but wrong in ascribing this to any 'confidence in the ability and loyalty (to whom?) of the Empress Dowager'. He and his colleagues simply refused to believe that the Boxers were enough of a menace to be taken seriously.

Finally, it is amusing to note that when Sir Claude's 'second' obituary came to be written on his death in 1915, no mention was made of the first although large parts of it were re-used verbatim!

## Dr G. E. Morrison

After a lengthy description of his adventurous life, the obituary continues . . .

'Whilst our readers can realise how grievous is the loss which has befallen *The Times*, only those who knew Morrison personally can appreciate the loss that has befallen his friends. His was in every way a striking personality, essentially modest and unassuming yet at the same time resolute and virile. Even in familiar conversation his precision of expression combined with a peculiar deliberateness of speech conveyed a sense of intellectual strength and lucidity of thought which the saving grace of a quaint and kindly human redeemed even the faintest suspicion of priggishness . . .

Both as a man and a journalist Dr Morrison leaves an honoured name to be added with sorrowful and affectionate regret to the memorial roll of those who have died in the service of *The Times*,\* died, as our French neighbours happily express it – *au champ d'honneur'*.

---

\* It seems that the *Times* correspondent with the Anglo-French invasion force of 1860 was taken prisoner by the Chinese and 'cruelly done to death in the dungeons of the Peking Board of Punishment'.

# Appendix D

## The Taiping Rebellion
## (1850–64)

The Taiping movement, which developed into China's longest and bloodiest civil war, was led by a Hakka called Hung Hsiu-ch'uan (1813–64).

In his youth Hung had come under the influence of the Protestant Church, but at the age of about thirty he invented his own deviant form of Christianity and, as a result of certain visions, declared himself the Son of God and the Brother of Christ.

His reformist policies and opposition to the Ch'ing (Manchu) dynasty attracted many followers from the poorer classes, particularly of his own Hakka racial group. Also he was successful militarily, seizing Nanking as his capital in 1853, having been proclaimed King and founder of a new dynasty to replace the Ch'ing.

Although imposing strict rules of austerity and morality upon his followers, for himself he preferred the life of a voluptuary. The dynamism of his movement gradually degenerated through nepotism, internal feuding and his failure to take Shanghai where he was defeated by Gordon's Ever-Victorious Army officered by western mercenaries.

The Taiping were finally crushed by Ch'ing troops after the two-year-long siege of Nanking in July, 1864, and Hung committed suicide. The religious aspect of his movement died with him but his reforming influence was not entirely absent from the philosophies of later Chinese revolutionaries.

# Bibliography

**Some Published Sources**

Barnes, A. A. S., *On Active Service with the Chinese Regiment*, 1902

Bazin, Réné, *L'Enseigne de Vaisseau Paul Henry*

Beeching, Jack, *The Chinese Opium Wars*, 1975

Bigham, Clive, *A Year in China*, 1901

Bland, J. O. P. & Backhouse, E., *China under the Empress Dowager*, 1910

Brown, Fred R., *The History of the 9th U.S. Infantry*, 1909

Dix, C. C., *The World's Navies in the Boxer Rebellion*, 1905

Fairbank, John K. & Kwang-Ching-Lu, *The Cambridge History of China*, Vol. 11, 1980

Field, C., *Britain's Sea Soldiers*, 1924

Fleming, Peter, *The Siege at Peking*, 1959

Glover, Michael, *That Astonishing Infantry*, 1989

Keyes, Admiral of the Fleet Lord, *Amphibious Warfare and Combined Operations*, 1943

Lo Huil-Min, *The Correspondence of G. E. Morrison*, 1976

Lunt, James, *Imperial Sunset*, 1981

Oliphant, Nigel, *Siege of the Legations in Peking*, 1901

O'Neill, Hugh B., *Companion to Chinese History*, 1987

Pearl, C., *Morrison of Peking*, 1967

Richards, Frank, *Old Soldier Sahib*

Smith, A. H., *China in Convulsion*, 1901

Sorley, L. S., *The History of the 14th U.S. Infantry*, 1909

Tan, Chester C., *The Boxer Catastrophe*, 1955

Trevor-Roper, Hugh, *Hermit of Peking*, 1976

*Globe and Laurel*, Journal of the Royal Marines

*RUSI Journal*, 1898 and 1914

*The Daily Mail*

*The Times*

**Manuscript and Unpublished Sources**

The Archives of the United States Marine Corps Historical
  Centre, Washington, DC
The Archives of Le Service Historique de l'Armée de Terre,
  Chateau de Vincennes, Paris
The Archives of Le Ministre des Affairs Etrangers, Paris
The National Army Museum, London
The Archives of the Royal Welch Fusiliers
The Archives of the Royal Marines
The Royal Engineers Institution
The Royal Artillery Institution
The India Office Library
The Foreign and Commonwealth Office Library
The Japan Information Service, London
Letters and Diary of Sub-Lieutenant Maurice Cochrane, RN
Notes by Lieutenant J. R. Gaussen, Bengal Lancers

# Index

266

China Medal (British), 125n, 209
Chinese Regiment (British), 38, 100, 126; description, 127; in action at Tientsin, 140; 141, 158, 167; drag guns to Peking, 179
Ching-shan, 183; 'diary', 209–13
Ch'ing, Prince, President of Tsungli Yamen, 48, 88, 143, 147, 154, 228; death, 243
Chuang-Yung or Fighting Braves, 35–40, 59, 84, 159; defend Peking, 183; 239
Chuang, Prince, 221; suicide, 223
Clemenceau, G., 41
Cochrane, Sub-Lieut M., describes Boxers, 65; 65n, 96, 99–100
Cohong, 11–12
Cologon, Senor, 75, 83
Confucius, 9, 20
Conger, E., character, 42–3; 46, 57; visited by mandarins, 72; 75, 86, 87; distrusted by US Marines, 121; cables State Department, 152; replaced, 221; later career and death, 245; 248
Congressional Medal of Honor, 178n
Cordes, Herr, 86
Cossacks, 50, 52, 101, 176
Cradock, Commander, 78, 80
Crozier, Capt, 186
Currie, Mr, 97


D'Arcy, Enseigne, 131, 134, 194, 195
Daggett, Col, 186
*Daily Mail*, 144–5
De Giers, M., Russian ministers, 59; visited by mandarins, 72; prepared to accept ultimatum, 74–5; 86, 87, 152
De Pelacot, Col, 136, 152
Delcassé, T., 57; warned of supposed British intentions, 112
Delmas, Leading Helmsman, 201
*D'Entrecasteaux*, French ship, 192
Di Martino, Signor, 18, 43
Di Salvago Raggi, Marquese, 43
Distinguished Conduct Medal (DCM), 117, 129, 141&n, 165, 246
Distinguished Service Order (DSO), 53, 103, 129, 170, 216
Dix, Lt C. C., 80
Dobrolovsky, Capt, 78
Doig, Capt, 97
Dore & Garregue, Fathers, 194
Dorward, Brig-Gen A., arrival & career, 103–4; problems with Allies, 126–7; 130; strengths of Allied columns, 136&n; handling of attack on Tientsin, 137–41; 150, 216


East India Company ('John Company'), involvement in opium trade, 10–11
Eight Diagram Sect, 27
Elias, Petty Officer, 193, 202
Empress Dowager (Tsu Hai), 4; plunders defence budget, 17; 18; the Hundred Days, 23–32; ignorant of outside world, 29; attitude to Boxers, 30; 32, 47, 55, 58, 67, 69; sends 'message' to Lady MacDonald, 71–2; 73, 143, 147; influenced by Li Ping-Heng, 148; losing control of China, 149; rumoured poisoned, 149; 172; murders Pearl Concubine, 185; 186, 187, 196, 212; admires murders of missionaries, 215; 220, 223, 224, 228; Tour of Inspection and Return to Peking, 230–6, 238, 239; mysterious death, 241–2; a minor monster, 243; suitable epitaph, 249
En Hai, Corporal, 87–8
Esdaile, Midshipman F., 125
Ever Victorious Army, 1

Fanning, Sergt, 121
Fashoda Incident, 113
Favier, Bishop, warns diplomats, 31; 42, 47, 57, 111; at the Peit'ang, 191–204, 215; no
    grudge against Boxers, 218–19; 240; death, 248–9
First World War, 176, 245, 249
Fists of Righteous Harmony – *see* Boxers
Forbidden City, 3, 29, 48, 61, 67, 73, 84, 96, 143, 148, 149, 172, 183; American attack
    on, 186–8; 203, 239, 242
Frank, Stoker, 198
French/France, 2, 3, 9; involvement in Second Opium War, 12; relations with China,
    13–14; 15, 17; Sphere of Interest, 24n; good relations with Yuan, 38; 41, 45;
    legation guards, 52–5; 60; disobey Seymour, 66–7; 74, 78, 93, 94; decline to attack
    arsenal, 95, 100; suspicion of British, 111–13, 115; bayonet prisoners, 116; 117,
    120, 123, 126, 127; legation mined, 131, 136&n; 138; casualties at Tientsin,
    139–40; 150, 152, 159, 161, 163; left behind, 165; 'beneath contempt', 166–7; 172,
    173, 175; overtake Americans, 177–8, 183, 187, 188; nuns, 191; sailors in defence
    of Peit'ang, 192–204; priests killed, 204n; 'best looters', 207–8; resent German
    commander, 207; 216, 217; proposals for Protocol accepted, 223; share of
    Indemnity, 225; give banquet, 228–9&n; 239
Frey, Major-General H., 152, 165, 228
Fu (Su Wang Fu), occupied by Allies, 92; held by Japanese and Italians, 110; 111, 113,
    118, 120, 131, 132, 147; last fighting in, 182; 192
Fuckie Tom, English pirate, 1
Fukushima, General, role in victory at Tientsin, 136–9; 150, 156; message to Shiba,
    170; only memorable general, 243


Gamewell, Rev F. D., 90
Gartner, Brother, 193; leads patrol, 200
Gartside-Tipping, Col R. F., 166, 167
Gaselee, Lt-Gen Sir Alfred, 141; arrives in China, 151; 152, 155; character, 156; fumes
    at Allies, 166; receives despatches from MacDonald, 169–70; 173; first to enter
    legation quarter, 180–1; tries to organize looting, 205
Gaussen, Lt J. R., 215–16
George III, 10
Gerbillon & Pereira, Fathers, 15n, 20
Germans/Germany, 2, 9; relations with China, 17, 20, 24n, 29, 41; legation guards, 52;
    60, 61; disobey Seymour, 66–7; 78, 79; attacked at Langfang, 84–5; 88, 92, 93, 95,
    100; first casualties of siege, 105; 106, 116, 117, 120, 121, 123, 126, 131, 136;
    behaviour at Tientsin, 142; 151, 159, 172, 173; terrorize north China, 207–8; fight
    Welsh, 217; bombastic, 222; share of Indemnity, 225; 226
Gi Dien Kwee, Sergt, 141&n
Gilpin, Lt, 96
*Gilyak*, Russian gun-boat, 76; hit, 79, 82
Gladstone, Mr, 11
Gordon, Major-General C., 1, 29, 47, 63
Gowney, Corp D. J., 55, 64, 117; describes Japanese, 122; later career, 245–6
Great Hunting Park, 65, 84
Gregory, Corp W., 121
Griffin, Capt, 169–70
Groves, Chaplain L., 165, 166
Guerin, Consul, 100, 111
Guy, Midshipman B., wins VC, 140
Gwynne, Capt, 137


Hall, Capt N., 121; accused of cowardice, 247–8
Halliday, Capt L. S. D., wins VC, 108–10; 134, 199; later career, 245
Han-lin or Great Library, burns, 106–8; 118, 122

Russia, 228; effect of Boxers on, 241; use P'u-I, 242; international reputation, 243–4; Ango–Japanese Alliance, 245
Jardine Matheson, 11
Jarlin, Monseigneur, 191–204
Jellicoe, Capt, 61, 65&n; wounded, 94
Jen Tz'u T'ang, 191–204
Jesuits, 15n, 19, 20
John of Monte Corvino, 9
Johnstone, Major R. J., 95, 127
Joseph-Felicité, Brother, 197
Jouannic, Petty Officer, 193; killed, 195–6
Jung Lu, Grand Secretary, 25, 32; army reforms, 36–7; Macdonald's message to, 146–7; 151, 159; rumoured suicide, 172; 185, 186; exonerated by 'diary', 212–13; joins Tour of Inspection, 230; 232, 239

K'aifeng, 233
K'ang Yu-wei & Weng Tung-ho, 24
Kansu Province & Rebellion, 35; 'the Colonel', 146–7
Kelly, Col-Sergt, 175
Kempff, Admiral, 76n, 78
Kennedy, Private, 117
Ketteler, Baron K. von, character, 42; 57; reckless behaviour, 58; rejects ultimatum, 75; murdered, 85–6; enigma of his murder, 87–9&n, 92; China apologizes, 226, 245
Keyes, Lt, 61&n; captures destroyers, 78–81
King, Private, 108
Kitchener, Field-Marshal Earl, 102, 129
Korea, 16, 61, 100, 243; War, 244
*Koreytz*, Russian gun-boat, 76; hit, 78
Kuang Hsu, Emperor, 4; his Hundred Days, 23–32; 58, 74, 88; rumoured poisoned, 149; 172; favourite concubine murdered, 185; 187; blamed for Boxer catastrophe, 230; 231; apologetic decree, 232; 233, 234; mysterious death, 241–2; 243
Kup, Mr B., 180

Labrousse, Capt, 172
Langfang, 64, 83–4
Lanterns, 27
Learnard, Capt, 178
Lee, Major, 139
Li Hung-chang, appeals to, 68, 69; 188; negotiates Boxer Protocol, 220–3; dies, 227; 228, 232, 248
Li Ping-heng, 148, 152, 240
Li Shan, 71
Lien-chun or Disciplined Troops, 35–40, 59, 159
Lincoln, Trebitsch, 2
Linievitch, Gen N. P., 152&n; dispute with Japanese resolved, 156; his plan of attack on Peking, 173–5; and implementation, 176–7
*Lion*, French gun-boat, 78, 80
Lippett, Dr, 248
Liscum, Col E. H., 137; killed, 139
Lofa, 64
Loti, Pierre (Capt Louis Viaud), 229&n
Luh-ying or Green Regiments, 34, 37, 136, 159
Luke, Major, 101, 137

Ma Yu-Kun, Gen, 37
Macao, 9

Opium War, Second (Arrow War), 12, 15, 61, 123, 222
Owen, 2nd Lt C. S., 102&n


Paolini, Lt, wounded, 118, 134
Paoting, 235
Pearl Concubine, murdered, 185; posthumously honoured, 232
Pei-ho River, 13, 75–6, 78, 83, 93, 95, 98, 157, 161, 163
Peit'ang Cathedral, 52, 55, 183, 188; under siege, 191–204; 216; repaired by ex-Boxers, 218; 237, 238, 239, 245
Peits'ang, Battle of, 156, 161–3, 168
Pethick, W. N., 248
Philippines, 53, 100, 130, 248
Phillips, Private C. W., 116; memorial, 246
Pichon, Monsieur S., career, 41–2; reports to Paris, 57–8; favours acceptance of ultimatum, 75; changes mind, 87; 88; burns files, 134; receives Legion d'Honneur, 152; 192; leads sailors to Peit'ang, 193; achieves high office, 243
Poole, Capt F., 53&n; opinion of Pichon, 57; 59, 70, 105, 107, 108; opinion of Wray, 134; 209
Poole, Dr W., 53, 110
Port Arthur, 100, 127n, 168
Portuguese, 9
Protestants, 14, 17, 19, 20; murders of, 214–15
Prussian (see German)
P'u-I (Emperor Hsun-t'ung), 242
Purdon, Col-Sergt R., 141


Raden, Lt Baron von, leaves gun at station, 57–8; 59, 106
Ragsdale, Consul-General, 157
Red Fist Society, 27
Reilly, Capt, killed, 186–7
Rendel, Lord, 3, 11
Repington, Col C., 168
Reuters, 145
Ricci, Father M., 20
Richards, Private F., 176n; tales of Boxer campaign, 217
Robinson & Norman, murdered missionaries, 55
Rockhill, Mr, 221
Roman Catholics, 3; used by France, 13; privileges, 14; 15, 17, 19, 20, 31, 42, 45, 191; murders of, 214–15; 219
Roshan Khan, Havildar, 129
Rowcroft, Capt E. C., 129
Royal Marines (RMLI & RMA), legation guards, 50–5; 58; with Seymour, 61n, 78, 81; admired by McCalla, 95; 96; attempt to reach Tientsin, 97; 101&n, 104; operations in Han-lin, 108–10; 115, 116; operations on Tartar Wall, 117–21; 127, 132, 137; casualties at Tientsin, 140; 153; in relief expedition, 158; 173, 209, 245; memorial to fallen, 246
Royal Navy, 2, 12, 50 61n, 66, 76, 81, 97, 98, 112, 127, 137; casualties at Tientsin, 140; 209, 223
    HMS Algerine, in Taku operation, 76; direct hit on fort, 80
    HMS Barfleur, 125, 140
    HMS Centurion, 65
    HMS Fame, 61n; in Taku operations, 76–82
    HMS Orlando, 100
    HMS Terrible, 125&n, 127; 12-pounders at Tientsin, 137; sailors drag guns to Peking, 179
    HMS Whiting, in Taku operation, 76, 79; damaged, 80, 82
Russell, S. M., 118

Russians/Russia, 2, 9, 12; relations with China, 15, 16, 20; Sphere of Interest, 23n; 50; legation guards, 52–5; forget gun, 57; 59–61, 68; officer delivers Taku ultimatum, 76–9; 80, 82; decline to attack arsenal, 95; 97; rescue Seymour, 98; reinforcements, 100; 101, 104, 106n, 116; operation on Tartar Wall, 117–1; student killed, 123; 126, 129, 131, 136, 139; called 'savage', 142; 150, 156, 159, 161; fire on Allies, 163; 165, 166; ill-treated by officers, 169; 181, 172, 173; premature attack on Peking, 175–8; 179, 180; severe casualties, 182–3; 186, 187; strip Summer Palace, 207; 211; relations with Allies, 217; with Li Hung-chang, 220; Manchurian policy, 221&n; pose as China's friend, 223; largest share of indemnity, 224–5; 227; bad faith and war with Japan, 228; 242, 243
Russo–Japanese War, 15, 168, 228


Salisbury, 3rd Marquess of, relations with French, 112–13; 223
San Men Bay, 17
Sandercock, L., 68
Satow, Sir Ernest, replaces MacDonald, 221; 245
Sawyer, Private A. G., mortally wounded, 110; memorial, 246
Scadding, Private A. W., first British casuality, 106; memorial, 246
Second World War, 168, 205, 244
Seymour, Admiral Sir Michael, 61
Seymour, Vice-Admiral Sir Edward & his expedition, 60–7, 71, 83–4; retreating on Tientsin, 93–9; 100, 101, 111; in Shanghai and Hankow, 112–13; 115, 150, 179, 238
Sha k'ou Men, 179, 180
Shanghai, 111; Seymour's visit, 112; 144–5, 152, 213
Shansi Province, 28, 30, 111; missionaries murdered, 185; 215, 230; famine, 231
Shantung Province, 24n, 27; earliest Boxers, 28; Yuan crushes Boxers, 30; 100, 145
Shensi Province, 231, 233
Shiba, Col G., 34, 70; holds Fu, 110; 118, 120; outstanding officer, 121–2; 131, 132; receives message, 170, 172; final attack in Fu, 182; 199, 243; McCalla's opinion, 248
Shih Che Men, 183
Shirinsky, Capt, 98
Sian, 223; Imperial party at, 231–2
Sino–Japanese War, 32, 53, 222, 243
Smith, Oiler, 65
Smith, Rev A., 14, 45; opinion of Royal Marines, 53; 115, 173; condemns Allied behaviour, 214; sermon, 241; 245
Spanish/Spain, 18, 52, 120
Squiers, H., 121; replaces Strouts, 133&n; 145; loses turkey, 149; 169, 179; amasses loot, 205; death, 245; in Hall case, 248
St John, Major, 129
Stossel, Gen A. M., 127&n, 152
Strouts, Capt B. M., 106, 110; mortally wounded, 132–3; 134, 143, 199; memorial, 246
Su Wang Fu (see Fu)
Sugiyama, Mr, murdered, 64, 74; Chinese apologize, 226; 245
Sullivan, Private, 167
Summer Palace, 13, 58, 183–5; stripped by Russians, 207; vandalized, 231
Summerall, Lt, 186
Sun Yat Sen, Dr, 2, 243
Sung Ching, Gen, 37
Surdar Khan, Subedar-Major, 129
Sutterlee (alias Silvester), 145
Swannell, Ldg Sigmn H., 173


T'ai-yuan, 230, 231
Taiping Rebels/Rebellion (see Appendix D), 1–2, 13, 29, 35, 238

Taku/Taku Forts, 13, 50, 59, 61, 67, 68; threatened by Allies, 73; Allied ultimatum and seizure of forts, 74–83, 95, 100, 101, 102, 126, 130, 152, 155, 159, 192; forts to be fazed, 226, 229n
T'angku, 60, 65n, 79, 80, 127, 159
Tartar Wall, 106&n; most dangerous, 113&n; 114, 116; vital to defence of legations, 117; operations on, 117–21; MacDonald meets 'colonel', 145–7; 149, 171; flags raised on, 173; 180, 187; Hall accused to abandoning, 247–8
Thomann, Capt, 104–5; killed, 123, 134
Thomas, Armourer's Mate J. T., 123, 173
Thomas, Private, 121
Tientsin City/Settlements (Concessions) and Battle of, 14, 25, 50, 55, 57, 60–3, 64, 65n, 66, 67, 68, 71; legates ordered to, 74; 75, 83, 84; Seymour retreats on, 85–98 passim; under seige, 99–104 passim; Concessions reported fallen, 111, 115; seige continues, 124–31; assault on Walled City, 134–41; 143, 147–52, 154; under foreign government, 155, 156; Allied advance from, 157; 159, 163, 169, 182, 214, 215, 218, 220; stationing of foreign troops at, 226, 240, 243
*Times, The*, 43, 49; last despatch to, 71; publishes 'obituaries', 145; 168, 208, 212, 233, 249
Titus, Musician C. P., 178&n
Townsend, W., killed, 118; memorial, 246
Treaties
  Nanking, 12, 16
  Nershinsk, 15
  The Bogue, 12
  Tientsin, 13–16
  Versailles, 42
  Whangia, 16
Treaty Ports, 2, 3, 12, 15, 30
T'sait'sung, 169–70
Tsar of Russia, 4
Tsu Hai, *see* Empress Dowager
Tsungli Yamen, 17–18, 45, 48; mandarins visit legates, 71–2; 75, 83; von Ketteler murdered en route to, 85–6; 92, 143, 146, 147, 151; mandarins beheaded, 152, 172; re-named, 228
Tuan, Prince, 25; principal supporter of Boxers, 30; appointed President of Tsungli Yamen, 48; forges Note, 72; suspected of von Ketteler's murder, 87–8; 143, 144; death penalty demanded for, 221; banished, 223–4; son disinherited, 232
Tuchter, Private, 116
Tung Chih Men, 178, 182
Tung Fu-hsiang, Gen, 'savage ruffian', 35; commander of Braves, 37; 84, 134, 146, 154; executed traders, 156; 157, 159; defends Peking, 183; denied artillery, 212; execution demanded, 221; relieved of command, 223–4; 239
Tung Pien Men, 175–8, 183, 186
T'ungchou, 172–3, 175
Turner, Private, 120, 121


United States Army
  Artillery, 158; in attack on Forbidden City, 186–8
  6th Cavalry, 152, 158, 177, 186–8; at Tientsin, 215–16
  9th Infantry, 130; in assault on Tientsin, 136&n, 137, 138; CO killed, 139; casualties, 140, 158; at Yangts'un, 163–5; 169; in attack on Forbidden City, 186–8
  14th Infantry, 150, 158; at Yangts'un, 163–5; help Russians at Peking, 176–8; disappointing reception at legations, 181–2; in attack on Forbidden City, 186–8
United States Marines, legation guards, 52–5; 98; friendship with RWF, 102; dislike of MacDonald, 106; first casualty, 108; 113, 116; operations on Tartar Wall, 117–21; looting of Tientsin, 141; 145; turkey incident, 149; disliked by Chaffee, 152; 153, 158, 167, 171; in attack on Forbidden City, 186–8; 244; Hall accused of cowardice, 247–8

United States Navy, with Seymour, 61; takes no part in Taku operation, 82; 97, 98, 99, 248
  USS *Monacacy*, 78, 82
  USS *Newark*, 98, 247
Upham, Private O., 52, 114, 116, 117, 147; opinion of MacDonald and Squiers, 149; Russians 'OK', 171; hears Maxim fire, 179
Usedom, Capt von, 61; disobeys Seymour, 66–7; attacked by Tung, 84–5; leads retreat, 93; 94, 96


Vassilievsky, Gen, 176, 178
Victoria Cross (VC), 108, 110, 140
Victoria, Queen, 123
Vidal, Commandant, reports on Chinese Army, 32–9; 61, 66, 94; calls for French troops, 100; 101&n, 136, 137, 150
Vogack, Col, 50
Voyron, Gen, 228


Wagner, Monsieur, 117
Wai-Wu-pu (*see* Tsungli Yamen)
Waldersee, Field-Marshal Graf von, appointed Allied C-in-C, 207–8; 222
Warren, H., dies of wounds, 131; 143; memorial, 246
Watts, J., 101
Waymouth, Capt E. G., 129
Weaponry (*see also* Appendix B), available to Chinese army, 39–40; 55, 61n, 65&n, 76–8, 81; at Hsiku Arsenal, 95–6; with legation guards, 115–16; Japanese rifle, 122; 'home-made' shells, 123; construction of 'Betsy', 123–4; 125, 129, 137, 147, 173; Maxims, 179
Wei-hai-wei, 100
Wilhelm II, Kaiser, 17; bloodthirsty speech, 88; 151, 207
Winter Palace, 207
Wood, Capt C., 100
Wood, Field-Marshal Sir Evelyn, 100
Wray, Capt E., 58, 70; wounded, 117; 134


Yamaguchi, Gen, 131, 136; arrives in China, 152; dispute with Linievitch, 156; enters Peking, 182; objects to foreign command, 207
Yangts'un, Battle of and Station, 64, 66, 83–5, 163–5, 168, 172
Yangtze River, 24n, 112, 148
Yellow River, 24n, 234
Yu Hsien, Governor, supports Boxers, 30; murders missionaries, 185; 215; execution demanded, 221; executed, 223–4, 230
Yu-Lu, Viceroy, 31, 61; suicide, 172
Yuan Shih-k'ai, Gen, betrays Emperor, 25; opposes Boxers, 30; his Division, 37–40; 96, 111, 136, 145, 150; remains neutral, 159; 176; approves Protocol, 223; later career and death, 243; 249